FRS YORKE
AND THE EVOLUTION OF ENGLISH MODERNISM

FRS YORKE
AND THE EVOLUTION OF ENGLISH MODERNISM

Jeremy Melvin

With a memoir by **David Allford**

WILEY-ACADEMY

ACKNOWLEDGEMENTS

Many people contributed to, helped and encouraged this monograph on FRS Yorke since David Allford asked me to work on it in the summer of 1991. My first and very substantial debt of gratitude is to David Allford himself, for giving me the opportunity, patience, gossip, advice – and fine food and wine – and since his untimely death in 1997, to his widow Beryl, their daughters Jane, Sally and Ruth and son Simon for continuing the support with enthusiasm.

Professor David Dunster first introduced me to David Allford, with the words, reassuring to Allford at least, 'he's a capitalist'; before and since this occasion he and his wife Charlotte and son Arthur have been very generous with support and hospitality. Other friends and former colleagues from the Bartlett School of Architecture and Planning at University College, London also helped: Joanna Saxon and Iain Borden gave me a pristine (though no longer!) first edition of *The Modern House*; Professor Adrian Forty invited me to try out some of the early ideas for Chapter One in a research seminar with students on the history of modern architecture masters programme he established and directed for many years, and as a graduate of it, I am further grateful to him and to his former colleague Mark Swenarton. Margaret Richardson, Christopher Woodward and Will Palin of Sir John Soane's Museum also gave me the opportunity to present a research seminar at the Museum which helped to form the theme for Chapter Three.

A number of people gave up time to share memories of FRS Yorke: in particular his former partners Cyril Mardall, Randall Evans and Brian Henderson; his former lodger and colleague at the Architectural Press, Sir James Richards; Barbara MacDonald for whom Torilla was built and her sister Christabel Bielenberg who introduced him to her family; and Yorke's close friends Beryl Hope and Penelope Whiting. Richard Burton, of architects Ahrends Burton and Koralek, shared memories of Yorke and his buildings, which he experienced from a young age as a grandson of Christabel Burton and stepson of Gerald Barry. I am also indebted to people who showed me around buildings designed by FRS Yorke, especially Alan and Lesley Charlton, Nigel Goodman and David Bottom, as well as the architect John Winter, whose sympathy for the ideals of early modernism remains undimmed.

Neil Bingham, of the RIBA Drawings Collection, edited *Twentieth Century Architecture* volume 2, which included an early and edited version of Chapter One. His colleagues in the British Architectural Library and drawings collection, especially Ruth Kamen, Charles Hind, Eleanor Gawne and Lucy Porten were unfailingly helpful in locating the not always coherent Yorke archive. Other librarians and archivists who helped include the staff at the Shakespeare Centre in Stratford-upon-Avon; Trish Noble and her team at the Faculty of the Built Environment, South Bank University, London. Past and present colleagues at South Bank University who have helped include Peter Blundell Jones, Marina Adams, Nic Pople and Katherine Shonfield; Penny Hatfield at Eton College; staff at the Aalto Foundation in Helsinki, Finland; and in the early stages of research, Ruth Dar and Anna Piet of the Bartlett Library, University College, London.

With thanks to Gail Novelle, who read and corrected the text, and especially David Allford for his memoir; my father Peter Melvin who has also read the text and claimed ownership of the first copy I saw of *The Modern House*; my mother Muriel Melvin who actually owned it; Cedric Price and Paul Finch who provided various forms of encouragement; and David Gossage who explained the significance of Edgbaston. At Allford Hall Monaghan Morris, Jayne Chisnall deciphered tapes and Sonia Grant redrew plans.

Finally I would like to thank my wife Lisa Ekman Melvin, and twin children Naemi and Thomas for, respectively, tolerating FRS Yorke and creatively misunderstanding what the book is about.

Jeremy Melvin, Highgate, January 2003

Cover: Modernism gained: the dramatic play of cubic forms, light and shadow of FRS Yorke's house, Torilla, outside Hatfield and finished in 1935. Photo: Courtesy of *The Architectural Review*.

Frontispiece: By the end of the 1930s, Yorke was able to add modernist spaces to traditional buildings, as at Forge Cottage in Sussex. Photo: Cracknell.

Other Wiley Editorial Offices

John Wiley & Sons Inc., 111 River Street, Hoboken, NJ 07030, USA

Jossey-Bass, 989 Market Street, San Francisco, CA 94103-1741, USA

Wiley-VCH Verlag GmbH, Boschstr. 12, D-69469 Weinheim, Germany

John Wiley & Sons Australia Ltd, 33 Park Road, Milton, Queensland 4064, Australia

John Wiley & Sons (Asia) Pte Ltd, 2 Clementi Loop #02-01, Jin Xing Distripark, Singapore 129809

John Wiley & Sons Canada Ltd, 22 Worcester Road, Etobicoke, Ontario, Canada M9W 1L1

ISBN 0471-48960-3

Design and Prepress: ARTMEDIAPRESS Ltd, London
Printed and bound in Italy

CONTENTS

FOREWORD

This book is the outcome of the first of two projects that my father, David Allford, invented for his retirement from his role as chairman of YRM – Yorke Rosenberg & Mardall. The other, second project, was 'the poolhouse', which was designed to ensure that he and my mother Beryl could hospitably banish guests from their house to the new facilities in the garden.

The two projects, although very different in outcome, both demonstrate his love of architecture and his belief in collaboration and the benefits of giving others their heads. In the case of 'the poolhouse' the others were my partners and myself, with the book the singular other is Jeremy Melvin. That the second project was completed almost ten years ago reflects both our need for fees and a first building, and his determination to enjoy his retirement projects – as he often stated, he did not retire to be busy.

Having met Jeremy in 1988, David commissioned him to collaborate on the project on the understanding that David would contribute a personal memoir and Jeremy a critic's assessment of Yorke's importance as a historical figure. This role definition clearly reflected and suited both men's experience and expertise. I believe that this division of labour also dealt with the issues that concerned David; he was too close to, and fond of, 'Kay' to assess his merits as an architect; and indeed whilst certain of Yorke's importance as a writer, publisher and leader, he was uncertain of the status of Yorke the architect. Indeed it was only shortly before his death, long after he wrote the piece published in this book, that he came to some form of very relaxed conclusion.

In the summer of 1997 Beryl, Judith, David and I visited 'Torilla' with The Twentieth Century Society. It was a magnificent summer's day and the building, carefully restored by John Winter, was significantly more inventive and sophisticated than any of us had anticipated. Allied to this, the owner, an eminent artist, not only shared David's interest in Yorke the man but like my father was a native of the city of Sheffield and a Sheffield Wednesday supporter. I remember David remarking with real pleasure that 'Torilla' was 'rather good' – perhaps he was reflecting that it was something of the arrogance of youth and Yorke's generous recognition and support of his own talent that had led him to under-rate Yorke as an architect. This revised view of Yorke was one he shared with Jeremy a few weeks later at a wedding reception the night before he died.

Nevertheless his written contribution was never intended to be an assessment of Yorke the architect, but a recollection of Yorke the man; whose books he had read as a student and who later became his employer and eventually invited him to become the fourth partner of the practice, Yorke Rosenberg Mardall.

Of course, as great Epicureans, Jeremy and my father had numerous lunches to discuss the context and structure of the book and enjoyed a number of 'tours' encountering buildings and individuals who were friends and colleagues of Yorke. These were undertaken together, separately and with my mother. On these occasions ideas were exchanged, introductions to people, events and issues made, and the current form of five critical chapters established.

On assembling the book Jeremy and I, after completing the difficult task of deciphering David's texts – which was ironic as he was always proud of the elegance and legibility of his handwriting! – had only to choose which of his two texts to include. The first was written on holiday and later amended and is the one we have chosen. In the end it was a relatively easy choice and one with which we believe he would have agreed. As already stated, he found it difficult to write about Yorke, yet this text is an intriguing tale of a working relationship, a friendship and the evolving nature of practice set in the vital context of post-war reconstruction. It is the more personal of the two texts and communicates a lot about the two men, painting a vivid picture of Yorke. It does not touch too closely on Yorke's domestic circumstances (he was married and had twin daughters), lived a life often distant from his family. Indeed, in neither text did David choose to dwell too much on Yorke's private life, as interesting as it no doubt was, except as he experienced it through their intriguing collaboration.

The structure of the book offers another model for the architectural monograph – one which satisfies those of us intrigued by the personal history of architecture and the 'other' events and circumstances which help to define it.

Simon Allford

David Allford in convivial mood, with his friend the architect Cedric Price.

INTRODUCTION

Modernist architects in Britain during the 1930s saw their lives as a Sisyphean struggle against apathy, parsimony and bureaucracy. They had few clients, even fewer with large budgets; apart from a few exceptions they failed to galvanise progressive social movements with their message, and they often had to fight local authorities for permission to build their designs — even, on occasion, having to find different sites. Yet as World War II ended in 1945, and a Labour government committed to establishing a new society was elected, modern architecture became the idiom of its Welfare State, the visual mode for new hospitals, schools, housing and civic buildings. Whether in new towns or reconstructed cities, modernism touched everyone: children were educated in modernist schools; the sick were treated in modernist hospitals; many people moved into modernist housing; they went shopping in modernist shopping precincts and they moved about on modernist road systems. They lived, worked and found entertainment where the planning policy of 'zoning' dictated. Almost every aspect of post-war social policy had some manifestation in architecture. Only death offered escape: few people were buried under modernist tombstones or consumed in the fires of modernist crematoria.

If this extraordinary rise in the fortunes of modern architecture in Britain can be illustrated through a monograph on one of its protagonists, then Francis Reginald Stevens Yorke (1906–62) is the most appropriate subject. He was the only architect to be prominent in the emergence of modern architecture in the 1930s, and to enjoy the fruits of its success in the 1950s. If the firm he founded with Eugene Rosenberg and Cyril Mardall in 1944 designed more than its fair share of modernist homes, schools and hospitals, progressing to universities and airports, his career beforehand foreshadowed and informed the way this transformation evolved.

There are several readily available explanations for the triumph of modernism. Indeed, before it actually happened Nikolaus Pevsner argued that an ineluctable *Zeitgeist* made the adoption of modern architecture historically inevitable.[1] Others, often with political objectives, seem to claim that a coherent and conspiratorial architectural community foisted it on naive post-war politicians to make the public suffer.[2] An alternative view to either is that something as complicated as the trajectory of modern architecture in Britain is a tangled skein of influence, intention, chance, habit and opportunism with no coherent pattern. Part of the aim here is to explain how Yorke and his close colleagues did not determine that modernism would inevitably dominate post-war reconstruction, nor that its doing so was entirely coincidental. Instead there was enough mutual connection to find some crooked timber of common cause between modernism and the Establishment. By extension, this also highlights several episodes in Yorke's career which suggest that the engagement between modernism and social policy came about because several events, without necessarily a direct causal relationship between them, gradually revealed a degree of affinity — perhaps contingent and transitory. Nothing exposed that affinity more than the social and economic circumstances of World War II.

In the summer of 1939, the imminence of war shook the network of international contacts and small construction projects which had formed Yorke's career since he began independent practice

FRS Yorke on the steps of the Yorke, Rosenberg & Mardall Offices in Hyde Park Place, London, c1955.

Photo: Sam Lambert, courtesy of *The Architectural Review*.

as an architect and journalist eight years earlier. In July, Alfred Roth sent him a letter from the Doldertal flats in Zurich which Roth and Yorke's former partner Marcel Breuer had designed for Sigfried Giedion, asking, 'Pourriez-vous lui prêter votre assistance' for 'mon ami [Ernesto] Rogers … qui … est obligé de quitter l'Italie?'[3] On 25 August, the Czechoslovakian cartoonist and writer Adolf Hoffmeister wrote to Yorke from Paris. 'My dear and bloody Kay', Hoffmeister expostulated, 'As it usually is the case, in those days of bad humor and terrible mood, we write letters to good friends in bad english to say good bye and so long and I hope to see you on the front.'[4] Even Yorke's small architectural commissions, some taking no longer than a few weeks, required clauses in their contracts specifying what would happen if hostilities were to erupt.[5]

Yorke's friend, the Czechoslovakian writer and cartoonist Adolf Hoffmeister, who wrote an extraordinary letter to him on 25 August 1939.

It was precisely those contacts and activities that gave Yorke a unique position among pioneering British modernists, so war struck right at the heart of the persona he had constructed for himself. Since he had begun working for the Architectural Press in 1931 the company used his penchant for travel to assist him to establish a network of contacts with other modernists across Europe, which came to fruition with the publication of *The Modern House* in 1934, establishing Yorke's status as a modernist. In parallel with his activities in publishing he had also gained some reputation as a modern architect, though the projects were small and fees insufficient to provide a reasonable living. Yet he forged both aspects of his career into a complementary relationship, one supplying income and contacts, the other proving his standing as a modernist designer. In shaking those contacts and altering the nature of his design projects, war was not the ominous rumble of distant thunder but a real and visceral force in his circle of friends, colleagues and acquaintances. When the Prime Minister, Neville Chamberlain, characterised Czechoslovakia as a faraway country of which nothing was known, this must have seemed as inaccurate to Yorke as Chamberlain's announcement, broadcast over the wireless on 3 September, that a state of war existed between Britain and Germany was superfluous.[6]

Even with so much of his personal milieu in flux Yorke could not have foreseen how dramatically wartime conditions would alter the practice of modern architecture, from a struggle against public disinterest, small budgets and capricious local councils into an aspect of official government policy whose rewards could be lucrative. Paradoxically, war's drastic effects on his *modus operandi* of the 1930s brought about many preconditions which he had considered necessary for modern architecture to reach its full potential, such as the control of land development and research into industrial building techniques. Once reconstruction started in earnest it was these new and golden opportunities he perceived and pursued.

Many of these emerging openings grew out of circumstances which Yorke had experienced in the 1930s, though they did not come into focus until the wartime economy brought about a need for architects. Rather, as the suffragettes decided to suspend their civil disobedience for the duration of World War I to show that they were just as capable as men, and in return were enfranchised, so architects proved their capability for public service during World War II, and received their reward.[7]

With new legal recognition as a profession based on supposed technical proficiency, architects excelled; initially when working on facilities for munitions production and especially once the emphasis shifted to planning for post-war reconstruction: none more so than Yorke. The social, political and economic changes of wartime allowed him to turn the prominence he had achieved in pre-war modernist circles into prosperity, even if it meant adapting his views and eventually falling behind the most avant-garde design. Though still in its niche of complex building types like hospitals, law courts and airports, Yorke, Rosenberg & Mardall remained in the forefront for a generation after Yorke's death in 1962.

An investigation of the way Yorke fashioned his career during the 1930s, and how the circumstances of war absorbed and adapted it, sets the scene for understanding the firm's very existence and how and why he founded Yorke Rosenberg & Mardall. As this suggests, there was a demand for large stable architectural firms, it also helps to elucidate a crucial point in the wider history of architecture in Britain by looking at one episode where architecture, explicitly, became an instrument of public policy in constructing a new post-war society. Though this book does not attempt to explain fully this complex point, it does hope to offer some indications as to how it might be pursued further.

Two principal reasons make a study of Yorke a suitable vehicle for this historical explication. Firstly his career, dating from his qualification as an architect in 1930 to his death, aged 55, in 1962 fits well with the period when 'orthodox' modernism held sway in Britain. Had he lived another twenty or thirty years, as many of his peers did, he would have seen a significant reaction against modernism. How he would have responded cannot be assumed, though his response would certainly have obfuscated the clarity of his career as an example of modernism in Britain. Secondly, no other individual was so closely associated with the entire historical trajectory of modernism in Britain, from its origins in the 1930s to its flowering as the architectural idiom of the Welfare State in the 1940s and 1950s. After the war, many who had played active parts in modernist circles in the 1930s faded from the scene. Berthold Lubetkin, the driving force behind one of the finest firms, Tecton, took up pig farming. Godfrey Samuel, who introduced Tecton to many of its clients, left architectural practice to become secretary of the Royal Fine Art Commission, perhaps affected by the death of his partner Valentine Harding at Dunkirk. Maxwell Fry, to whom Yorke had slightly grudgingly conceded outright leadership of modernist architects in 1939, had more opportunities in West Africa and India than at home.[8] The Connell, Ward & Lucas partnership dissolved, with Amyas Connell working in East Africa and Basil Ward becoming a partner in the lower profile Murray, Ward & Partners, while Colin Lucas accepted relative anonymity in the London County Council's architects' department. Wells Coates never successfully re-established his practice after 1945.

Those who started to come to the fore after 1945 had experienced little, if any, of the pre-war tribulations. Ernö Goldfinger, who struggled to build his remarkably unassertive row of houses in Willow Road, Hampstead, in 1939, and Leslie Martin who co-edited *Circle* in 1937, do span the war years. But their reputations in the 1930s did not match Yorke's, nor did the levels theirs were to reach in the 1950s and 1960s. After 1945 other architects who had been virtually unknown in 1939 emerged quite rapidly, including Denys Lasdun, Gollins, Melvin & Ward, Powell & Moya, and Lyons, Israel & Ellis. Within a decade the Smithsons, Colin St John Wilson and James Stirling, all too young to have been active in 1939, had also achieved some repute, and contributed to the symbolic change of generation when Team X committed parricide against the *Congrès Internationaux d'Architecture Moderne* (CIAM).

As the only individual who successfully managed this change, Yorke's mode of practice encapsulates the elevation of modernism itself to a central role as the backdrop and crucible of public life in Britain. Through writing *The Modern House*, and as founding secretary of the MARS (Modern Architectural Research) Group, he was prominent among the pioneers of modernism in the 1930s. If Tecton's and Connell, Ward & Lucas' best houses are superior in composition and manipulation of canonic modernist forms, his finest work, at least, does not deserve the contempt Anthony Jackson showed for the house at Iver, Buckinghamshire, that Yorke designed in 1936.[9] By the end of the 1930s he had evolved a subtle and distinctive personal approach to design, as is shown by a glance at the curving, double-height, glass-fronted 'elephant room' he added in 1939 to a cottage in Sussex for the editor of the *News Chronicle*, Gerald Barry. Throughout the decade he also mingled easily with Berthold Lubetkin and others in the Tecton circle;[10] he was on intimate terms with the notoriously capricious Morton Shand and had an integral role in the Architectural Press.[11] He had friends outside architectural circles who were making significant contributions to modern life in their fields.[12] When refugees arrived from Nazi Germany he teamed up with Marcel Breuer, whose prestige was only slightly less than that of Fry's partner Walter Gropius, and probably equal to that of Erich Mendelsohn who worked with Serge Chermayeff. After Breuer left, Yorke had a partnership – albeit short-lived – with Arthur Korn, who had been a member of the Ring group of avant-garde architects in Berlin immediately after World War I. Yorke had travelled extensively in Europe and knew personally various continental architects, especially those in Czechoslovakia. His network of contacts supported his status as an *uomo moderno*. But with the formation of Yorke, Rosenberg & Mardall in 1944 he faced the post-war future with a stable, deliberately created and multi-skilled partnership. Exploiting opportunities which had not existed before, the firm soon began to give him and his partners the trappings of wealth.[13]

Yorke's ability to exploit what opportunities fell his way emerged before he became a committed modernist. He was adept at using his family background and connections to advance his ambitions. His father, Francis Walter Bagnall Yorke, was a successful architect in the Midlands and, though his design work differed considerably from his son's, they worked together on several occasions in the 1930s. When FRS Yorke was born in 1906 his father was about to start private practice and the milieu in which he operated influenced his son in several ways. Ultimately as a resident of a fairly grand house on one the best streets in Birmingham's most affluent suburb, Edgbaston, FWB Yorke belonged to the city's oligarchy whose unquestioned leaders in the early twentieth century were the Chamberlains. Following the ethos of this class, he did not send his son to a major public school and old university, but to school in Chipping Camden – perhaps for the town's Arts and Crafts associations which fitted FWB Yorke's architectural aspirations – and for higher education in his home city. The elite of Edgbaston, that had at various times included Chamberlains, Cadburys and Nettlefolds among its residents, rarely turned their wealth into land, and showed a lack of ambition for trappings of social successes like peerages that their counterparts in other industrial cities would have found baffling.[14] Yorke's views on this background are not recorded, but it would at least have suggested to him that education at Eton, Harrow or Winchester, followed by Oxford or Cambridge, was not an essential prerequisite for success. It might also have given him confidence in his own background and implied the existence of alternative power structures. His dealings with people from the conventional elite, whether his Westminster- and Oxford-educated MARS Group colleague Godfrey Samuel, whose father was a cabinet minister, or the provost and fellows of Eton, show little sign of a social inferiority complex.

Another strong aspect of Yorke's character was an extreme practicality. What theories he followed were generally adapted from other sources and, in his writings, are not especially interesting. His pragmatism comes out as much in the organisation of his life as in his design work. He arranged his lifestyle, pattern of work and domestic circumstances to suit his interests – not all of them strictly architectural – and when he arrived in London, following his marriage to Thelma Austen Jones in 1930, he showed an ability to splice together various sources of income to live well. Even in the 1930s, when his income from architectural practice was meagre, he ensured, largely through earnings from the Architectural Press and by persuading friends, colleagues and employees to become his tenants, that he could have a cottage in the country as well as a house in central London.

The most important of the early connections he made in London was the Architectural Press. It was crucial to Yorke's income, and played a significant part in the way modernism was introduced into Britain. Consequently the first chapter in this book analyses Yorke's activities in publishing in the 1930s, and especially the genesis of *The Modern House*. Through his friendship with Morton Shand, one of the Architectural Press's most important contributors at the time, Yorke augmented his contacts across Europe, and became the secretary of the MARS Group on its foundation in 1932. His connection with the Architectural Press was a fundamental component in his dual ambition of economic survival and proving his credentials as a modernist.

Much of Yorke's early work for the Architectural Press depended on his supposed understanding of construction techniques and materials, the subject of the second chapter. This helped to structure his perception of modernism, leading to an interest in industrial building methods and modern building products. Presenting modernism in this way helped to make it palatable to architects who were otherwise uninterested in its social or aesthetic theories, though such expertise also helped Yorke with clients who wanted to find cheaper means of construction or promote their products. Also, it was in his appreciation of construction and materials that Yorke developed his most personal designs. Even as his confidence that such an approach could yield appropriate solutions waned, his perception began to mesh with the Keynesian-inspired policies of the 1940s, which sought to provide full employment through industry which would produce all items necessary for the Welfare State. But Yorke had already been astute enough to realise that this approach would not, alone, solve the problem of housing.

Clients gave Yorke the chance to demonstrate the practical implications of his technical knowledge, and the third chapter looks at his client base. It adds to the range of reasons for commissioning modern architecture in the 1930s and helps to set out some basis for explaining why modernism was adopted so universally after 1945. While none of Yorke's projects in the 1930s was large, he did have to deal with wealthy, powerful and determined individuals, as well as with at least one venerable institution controlled by people who had more important matters on their minds than the small project he designed for them. Representing private wealth and public and cultural institutions, Yorke's clients in the 1930s cover in embryo the panoply of post-war clients. Their eventual acceptance of 'technical expertise' from defined 'experts' after 1945 is less of a bombshell and more of a continuation – albeit intensified – of existing trends.

Yorke forged these connections against the background of two major developments in the context of architectural practice which opened specific and contingent opportunities for him to exploit, and these form the subjects for the fourth and fifth chapters. Two Town and Country Planning Acts of Parliament, in 1932 and 1947, totally overhauled the statutory regulation of building controls across Britain. The first often seemed to create more problems than it solved, though the second brought about almost complete control of land development, creating new towns and enabling massive redevelopment of existing ones. Through Marcel Breuer, Yorke was associated with an early attempt in Britain to show that modernism could be compatible with the Garden City movement, which held an iron grip on many conceptions of planning both before and after the war. The Concrete Garden City they produced did not suggest a precise template for Yorke to follow, as it did for Breuer. Rather, it contributed to his formulation of a more personal attitude to planning which would come to fruition after the war, setting him slightly apart from the general view of the relationship between architecture and planning which held sway after 1945.

Similarly, two Architects Registration Acts in 1931 and 1938 heralded a significant change in the organisation of the architectural profession. These required anyone who wanted to use the

Francis Walter Bagnall Yorke striking a pose characteristic of a slightly dandified Arts and Crafts architect of the early twentieth century.

Yorke's parents and parents-in-law (from left to right) on the day of his wedding to Thelma Austen Jones, 13 August 1930.

title 'architect' to prove their qualifications and to register with the Architects Registration Council of the United Kingdom, and progressively they had a huge impact on architectural education and practice. Armed with this new status, architects made an easily defined body with what appeared to be an easily defined purpose, though the difficulties over accommodating refugees from Nazi Europe who might have been as distinguished as Walter Gropius and Marcel Breuer posed an early challenge to this cosy assumption. These circumstances set the material pattern within which Yorke began his career, the benefits of such a Kite mark of definable expertise meshed neatly with the label he slowly acquired as a technical expert, in the construction and planning of complex building types that would become common after 1945. As well as defining 'experts', registration helped to create an appreciation of the value their expertise might have. Even though Yorke did not make his views of professional politics explicit in the 1930s, the course of his career is eloquent testimony to its unfolding development. During the 1930s his lifestyle was close to that of an apocryphal Bohemian artist, implying he had little direct interest in professional politics. It was his war work, though tedious and frustrating, that exposed him to the inner workings of a large organisation and provided a model of how he could achieve success.

These five themes all deal with generic issues that might apply to almost any study of almost any architect in almost any context. But they are particularly relevant to understanding how Yorke's career relates to the circumstances of his time, and therefore help to generate an insight into his contribution to an important episode of British architectural history. They do not set out to be definitive studies of say, planning in Britain between 1930 and 1950, or of pre-fabrication and its impact on building production. Their terms are limited by the book's mono-graphical framework, but that has the advantage of helping to set the themes in relation to each other, which a study of a single aspect could not do. Nor are these themes the only ones that would be necessary to build up an accurate picture of architecture in Britain during the 1930s. Education, for example, especially at the Architectural Association, attracted considerable controversy, but this was one part of the architectural world in which Yorke seems to have had very little interest, perhaps because of unhappy experiences as a student. Overall this quintet of angles begins to offer a template for explaining how and why modernism became so important a factor in British society.

The book's final chapter is a memoir of Yorke written by David Allford, who first met him in 1952, having corresponded briefly with him in 1944. He joined Yorke, Rosenberg & Mardall shortly after that meeting and worked closely with Yorke. He became a partner in 1958 and chairman after the firm's incorporation in 1987 until his retirement two years later. He wrote his memoir in various phases between 1992 and 1996, and it remained incomplete when he died in 1997.[15] Naturally it draws heavily on personal memories, though he corroborated some of it with others who had known Yorke and more is borne out in the historical record. Allford was an architect rather than a historian and his appreciation of Yorke came from personal experience rather than the methods of history. His memoir gives a direct impression of Yorke's character, which in turn helps to suggest how and why he reacted to opportunities in the way he did, complementing the historical investigations of the earlier chapters. Allford's writing has an immediacy and perception that makes it a historical source in itself as well as an appraisal of Yorke's career and personality.

Clearly David Allford only knew Yorke after the partnership was founded and his memoir sets Yorke against its background. Yorke's career had already almost reached its halfway point when he formed the partnership, and his previous experiences were crucial in his decision to do so and in the pattern it took. This suggested that a study of the first part of Yorke's career would be essential to understanding the second, and that it begged different treatment to the story of the partnership, which remained open-ended. This task, forming the first five chapters, fell to Jeremy Melvin. As the book's form evolved, identifying which parts of Yorke's life might be relevant to the study became easier. It is not a biography and does not delve deeply into his family background, beyond the strong bond he had with his father; his private life, however colourful, had little bearing on his significance as an architect.

One aspect of this book's long gestation is a significant change in the possibilities for research. At the outset, in 1991, numerous members of Yorke's generation were still alive, including his partner from 1944, Cyril Mardall, his collaborator from 1936 and partner from 1958, Randall Evans, and Sir James Richards, a colleague from the Architectural Press and lodger in Yorke's house from 1933. As they died over the following few years, understanding the 1930s and 1940s became even less ambiguously an exercise of historical research rather than a collection of memories. To some extent that informed the decision that the book should be about Yorke himself rather than the Yorke, Rosenberg & Mardall partnership. In 1972 the firm commissioned a book on its first three decades, with an introduction by the historian Reyner Banham; and in 1992 Alan Powers curated an exhibition and wrote the accompanying catalogue, both of which deal with the partnership first and foremost. Individuals appear, where at all, fleetingly. In different ways these set markers for investigating the practice, but not the individuals within it.[16]

This is far from saying that Yorke's personality played no role in his career. Allford's memoir portrays someone who was determined but charming, at ease in any social group, a shrewd judge of character and of the tactics he might adopt to ensure the outcome he wanted. Surviving pictures of his parents suggest that they had these characteristics between them. His father appears gentle with something of the *fin-de-siècle* dandy about him, though he also had the ability to follow a successful career as an architect, while his mother, more foursquare, speaks of determination. If they mingled with neighbours in Edgbaston, Yorke would have been familiar with the names, at least, of several powerful and well-connected families, and Neville Chamberlain was the Member of Parliament for Edgbaston from 1929 to 1940.

Whatever he took from his family, there is no doubt that Yorke was a compelling person. With a gargantuan appetite, and not just for food, he had an ability to fascinate people of either sex. Even while dying he retained a sense of humour and hospitality. Colin Penn remembered a crate of beer somehow smuggled in, and Raglan Squire expressed regret that he had not accepted the invitation to see his ailing friend.[17] Christabel Bielenberg recalled Yorke and his wife Thelma as by far the most attractive and entertaining couple in a dreary Austrian hotel. Given her Harmsworth uncles, Astor colleagues and circle of friends in the doomed plot against Adolf Hitler, she has known some of the most fascinating personalities of the twentieth century. While learning to 'stenbogen' Christabel and the Yorkes obviously enjoyed each other's company.[18] Yorke's personality did not create the circumstances that shaped his career, however, it can hardly have hindered his ability to exploit them, just as his intelligence and experience enabled him to identify them. In his ability to adapt to the new circumstances during and after the war Yorke proved himself to be pre-eminent among his contemporaries. What makes that eminence all the more impressive forty years after his death is that it stemmed from an appreciation of the pitfalls of orthodox modernism, as much as its potential advantages.

Notes

1. Nikolaus Pevsner, *Pioneers of Modern Design*, first published as *Pioneers of the Modern Movement*, Faber (London), 1936.

2. One particularly influential attack is David Watkin's *Morality and Architecture*, first published in 1977 and reissued in revised form as *Morality and Architecture Revisited*, John Murray (London), 2001. Another is Christopher Booker's 1979 film for BBC television, *City of Towers*. Both took what were then unfashionably right-wing political stances.

3. The letter is dated 30 July 1939. On 3 August Yorke wrote to EJ 'Bobby' Carter, librarian of the RIBA and secretary to its refugees committee, to ask his help for Rogers. Both letters are among the papers of the RIBA's Refugees Committee.

4. Letter from Hoffmeister to Yorke, dated 25 August 1939 in the RIBA YoF/1/12. 'Kay', or just 'K', was the nickname which, following his wife Thelma, many of Yorke's friends used, supposedly because during Territorial Army camps in the late 1920s an adjutant called out 'Yor-kay'. To his family and other friends, especially those at the Architectural Press, Yorke was known as Reg or Reggie, presumably to distinguish him from his father, whose first name was also Francis. Yorke's mother's name was Mary Stevens.

5. See, for example a contract dated 3 August 1939 for £120 10s worth of renovations to almshouses in Hawkhurst, Kent, which contained a provision to terminate the contract within 28 days of the outbreak of war. RIBA YoF/1/2.

6. Chamberlain's exact words referred to 'a quarrel in a far away country between people of whom we know nothing', and '. . . unless we heard by 11 o'clock that they were at once prepared to withdraw their troops from Poland, a state of war would exist between us [ie Britain and Germany]'. *See The Oxford Dictionary of Quotations*, Oxford University Press, 1999, p 200, item 17; p 201, item 1. The items come from a wireless broadcast of 27 September, quoted in *The Times* of 28 September 1938, and a wireless broadcast of 3 September 1939 respectively.

7. And it was a reward. The mandatory fee scale which was in force until the early 1980s gave architects a minimum of six per cent of the construction cost of new buildings, more for refurbishments.

8. FRS Yorke and Colin Penn *A Key to Modern Architecture*, Blackie (London and Glasgow), p 45.

9. Anthony Jackson, *The Politics of Modern Architecture*, Architectural Press (London), 1970, p 103. Jackson comments about the house: 'Typical in its fussiness, the building uses 19 outside vertical angles to house a conventional set of rooms.' Mixing subjective measures like fussiness and convention with objective ones such as the number of outside angles hints at a critical filter that shows little empathy with the circumstances of the time, and in particular the difficulties of finding a site for this house. It also overlooks the fact that neither Yorke nor any of his colleagues would have held up this house as his best. Torilla's living room, for example, could hardly be called conventional. Judgement of modern architecture in Britain quickly became subject to normative prescriptions, especially narrow interpretations of Le Corbusier. For an analysis of this view see Adrian Forty, 'Le Corbusier's British reputation' in Michael Raeburn and Victoria Wilson (eds), *Le Corbusier: Architect of the Century*, The Arts Council (London), 1987, pp 35–41. Yorke was much less adulatory of Le Corbusier than some of his peers, and looked more to Germany and Czechoslovakia for formal influence.

10. Several letters from the late 1930s between Yorke and Godfrey Samuel exist among Samuel's papers at the RIBA. Though not obviously close friends, they are cordial and respectful, especially where Yorke held some promise of publishing Samuel's work. Clearly the patronage did not all come from sons of cabinet ministers. See letters dated 6 January 1937 and Yorke's reply of two days later: SaG/74/6 and SaG/75/1. The latter folder has several further letters between them.

11. Letters dated 13 November 1939, 21 June and 1 October 1940, and 20 April 1941 from Shand to Yorke are in the RIBA YoF/1/12.

12. The most notable of these was Patrick Blackett (1897–1978), a distinguished physicist who collected a Fellowship of the Royal Society, Nobel Prize, life peerage and the Order of Merit. A letter from him to Yorke dated 2 July 1940, clearly showing they were on friendly terms, is in the RIBA YoF/1/12.

13. Interestingly the wealth the three partners accumulated was channelled into very conventional magnets for successful bourgeois expenditure. The firm's accounts, surviving but as yet uncatalogued at the RIBA, record ownership in the 1950s of expensive motorcars like Bentleys, Alvises and Aston Martins, as well as a couple of Jaguars. Yorke himself became a landowner, having purchased a farm in Oxfordshire, Mardall became an enthusiastic yachtsman and Rosenberg collected contemporary art.

14. The story of Birmingham elites is a fascinating one. Often Nonconformist and frequently Unitarian, until well into the 19th century they were barred from official positions in British public life, yet many were making significant contributions to intellectual and business life. See Jenny Uglow, *The Lunar Men*, Faber and Faber (London), 2002 for a study of 'the friends who made the future', including the engineer Matthew Boulton, manufacturer Josiah Wedgwood, physician Erasmus Darwin (grandfather of Charles), and chemist and Unitarian minister Joseph Priestley.

15. What appears in this book was put together from David Allford's drafts by his son Simon and Jeremy Melvin, with assistance from Gail Novelle.

16. *The Architecture of Yorke, Rosenberg, Mardall, 1944–1972* (with an introduction by Reyner Banham), Lund Humphries (London), 1972. Alan Powers, *In the Line of Development*, RIBA Heinz Gallery (London), 1992. The exhibition ran from 10 September to 17 November that year.

17. Discussion between Jeremy Melvin and Colin Penn, July 1992; and Raglan Squire, *Portrait of an Architect*, Smythe (Gerrards Cross), 1984, p 180.

18. See Christabel Bielenberg's letter to Yorke, dated 20 July 1934, in the RIBA Yorke archive, Box 1 Folder 7. On 14 January 1999, in a telephone conversation with Jeremy Melvin, Mrs Bielenberg recalled how she and her husband-to-be enjoyed the Yorkes' company in the 'terribly dull' hotel where they had met the previous winter. In *The Past is Myself*, Chatto and Windus (London), 1968, republished Corgi, 1984, she gives an account of her and her husband's friendships with the German plotters against Hitler, especially Adam von Trott. In the second part of her autobiography, *The Road Ahead*, Bantam (London), 1992, pp 124–31, she gives a typically vivid account of her Uncle Cecil, later Lord Harmsworth. Other uncles included Lord Northcliffe and the first Lord Rothermere.

CHAPTER 1

PUBLISHING ARCHITECTURE IN THE 1930s

The Architectural Press and *The Modern House*

By the end of 1934 the introduction of European modernism into Britain became irreversible. During that year several established but loose threads began to draw together, weaving the social and intellectual fabric from which modernism in Britain would take its distinctive course within the context of architecture. It may not have been apparent at the time, as 1934 drew to a close the seeds which shaped modernism had taken root. Among these threads – and reaching a far larger audience than the small number of modernist buildings – were the activities of publishers, especially the Architectural Press.

For the cover illustration of *The Modern House*, Yorke chose a drawing by the American architect HT Fisher, not a conventional icon of European modernism.

In 1934 the RIBA celebrated its centenary and moved to new headquarters, an event inevitably attended by a certain amount of navel-gazing. The construction industry began to emerge from the depression of the early 1930s, led largely by publicly funded and subsidised private housebuilding. Although very little was recognisably 'modern', it did at least increase the sparse opportunities for architects who aspired to CIAM's ideals.[1] It was the year of the BBC debate between the aged, cantankerous Sir Reginald Blomfield and the thrusting, young modernist Amyas Connell which appeared to institutionalise the confrontation between modernists and traditionalists along generational lines, a theme which would recur repeatedly.[2] It was also the year the first refugees started to arrive following the Nazis' takeover of power in Germany in 1933. *The Architects' Journal* threw down a challenge to the British Union of Fascists to explain their architectural views, anticipating the perception of modernism as progressive and socialist, and traditional architecture as reactionary and narrowly nationalist.[3] Although not yet recognised in mainstream politics, the threat of Fascism was beginning to be perceived in other quarters.

Against these broad and significant trends, the publication of a mere book might barely register. But many of the peculiarities which modernism adopted in Britain are foreshadowed in FRS Yorke's book *The Modern House*.[4] Its success was huge. By far and away Yorke's best and most widely read book, it went through three editions before 1939, two wartime editions, and three after the war, remaining in print until his death in 1962. It was the first introduction to European modernism for many people, including, at an interval of thirty years, the authors of this study.[5]

Widely reviewed on publication, its reputation endured. Writing a review in the *Spectator*, GM Boumphrey advised, 'Mr Yorke's book is by far the best on its subject [ie modern architecture] that has yet appeared . . . It would be expensive folly for any layman to think of building a house today without first reading this book – or seeing that his architect had done so'.[6] Much later, in an appreciation of Yorke written after his death, Max Fry recalled, '*The Modern House* . . . showed us where we stood, introduced us to architects . . . acted as an open sesame for a new type of continental tour . . . set standards of excellence by which we could measure ourselves . . . I find it hard to overestimate the value of that book'.[7] At either end of its published life, The *Modern House* was recognised as one of the most important documents of its time.

There are many reasons why *The Modern House* made such an impression. Clearly it appeared at a propitious moment, when people were hungry for a book on modern architecture and just

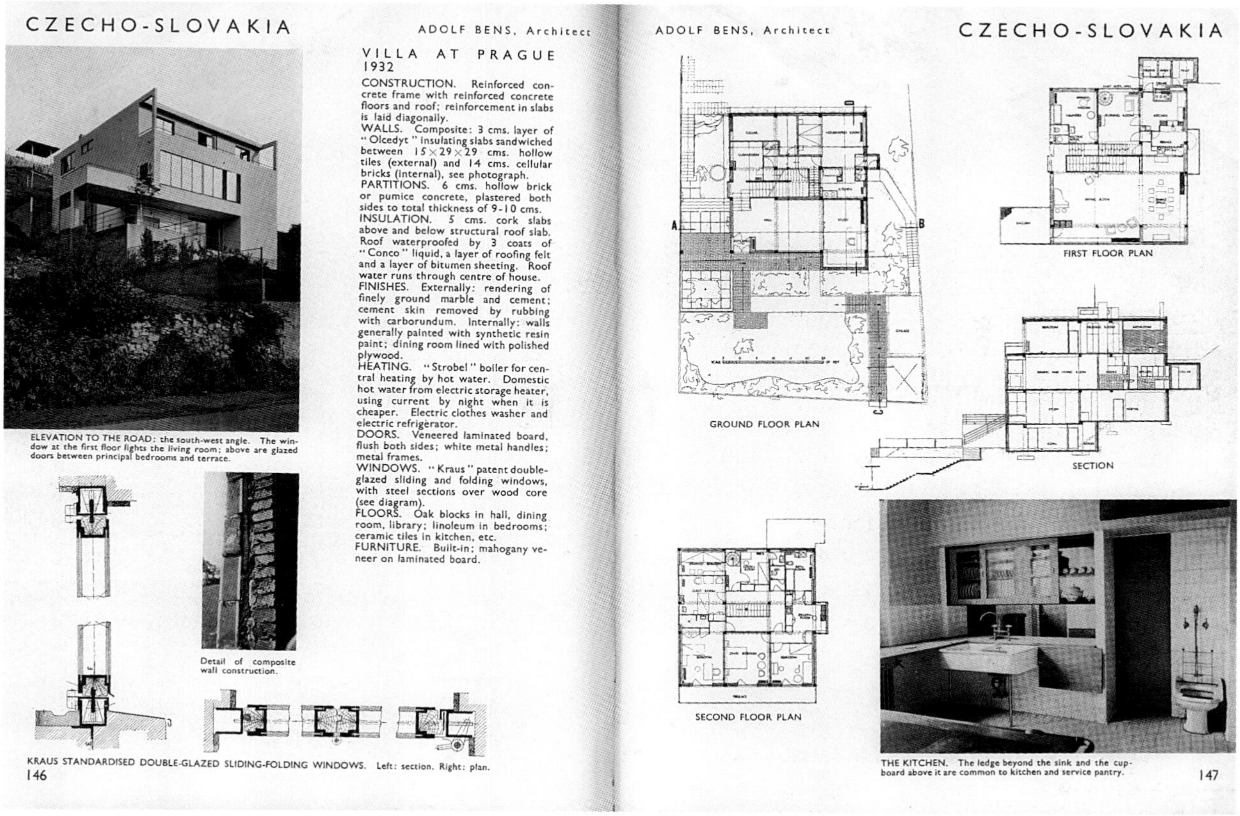

CZECHO-SLOVAKIA

ADOLF BENS, Architect

VILLA AT PRAGUE
1932

CONSTRUCTION. Reinforced concrete frame with reinforced concrete floors and roof; reinforcement in slabs is laid diagonally.
WALLS. Composite: 3 cms. layer of "Olcedyt" insulating slabs sandwiched between 15×29×29 cms. hollow tiles (external) and 14 cms. cellular bricks (internal), see photograph.
PARTITIONS. 6 cms. hollow brick or pumice concrete, plastered both sides to total thickness of 9-10 cms.
INSULATION. 5 cms. cork slabs above and below structural roof slab. Roof waterproofed by 3 coats of "Conco" liquid, a layer of roofing felt and a layer of bitumen sheeting. Roof water runs through centre of house.
FINISHES. Externally: rendering of finely ground marble and cement; cement skin removed by rubbing with carborundum. Internally: walls generally painted with synthetic resin paint; dining room lined with polished plywood.
HEATING. "Strobel" boiler for central heating by hot water. Domestic hot water from electric storage heater, using current by night when it is cheaper. Electric clothes washer and electric refrigerator.
DOORS. Veneered laminated board, flush both sides; white metal handles; metal frames.
WINDOWS. "Kraus" patent double-glazed sliding and folding windows, with steel sections over wood core (see diagram).
FLOORS. Oak blocks in hall, dining room, library; linoleum in bedrooms; ceramic tiles in kitchen, etc.
FURNITURE. Built-in; mahogany veneer on laminated board.

ELEVATION TO THE ROAD: the south-west angle. The window at the first floor lights the living room; above are glazed doors between principal bedrooms and terrace.

Detail of composite wall construction.

KRAUS STANDARDISED DOUBLE-GLAZED SLIDING-FOLDING WINDOWS. Left: section. Right: plan.

146

ADOLF BENS, Architect

CZECHO-SLOVAKIA

GROUND FLOOR PLAN

FIRST FLOOR PLAN

SECTION

SECOND FLOOR PLAN

THE KITCHEN. The ledge beyond the sink and the cupboard above it are common to kitchen and service pantry.

147

Pages from *The Modern House*, showing a villa in Prague by Adolf Bens, one of the architects of the remarkable Czech Functionalism movement that Yorke brought to the attention of English-speaking readers.

as the conditions for practising architecture were irrevocably changing. *The Modern House*, although not the first work on the subject, was easily the most digestible, with striking graphic design and relatively unencumbered by text.[8] It could be read purely as a picture book with 128 pages devoted to illustrations of fifty-seven house designs from fourteen countries, while a more literary reader could plough through the written chapters at the beginning and end. These give a clear, if somewhat limited and not entirely original, account of the nature of modern architecture. As Fry implies, an impoverished, inexperienced architect could turn to *The Modern House* as a source book, almost a religious text.

The Modern House is a critical event in the architectural maelstrom of 1934. Derived from background and education, his ideas were moulded by subsequent experiences and contacts, and in producing *The Modern House*, by a publishing policy which tempered enlightenment with commercial shrewdness. Although it appropriated an established genre of books about domestic architecture, *The Modern House* was refreshingly cosmopolitan and introduced new graphics and buildings to British readers – many of the architects and their repertoire of houses had never been published in the UK before.[9] *The Modern House* was a publishing and architectural achievement: just as a definition of architecture has to cover more than modernism, so it also segues into publishing. The book's triumph was that the strictures of publishing, its mode of production, did not absolutely dominate reader's perceptions. The skills and experiences of an individual meshed with the context of architectural practice, theory and publishing helped shape a uniquely influential document in the early development of modern architecture in Britain.

RIGHT: Lois Welzenbacher's Haus Rosenbauer, overlooking the Danube Valley, was the first house of those Yorke picked for *The Modern House* which he described in *The Architectural Review*.

BELOW: Yorke made this measured drawing of the Landor House in Warwick (named for the poet Walter Savage Landor) as a student at the Birmingham School of Art, and reused it for his earliest traceable publication in *The Architects' Journal*.

British Architectural Library, RIBA, London.

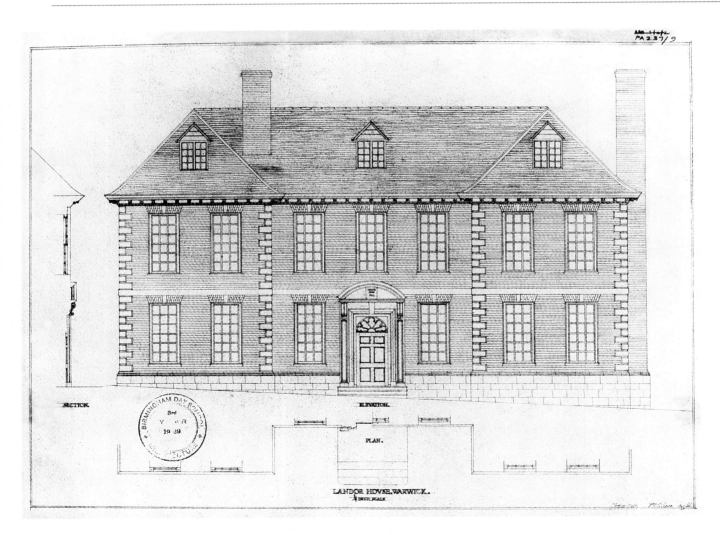

To invert David Watkin's comment on the failure of Blomfield's *Modernismus* published in the same year, *The Modern House* could be described as written by the right person at the right time.[10] In 1934, just as the construction industry was picking up, the seeds of political questions which became crucial by the end of the decade were being sown, and the British architectural world was receptive to a specifically national interpretation of the phenomenon of European modernism, well publicised, widely available and attractively presented.[11] It did not want a grouchy, reactionary attack on modernity written by an aged architect who could, with a certain amount of justification, be accused of hypocrisy. *The Modern House* happened, or at least took its form, as a result of Yorke's areas of knowledge coinciding with his publisher's commercial and ideological needs, which in turn both suited and shaped the contemporary mood.

But the book is not without its flaws. *The Modern House* combines three themes that later haunted architectural thought: determinism, both historical and materialist, and a subliminal impression that architecture is about skilful composition of form and little more. All have their origins in the book's genesis and were resolved to suit the needs of publishing, rather than an altruistic view of modern architecture and its potential for social amelioration, whatever the text might appear to say. Examining the book's origin, from the point of view of its author, publishers, and the context into which it was assimilated, is no less than a dissection of the architectural attitudes of its generation.[12] Both a recipient of and an active contributor to historical circumstances, it is influenced as much by the exigencies of experience as by a grand vision of the future.

Why was Francis Reginald Stevens Yorke the 'right person'? By 1934 he was already established as an advocate of contemporary architecture. At the recommendation of Morton Shand – whose enthusiasm for things continental and knowledge of languages placed him in the first rank of British commentators on European modernism – Yorke became secretary of the MARS group, established in 1932 as the British branch of the *Congrès Internationale d'Architecture Moderne* (CIAM) following an approach to Shand from CIAM's redoubtable secretary Sigfried Giedion. In 1933, *The Architects' Journal* described Yorke as '. . . well-known as one of the most progressive younger architects'.[13] Yorke's reputation rested almost entirely on publishing, as at this stage his credentials as an experienced architect were tenuous: the few buildings to which his name can be attached were designed in partnership and are undistinguished.[14]

Yorke's background was actually far more interesting and complex than his reputation as a young expert on modern architecture suggests. From an early age he was immersed in the influences which shaped the Arts and Crafts architects. He was born on the 3 December 1906, the son of a proficient architect, FWB Yorke, whose work veered gently between neo-Georgian and Arts and Crafts and was occasionally published in architectural periodicals.[15] Yorke junior went to school in Chipping Camden, a hotbed of Arts and Crafts thinking, and a town whose buildings appealed to Arts and Crafts architects. Later he studied at Birmingham School of Art (1924–30), whose principal in architecture, George Drysdale, had studied at the École des Beaux Arts in Paris.[16] Despite the formal classical basis of the course, an Arts and Crafts influence was also filtering through tenuous links with WR Lethaby. Throughout his life, Yorke retained an interest in craft, although it is more visually obvious in work of the late 1930s and post-war period.[17]

When Yorke came to London on leaving Birmingham in February 1930, he began to ally these interests with the embryonic avant-garde enthusiasm for modern architecture. After a year with Campbell-Jones, Son & Smithers, he established a relationship with the Architectural Press, the leading but not the only publishers of modernism. His first traceable publication was a measured drawing of the Landor House, an attractive eighteenth-century building on Leamington Road, Warwick, in *The Architects' Journal* of April 8 1931.[18] The following year Yorke and the engineer

WEJ Budgen provided primers for architectural students sitting their intermediate and final structures exams set by the RIBA.[19] Yorke was acquiring a reputation as a technical expert, to the extent that on 22 March 1933, *The Architects' Journal* was able to announce that he would write the weekly 'Trade Notes' column – a review of new materials and products – as he possessed a '. . . unique knowledge of materials and is in close contact with the work of British manufacturers'.[20]

Within three years Yorke had 'modernised', or at least 'industrialised' the knowledge of materials he brought from his background and education. Retaining an essentially Arts and Crafts view that architecture derived from components, their manufacture and assembly, he had embraced the process of industrial production and its products. This was fundamental to his interpretation of modern architecture, and to the formation of *The Modern House*. Sir James Richards, who joined the Architectural Press in 1933, remembered Yorke's role there primarily as a technical expert, seeking this knowledge from him rather than his opinion as a straightforward critic.[21] Technical expertise, particularly relating to industrialised production of building components, is one aspect of *The Modern House* where Yorke's skills neatly matched the Architectural Press's programme.[22] Chapter titles like 'Wall and Window', and 'Roof', and a section on 'Experimental and prefabricated houses', suggest Yorke's approach was to present modern houses through their construction, rather than the dynamic play of platonic solids in light, or social amelioration.[23]

Here lurks a belief that architectural form derives from its materials and construction techniques. Yorke wrote, 'The new materials are light, strong, mobile; their aesthetic is other than that of piled-up mass masonry . . .'; 'Modern materials and construction and the shapes produced by them have an intrinsic beauty which needs no embellishment . . .'. There is plenty of ammunition in the book for anyone wanting to accuse Yorke of simple, reductivist and derivative arguments.[24] For Yorke, the starting point is 'the *new functional plan*' [his italics]. 'There is only one law for [the typical form of an industrial product]; that it shall be entirely appropriate to its purpose', he opined, to the accompaniment of pictures of North Michigan Avenue in Chicago and the liner *Europa*.[25] He had learnt his lessons and sources well. Knowledge of the products on the market did not necessarily give him licence to transcend the received wisdom of progressive architecture of the time.

Yorke's international contacts were also valuable to the Architectural Press. Between 1929 and 1932 he spent a total of five months travelling on the European mainland, visiting Italy, Germany and Czechoslovakia.[26] That these voyages began before he arrived in London attests to his parents' affluence, but also suggests some shrewd self-motivation. Contacts with architects in these countries were facilitated after he joined the Architectural Press, especially through Morton Shand. Their fruits occasionally became apparent in the company's flagship publication, *The Architectural Review*. In February 1932, for example, there was a feature on Lois Welzenbacher's Haus Rosenbauer overlooking the Danube valley, which was included in the book two years later.[27] This feature makes a change from most of Yorke's other contributions to *The Architectural Review*, which started in the second half of 1931 and tended to be on craft and trade matters.

It is remarkable how the Architectural Press managed to exploit, nurture and bring to fulfilment Yorke's particular interests and experiences.[28] English by background and education, yet as knowledgeable as any contemporary architect about developments abroad, Yorke's experiences shaped the book. He virtually introduced Czech modernism to Britain, and showed that German modernism was deeper than Gropius and Mendelsohn. Of the fifty-seven house designs featured in the first edition, thirty-nine come from the Europe including one from the USSR. Thus Heinrich Lauterbach rubs shoulders with Mies, Ladislav Zak with Le Corbusier. Although paying lip service to the CIAMesque view of modern architecture – already firmly established by 1934 when political circumstances in Germany ended any real debate about the nature of modernism and

OPPOSITE TOP: A small villa in Prague designed by Yorke's friends Josef Havlicek and Karel Honzik. Honzik collaborated with Yorke on the early stages of *The Modern House*, and although they ultimately disagreed on its precise emphasis his influence is apparent throughout.

BOTTOM LEFT: Yorke was fascinated by novel forms of construction, such as that used by Richard Neutra for the Lovell House in Los Angeles.

BOTTOM RIGHT: This house by Gudolf Blaksted and Herman Munthe-Kaas for a doctor near Oslo survived many editions of *The Modern House*, despite its variance from CIAM's proscriptions.

Photo: O Vaering.

Heinrich Lauterbach's Haus Hasek in Gablonz, now Jablonec in the Czech Republic, which Yorke featured in his book and whose raised main floor with wrapping terrace later inspired an early scheme for his first house, Torilla.

Sigfried Giedion's deft handling had more or less elided the so-called 'other tradition' represented by Scharoun and Häring – Yorke did retain a catholic range of examples.[29] Blaksted & Munthe-Kaas's house, for example, would hardly make a conventional CIAM text book.

The main departure from a CIAMesque line was again informed by Yorke's interest in construction. Each architect was asked to supply details of: type of construction and general structural materials; walls – filling walls and partitions; insulation against sound, weather, heat, roof construction and insulation; heating and ventilation systems; water heating in kitchen and bathroom, type of kitchen range; windows; doors, handles, frames etc; floor and pavings; furniture if built in, type and material; internal/external wall finish; and special arrangements.[30]

Yorke also showed enthusiasm for developments in America, although he did not visit the United States until after the war. Lawrence Kocher, editor of *The Architectural Record*, received a generous acknowledgement from Yorke. Yorke appreciated America's technical prowess, as shown by the predominance of American examples in the section on 'Experimental and prefabricated houses'. He favoured European immigrants such as Richard Neutra, William Lescaze and Kocher's partner Albert Frey rather than native Americans. Kocher & Frey, for example, are featured fourfold while Frank Lloyd Wright is represented by one small illustration.

Yorke particularly liked the prefabricated houses, and his tastes were gratified by his contacts with Lawrence Kocher, and the *Architectural Record*. Their dominance of the section on 'prefabricated and experimental houses' and Yorke's lack of first hand experience of the United States is yet more evidence of his dual interests shaping the book. Through Kocher he had access to work by Buckminster Fuller, Kocher & Frey and especially General Houses, one of whose examples graced the dust jacket. This is a significant decision, for Yorke could easily have chosen the Villa Savoye or the Haus Tugendhat, both of which were included in the book. Either would have been in line with the CIAM version of modernism. But for the principle image of *The Modern House*, he selected a drawing by the almost unknown HT Fisher, founder of General Houses, because it was the apogee of his reading of modern architecture. Yorke's interest in modern materials and construction overrode the already established European canon. An article about General Houses, probably by Yorke, had been published in *The Architects' Journal* in 1933, and explained something about this Chicago-based supplier of prefabricated homes.[31] William Lescaze was another European-born American architect to receive considerable coverage, whose book *What is Modern Architecture?* Yorke cited in 1933.[32]

By privileging prefabrication and industrial construction over an architect of the distinction and reputation of Wright, *The Modern House* began to shift an understanding of modernism towards an interpretation which could be broken down into an emphasis on materials and products, a development whose commercial benefits could hardly have been lost on the Architectural Press. Here lurked both the ghost of the Arts and Crafts movement, and the embryo of materialist determinism. But there was another equally important component of the publishing strategy, the decision to make the book about modern houses, rather than modernism in general.

Clues about this decision can be found in an undated letter to Yorke from Karel Honzik, of the Prague architectural firm Havlicek & Honzik.[33] In his acknowledgements, Yorke placed on record his '. . . indebtedness to . . . Honzik, who has supplied me with much of the material that has made the production of this book possible'.[34] Havlicek & Honzik were among the talented architects first published in Britain in *The Modern House*. Honzik's letter shows that some misunderstanding had arisen. 'I really supposed till to day, that the book is to deal with architecture generally, not only with the domestic house', wrote Honzik, a subject which with a curiously central European combination of charm and pessimism, he considered 'ten times greater . . . than about the architecture generally'. He gave Yorke much food for thought. 'We cannot estimate the villa, which is built in the modern stile [sic] as a definite [sic] result of the functional architecture. A villa is a descendant of a medieval aristocratic castle . . . the greatest part of the population does not live in them, they have not enough money for it . . .', points which Yorke implicitly acknowledged in his introduction to *The Modern House*, '. . . the author does not pretend that the building of villas is a good or even a possible solution to the problem of housing the people''.[35] Yorke circumvented this problem by claiming the villa as a vehicle for experiment and including much on prefabricated buildings, a line that Honzik had implicitly suggested by mentioning American 'steel houses which are built in six days'. Honzik however, sought greater comprehensiveness by looking at flats and houses, and obviously saw no real distinction between the two types of domestic architecture. To Yorke, or at least his publishers, there was both a distinction and a commercial opportunity, as in 1938, with Frederick Gibberd, Yorke was to write *The Modern Flat*.[36]

Honzik concludes with several suggestions: taking another year at least to work on a book about domestic architecture, including both flats and houses; or limiting themselves to either the villa, or modern architecture generally. Villas do not 'need such long studying' while a less specific theme would 'permit us . . . to make the book more belefistic [sic]'. For a young architect in a hurry, and moreover one whose cultural and personal background made ideology suspicious, and a shrewd publisher in the background, there was only one choice. Although the collaboration did not go ahead as planned, Yorke and Honzik remained on friendly terms and Honzik's influence in the book is strong, both in the numerous central European examples and in the way Yorke worded the text to deal with the issues Honzik raised.

The introduction to *The Modern House*, Yorke acknowledged 'the housing problem', and suggests 'the solution . . . lies . . . in a reformed type of flat dwelling and controlled land development'.[37] Had Yorke wanted to write about domestic architecture, by 1934 he could have chosen examples of housing schemes as opposed to individual houses. There were the Hofeisenseidlung, Onkel Toms Hutte and Siemenstadt in Berlin; numerous *seidlungen* from Frankfurt; at a pinch he could have included Le Corbusier's Pavillion Suisse, and he even hints darkly at 'a thorough analysis of the situation followed by extreme experiments' in the USSR.[38] Honzik explicitly mentioned Frankfurt and Milyutin's work in Russia. So Yorke's assertion that, 'There have been many projects for the lay-out of groups of flat blocks . . . but there has been little actual development', is a trifle disingenuous.[39] The reasons why *The Modern House* took its format lie elsewhere.

There were numerous international precedents for such a theme. *The Architectural Record* carried frequent surveys of domestic architecture. More specific was 'Die Wohnung Unserer Zeit' (The dwelling of our Time) by Ludwig Hilberseimer and published in *Die Form* in 1931.[40] Several buildings featured in *The Modern House* were also shown by Hilberseimer, including a house by Adolf Rading, the Berlin Bauaustellung flat by Lilly Reich, and both used the same Gropius illustration of Tortensiedlung development in Dessau.[41] Themes of the internationalism of modern architecture and the suitability of modern components are not the only constituents of the book. Yorke, like many of his MARS contemporaries, did believe that architecture had a social role.

The strongest clues for the format of *The Modern House* can be found in the history of architectural publishing in Britain. During the first third of the twentieth century an vast number of books about English domestic architecture appeared. Herman Muthesius' seminal *Das Englische Haus*[42] was probably the most authoritative survey of English housing design of its date, but by no means the first. *Country Life*, founded in 1897, also devoted considerable attention to contemporary house design by architects like Sir Edwin Lutyens. By the end of the 1920s books about English houses had become a familiar genre, from a variety of publishers like the Studio,

Left: A house in Prague by Eugen Linhart, another fine example of Czech Functionalism.

Below: Yorke had to redraw the plans Linhart supplied for publication in a far cruder style.

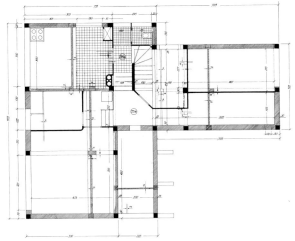

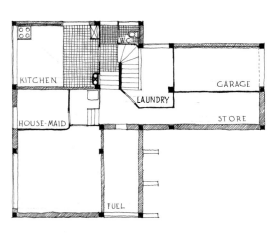

Country Life and the Architectural Press. The sentiments and examples in each are hard to distinguish. Many have titles in any permutation of the words 'modern', 'house' and 'English'.[43] What these words implied was often a long way from the interpretation of Yorke and his fellow modernists.

The plethora of these books must have caused a potential for confusion among the architectural book-buying public. At the opposite extreme from Yorke was Randal Phillips' *The Modern English House* published by Country Life in 1927. It contains the discovery that modern kitchen equipment allowed the scullery to be eliminated and the space saved to be used as a servant's sitting room. 'This arrangement', Phillips wrote, 'applies more particularly to the smaller type of house'.[44] This may have puzzled someone who understood small houses as *existenz minimum*. True there are dwellings in *The Modern House* have some servants' accommodation, but these are larger examples and planning for a servantless lifestyle is far closer to Yorke's political aims.[45]

In 1929 the Architectural Press published *Recent English Domestic Architecture*, by no less a person than Hubert de Cronin Hastings, son of the company's chairman Sir Percy Hastings.[46] Hastings junior was to establish himself as the presiding editorial genius and, in conjunction with the editor Christian Barman, was responsible for modernism's increased exposure in *The Architectural Review*.

The sheer volume of these publications suggests that there was a market for books about domestic architecture.[47] A small number of publications dealing with European modernism had already appeared: Frederick Etchells' translation of Le Corbusier's *Vers une architecture* had appeared as *Towards a New Architecture* in 1927, two years later Bruno Taut's *Modern Architecture* was published in English simultaneously with the German edition.[48] With the exception of Taut's sparse 'Notes concerning England', there was nothing about modernism in an English context. *Modern European Buildings* by Francis Yerbury gave a very Swedish view of modern architecture.[49] A book on modernist houses made modernism more palatable by introducing it through an adaptation of a venerable English publishing genre. Yorke's explanation of the 'relation of the villa to modern architecture . . .' is revealing:

> the villa has had, and will continue to have, a great importance as the cheapest complete building unit for examination and experiment, and it is most often in this small structure that modern architecture goes through its complete revolution . . . There are many new and untried materials . . . and the architect . . . is most likely to find in the villa the most easily accessible unit for research.[50]

Yorke's justification for writing a book about villas and their relation to modern architecture played directly to his fabled expertise in materials and construction. A not-so-subtle redefinition of the genre overcame an ideological problem and played to his strengths.

Sir James Richards suggested that the idea for *The Modern House* probably came from H de C Hastings himself. Certainly it was conceived at an early stage of Yorke's involvement with the Architectural Press.[51] If Richards was correct, it would explain why Yorke was chosen to write the book; his unique combination of knowledge of modernism and materials allowed him to reconcile the apparent discrepancy between writing a book about villas and modern architecture.

Further evidence of a coordinated strategy is implied by two other AP publications. Three years before *The Modern House* was published, the company produced Nathaniel Lloyd's seminal *A History of the English House*.[52] Written by an unabashed Lutyens-dweller, this book does not on the surface seem to have anything in common with *The Modern House*. However, Lloyd explained that the examples were divided into sections on: plans and exteriors; external wall treatment; entrances; windows; chimneys; interiors; internal wall treatment; ceilings; fireplaces; staircases; metalwork; various (including constructional drawings etc).[53] It may not fit Yorke's list like a glove, but it certainly shows an affinity in categorising buildings. Lloyd also credited Hastings: 'The inception of this history is due to the foresight and imagination of Mr de Cronin Hastings'.[54] There is some evidence, at least, that Hastings was marshalling his publishing forces towards comprehensive coverage of all types of housing.

Explaining the apparent anomaly between Lloyd and Yorke fell to P Morton Shand, the Architectural Press's most literate critic at the time. In his occasional series 'Scenario for a Human Drama', which started in *The Architectural Review* in July 1934, together with a preview for Yorke's book, Shand argued that something went wrong with architecture round about 1830 but through the agency of people like Peter Behrens, Henri van de Velde, Otto Wagner, Adolf Loos and CR Mackintosh, the true path was regained.[55] Lloyd's book had conveniently stopped at the Regency. Shand realised the potential of this concluding point, arguing that up until 1830 all architecture was necessarily nationally specific: hence the inevitably of 'English' in Lloyd's title. However the turbulent nineteenth century, with its technical, productive and transportational advances, rendered such regionalism obsolete: hence 'modern' in Yorke's title, and by implication the futility of books like Randal Phillips' *The Modern English House*. In 1937, when Yorke published his second book, about modern houses in England, it was carefully titled *The Modern House in England*.[56]

Shand explained the hiatus between Lloyd and Yorke, implying there was no discontinuity between them other than that caused by 'architecture ignoring structural technique' in the 19th century. *The Modern House* '. . . is a memorable book', Shand wrote 'for it is the first in English which liberates architecture from its narrower self, and shows the modern house as the technical product it really is . . .'.[57] Once this is understood, the implication runs, the rest of architecture will follow.

Some two years before Nikolaus Pevsner's *Pioneers of the Modern Movement* covered similar ground, Shand gave modernism a British lineage combined with a liking for heavy engineering.[58] Writing about CR Mackintosh, he said, '. . . for nearly a hundred years ships and locomotives were almost the only branch of creative design in which our formal tradition contrived to develop along the lines that the eliminative elegance of the Regency style had so surely traced . . .'.[59] Here the manifesto is at least partly shaped by the commercial strictures of publishing. 'A Scenario for a Human Drama' put theoretical flesh on what was a common belief among progressive architectural writers at the time. Yorke himself paid lip service to this historical determinism in *The Modern House*, but had anticipated the argument in a feature in *The Architectural Review* of December 1931, revealingly entitled 'From order through disorder to order'.[60] Its subject was shop fronts, and the theme that Regency shops were rather attractive, the Victorians cocked them up, but with modern design, shops were rediscovering their true destiny.

Here is the source of Yorke's historical determinism. Many of his sentiments match Shand's. 'There was a gradual evolution [in British architecture]', Yorke wrote, '. . . but the logical continuity ended with the Regency'.[61] Disaster. 'For more than a century man has been stumbling along the way of the machine, the way that is leading inevitably towards a new order'.[62] So far, perhaps, so good. But the only way out of this mess was '. . . a period of purification and, largely under the influence of Le Corbusier, the unnecessary was eliminated. A little more than a decade ago there appeared the first buildings of a new architecture, based on a scientific approach to building through an analysis of function'.[63] Modernism arrived as the true end of historical development.

Other writers and architects were also beginning to recognise the value of Regency architecture and town planning: 1934 saw first publication of Steen Eiler Rasmussen's charming paean to Britain's capital, *London the Unique City*, and the following year Sir John Summerson completed his biography of John Nash.[64] Sir James Richards articulated what seems to have been a common belief when in 1933 he reviewed *The Smaller English House of the Later Renaissance* by Sir Albert Richardson, first published in 1925.[65] 'It is not,' Richards wrote, 'that the book has changed, but

RIGHT: Top floor studio in the Linhart House.

BELOW: Interior showing the ramp between the dining room and sitting room.

that our own architectural intentions ... have become clearer'.[66] Richardson's own architecture may have been anathema to the modernists, but his scholarship could be called into service to reinforce their justification of their views. Yorke may not have been the first writer to perceive a link between the Regency and modernism, but his article 'From order through disorder to order' was in at the beginning of the formation of this popular view. Its popularity, too, shows what a chord *The Modern House* struck with contemporary thought.

The Architectural Press was uniquely placed to promote its books. In addition to receiving star billing in *The Architectural Review*, its sister magazine *The Architects' Journal* also noted publication of *The Modern House*'s with a critique by the most prominent émigré European modernist architect, Erich Mendelsohn. It must have been poignant, as the book included his magnificent house in Berlin's exclusive Wannsee district which he had had to abandon after living there for only a few years. Even so, he was complimentary, noting the book's importance for 'penetrating scientifically to the roots of the matter instead of treating it in a superficial, journalistic fashion', but expressed reservations over some layouts and Yorke's failure to see that a house is a small architectural unit.[67] 'A private house', he wrote 'is not an exhibition of architectural and technical devices'.

Mendelsohn identified a fair point. As outlined above Yorke was less interested in the house as a description of an agreeable bourgeois lifestyle or for its own sake, but more as 'an exhibition of architectural and technical devices'. Mendelsohn, despite his reputation as a modernist, had little to do with the social experiments of his contemporaries, Gropius, Martin Wagner, Bruno Taut or Ernst May. His clients were department stores and cinemas rather than progressive city or regional governments. However, Mendelsohn recognised that *The Modern House* gave only a partial view of European modernism.

Few of these problems were noted at the time. Most architectural reviewers gave the book good notices, although there were several reservations, and the spread of opinion suggests very varied attitudes to architecture. *Country Life* suggested that 'there is something to be said for Herr Hitler's objection to the "international" [ie modern] style ...', a comment that became more tasteless with subsequent events.[68] *Design and Construction* (forerunner of *Architectural Design*) accepted that 'the modern movement is here to stay' and that *The Modern House* was the best account of the 'functionalist' house, but regretted the few English examples and the lack of prices.[69] GM Boumphrey in the *Spectator* and John Betjeman in the *Evening Standard* liked it, but they should have done because both were contributors to Architectural Press publications, and Betjeman had been a colleague of Yorke's at the Architectural Press.[70]

A brief notice in the rival *Architect and Building News* was essentially approving, but the most serious criticisms were penned by EJ 'Bobby' Carter, legendary RIBA librarian and editor of the *Journal*.[71] He argued that the 'quasi-technical' aspects of the book were a sidetrack to the argument although conceded that they might have been necessary to its appeal – further circumstantial evidence that the marriage of Yorke's skills was seen as essential to the book's success. Carter did not like Yorke's writing style, taking issue with the 'rather timid, sermonistical unction of his delivery that makes the reader mourn the fire of Corbusier or Ruskin or the incisiveness of Lethaby'.

Carter, a Cambridge history graduate as well as a holder of an AA diploma, was looking for something more literate, with more conventionally presented arguments. Yorke's apparently uncritical stance disappointed him, especially over 'functionalism' and economics. 'Neither Mr Yorke nor the architects know if these buildings are "functional" ... he does not know if the buildings are structurally sound', and 'Do economic demands allow the use of slabs and concrete when brick is the cheaper simply because "brick is not aesthetically a good material for the filling wall?"' But Carter was not entirely fair, as Yorke's sentence continued '... but economically [brick] remains the most satisfactory surfacing material in general use'.[72]

For obvious commercial and ideological reasons, it was hardly surprising that the Architectural Press and its contributors should praise *The Modern House*. The Architectural Press's reception of the book marks one pole of architectural thought, while *Country Life*, with its chilling approval of Hitler's nationalism, marks another. In between, other architectural publications recognising that modernism had taken root, but implying that it was one of several alternatives. Then there was Carter: a trifle harsh perhaps, but picking up on Yorke's propensity to make statements without justification, suggesting that Yorke's ambitions outrun his capacity, and looking for a definition of modern architecture which is not so dependent on Yorke's knowledge of Europe or materials.

The revised later editions also comment on its position in the evolution of modernist thought. The most obvious change is the replacement of eight English examples spread across fourteen pages in the first edition. Yorke later admitted that filling this space was hard, and he had resorted to dull houses by architects like William Wood, Frederick Etchells and Marshall Sisson. In 1934 there was a small field, but as the construction industry started to pick up, numbers grew fast. By the end of 1936, there were enough to fill Yorke's second book, *The Modern House in England*, a pot-boiler into which some of the unsatisfactory British examples included in *The Modern House* could be decanted. In 1943, a wartime edition of *The Modern House* included several new American examples, reflecting Yorke's work on the prefabricated housing programme.

Even though the text remained essentially the same, the examples changed significantly. Post-war editions differ in two main ways from earlier ones: firstly there are more housing schemes, including the Stratford brewery cottages designed by Yorke and his father in 1938, and the 'experimental' house at Codicote of 1945. This would imply that the massive house building programme of the Welfare State meant that Yorke's justification for a book on villas was no longer tenable: his work as an architect during the war and afterwards in partnership with Eugene Rosenberg and Cyril Mardall contributed to the new housing programme.

The early editions had one glaring omission among the leaders of European modernism. Until the last edition there are no examples of Alvar Aalto's work, even though he and Yorke were on friendly terms from 1933. On 4 November 1955 Yorke wrote to Elissa Aalto, 'For the last twenty years I have tried to obtain from Alvar Aalto photographs of your own house and for the Harry Gullichsen house [ie the Villa Mairea] so that I could illustrate them in *The Modern House* book, but Aalto never sends them so I am hoping I will have greater success by asking you . . . A new edition of the Modern House is being published and it will probably be the last one'. And in a desperate last plea, he handwrote, 'It really is twenty years but not always the same houses'. Yorke's tactic of writing to Mrs Aalto paid off: the final edition included examples of Aalto's work.[73]

The second major change is an increase in the number of American examples. Initially, this was in tune with the origin of the book, as the wartime editions carried several more prefabricated houses. But after 1945 they became increasingly luxurious with houses by Gropius and Breuer and their student Hugh Stubbins. This trend continued in the eighth and final edition of 1956, where the section on 'Experimental and prefabricated houses' was dropped, and examples like the Rockefeller guest house in New York City by Philip Johnson were included.

By 1956, and probably earlier, *The Modern House* had run its course. In 1934 Yorke could just about get away with arguing that the villa was the only available means of the experimentation necessary to develop modernist housing, but by the 1950s, modernist housing was for better or worse established, while the single family house prospered in affluent America.[74]

Losing its radical edge was probably necessary to perpetuate the book's life. Once the welfare state had gone some way to addressing Yorke's social aims, and disillusionment with prefabrication

had rendered that part of the book obsolete, its original *raison d'être* must have seemed tired. Instead it became a picture reference book with, by Yorke's own admission, a rather curious piece of text. It is here that the 'picturesque' aspects of its portrayal of architecture become most apparent.[75] Shorn of its polemic, *The Modern House* is a collection of images, dissociated from their national and historical context, and from their architectural intent.

The Modern House's published life coincides almost exactly with the period when orthodox modernism held sway in Britain. It is not surprising that it should reflect the strengths and weaknesses of that movement. Adapting the genre of books about houses, through Yorke's skills, into a book about modern houses was itself as great an anglicisation of modernism as the dubious historical ancestry put forward by Shand and Pevsner. Ironically, Yorke's knowledge of materials did give his interpretation of modernism an English ancestry, for it came straight out of his Arts and Crafts background. In one sense *The Modern House* is an important link between the Arts and Crafts movement and modernism in Britain. By a few sleights of hand, graphic design and textual argument, it shoehorned modernism into a familiar English publishing context, and in this format, with the book's potential for being read in many different ways, it was one of the formative elements of modernism in Britain.

That *The Modern House* contains some of the now familiar failings of Yorke's generation is not surprising. That it can transcend them, and even after the original motivations for the book seemed outdated it can appear to be an original, sympathetic and surprising selection, is a testament to the editorial skills of its author. Selecting the houses was probably the one area where the web spun by the Architectural Press, marrying genre with technique to frame perception of a movement, gave Yorke a free rein, and it played to his characteristics: perceptive though taciturn and uninterested in dogma.

In *The Modern House*, Yorke illustrated these examples of the Regency Lloyd Baker estate in London, and a row of modern workers' houses in Barcelona, reiterating the by then common belief that modern domestic architecture merely completed the seamless line of development which had evolved up to the Regency period, only to fall apart in the Victorian age.

Notes

1. The *Country Life* editorial, 29 December 1934, p 682, says, 'we can look back over a year of marked improvement in the building industry' and this is borne out in secondary literature. See for example 'Expansion and change in the building industry' in Marian Bowley, *The British Building Industry*, CUP 1966, pp 383–92.

2. See *The Builder*, 30 November 1934, p 930 for an edited transcript of the 'debate'. Another example of dispute between an old traditionalist and young modernist can be found at the end of Raymond MacGrath's book, *Twentieth Century Houses*, Faber (London), 1934.

3. See the editorial *The Architects' Journal*, vol 79, p 269, 22 February 1934, and the 'replies' from 'a number of fascist architects', and the British Union of Fascists' deputy director of policy A Raven Thomson, in the issue of 19 April 1934, vol79, pp 566–7.

4. *The Modern House* by FRS Yorke was published by The Architectural Press, London, 1934. Subsequent editions were 1935, 1937, 1943, 1944, 1948, 1951 and 1956. With each edition, particularly the third, and fifth, exemplars of modernist design improved, especially after the publication of *The Modern House in England,* Architectural Press (London), 1937. Some revisions were made for the third edition; more American examples and prefabricated houses were included in the fourth and fifth editions respectively. Later editions introduce some post-war examples, to the extent that the final edition is dominated by the houses of wealthy Americans.

5. Jeremy Melvin first became aware of *The Modern House* as a small child, when he admired a copy owned by his parents, bought when they were architectural students in the early 1950s. David Allford was introduced to it by his art master at High Storrs Grammar School in Sheffield as a teenager in the 1940s. See Chapter Six.

6. *The Spectator*, 17 August 1934, p 231. The following year Boumphrey commissioned Yorke to design a house in Bredon, Worcestershire. Drawings survive in the RIBA Drawings Collection, PA 238/8 (1–24).

7. *The Architectural Review*, vol 132 no 788, October 1962, p 279–80.

8. Le Corbusier's *Vers une Architecture* had, for example, been translated in 1927: *Towards a New Architecture*, trans Frederick Etchells, John Rodker (London) 1927. Bruno Taut *Modern Architecture* The Studio (London), 1929 is another early publication on modernism. It was simultaneously published in German as *Die Neue Baukunst*, Stuttgart Julius Hoffmann Verlag (Stuttgart), 1929.

9. Such studies as have been undertaken on the 1930s, with few exceptions, tend to be monographical or biographical. The most thorough monograph is John Allan's magisterial study of Berthold Lubetkin, *Lubetkin*, RIBA Publications (London), 1992. One exception is Anthony Jackson's now rather dated *The Politics of Architecture*, the Architectural Press (London), 1970. There was also Gavin Stamp (ed), 'Britain in the Thirties', *Architectural Design* (London), 1979.

10. Sir Reginald Blomfield, *Modernismus*, Macmillan (London), 1934. Watkin's comment comes from 'Architectural Writing in the Thirties' in Britain in the Thirties, op cit p 84–9. It runs '. . . *Modernismus* failed because it was written by the wrong man at the wrong time'. p 85.

11. Jeremy Melvin's first edition of *The Modern House* was originally purchased by Fred Vaux FRIBA of Bridlington. Despite designing a large housing estate (in a more or less traditional idiom) for the local authority, he was no more than a minor provincial architect. This suggests that the book had a larger readership than the metropolitan avant-garde. The RIBA biography file on Vaux (1888–1954) has brief details on his career.

12. Roy Landau, in 'A History of Modern Architecture that still needs to be Written', *AA Files* 29, Spring 1991, pp 49–54, suggested an approach to studying architecture of the 1930s based on Michel Foucault's concept of 'discourse' might help to conceptualise the position of modern architecture in Britain.

13. *The Architects' Journal*, vol 77, 22 March 1933, p 408

14. They include a house in Gidea Park of 1933, for which Yorke was the executive architect to two Liverpool University lecturers, William Holford and Gordon Stephenson. It was published in the *Listener*, 8 August 1934, p 243, a cutting of which is preserved in the Allford Yorke archive, folder 11, p 12, with further illustrations pp 13–4. Another was a drab neo-Georgian council office in Romsey, designed with his father. See *Architects' Journal*, 6 December 1934, p 848.

15. See for example, *The Architects' Journal*, vol 71, 1930, p 108, in which is illustrated an Arts and Crafts, neo-Tudor house by FWB Yorke in Luttrell Road, Four Oaks, Sutton Coldfield. This is the year before FRS Yorke's first contribution to the magazine.

16. An impression of Yorke's studies at Birmingham School of Art can be found in his surviving student work in the RIBA Drawings Collection, PA 237/3, /7, /9, /10, and /11. They include measured drawings of historic buildings, Beaux Arts-type watercolour renderings and a town planning project of a housing development at eight houses to the acre. There is little to suggest a latent interest, still less a pedagogic one, in modernism, except perhaps for a design for a market hall for the City of Birmingham, PA 237/5, dated January 1929, that has a passing resemblance to Giacomo Matte Trucco's FIAT Factory in Turin. See also Alan Powers, *In the Line of Development* RIBA Heinz Gallery (London), pp 1–2 for some information on Drysdale and Birmingham School of Art.
For a picture of the Arts and Crafts movement in Chipping Campden see Alan Crawford, *CR Ashbee*, Yale University Press (London and New Haven), 1985. Ashbee moved his Guild of Handicraft to the town from London's East End in the early years of the 20th century. Although the Guild was formally dissolved in 1919, Crawford wrote about a revisit to Chipping Campden in 1924, 'Quite a colony of craftsmen was growing up in the town and that Summer there was a big Arts and Crafts exhibition'. Crawford, op cit, pp 171, 200.

17. This aspect of Yorke's character can be shown in an anecdote. On one occasion, he brought a building site to a standstill by showing a mason how some work should be done. The unionised workforce was flabbergasted.

18. Architectural Press lore has it that Yorke was 'discovered' by an advertisement manager. This is not wholly unconvincing as ad managers would be likely to court specifiers who have an interest in materials and products. Another entrée could have come from his father, whose work had already been published by the AP. See footnote 15. The drawing was a piece of student work and the original survives in the RIBA Drawings Collection, PA 237/9.

19. See *The Architects' Journal*, vol 75, 11 and 18 March 1933, p 639, 665.

20. *The Architects' Journal*, vol 77, 22 March 1933, p 408. Previously 'Trade Notes' had been an irregular column.

21. Sir James Richards in conversation with Jeremy Melvin, 28 November 1991.

22. *The Modern House* was not the only place where the Architectural Press put Yorke's knowledge to sound commercial use. From 1935 until his death in 1962 he edited the annual, *Specification* a heavy responsibility which caused him to cease writing 'Trade Notes'.

23. These two ideas were, of course, current and could be typified by Le Corbusier against Ernst May.

24. *The Modern House*, op cit, pp 12, 14.

25. Ibid, p 14 (quote); pp 13, 15 (pictures).

26. See Yorke's nomination papers for his fellowship of the RIBA, held at the RIBA. There are also a large number of postcards to his parents in the Allford Yorke Folder 27.

27. 'Three new houses' *The Architectural Review* vol 72, February 1932 p 266–8. Yorke only described the Haus Rosenbauer. The other two houses are a vaguely 'moderne' example by Oliver Hill, and a thatched cottage style one by T Cecil Howitt, nothing if not eclectic.

28. Max Fry, See note 7, op cit p 280 mentions how *The Modern House* was an affordable substitute for travel.

29. Giorgio Ciucci, 'The Invention of the Modern Movement' in *Oppositions*

24, Spring 1981, pp 68–91, argued that 'modernism' was essentially invented as a coherent body of ideas from a disparate bundle of approaches between the first and second meetings of CIAM in 1927 and 1928. For an account of the 'excision' of the 'other tradition' of Alvar Aalto, Hans Scharoun and Hugo Haring from mainstream modernist thought, see Colin St John Wilson, *The Other Tradition of Modern Architecture*, Academy Editions (London), 1995.

30. This list is published at the end of the review of *The Modern House* in *The Architects' Journal*, vol 80, 12 July 1934, p 60.

31. *The Architects' Journal*, vol 77, 29 June 1933, p 875.

32. 'Trade Notes', *The Architects' Journal*, vol 77, 12 April 1933, p 506.

33. RIBA YoF/1/12. From a letter of 30 November 1932 (YoF/1/12) in which Adolf Hoffmeister asks Yorke to 'announce the day and hour of your arrival [in Prague] to my friend Charles Honzik' it is clear that Yorke first met Honzik late in 1932. Honzik's letter was evidently written rather later, after considerable thought and work had gone into developing the idea of the book, but some time before another letter from Honzik to Yorke of 23 April 1934 (YoF/1/12), which discusses how Honzik should be credited in the book on publication. All Honzik's quotes in this and the following paragraph come from his undated letter.

34. *The Modern House*, op cit, 'Acknowledgements' (no page number).

35. *Modern House* p 1.

36. FRS Yorke and Frederick Gibberd, *The Modern Flat*, London: the Architectural Press, 1938.

37. *Modern House* p 2.

38. Ibid, p 4. These are also mentioned in Honzik's undated letter, op cit.

39. Ibid p 2.

40. Ludwig Hilberseimer, 'Die Wohnung Unserer Zeit', in *Die Form* vol 6 no 7, 15 July 1931, pp 249–70.

41. *The Modern House*, op cit p 1.

42. Herman Muthesius, *Das Englische Haus*, Wasmuth Verlag (Berlin), 1904–5. The genre of books on house design could be said to go back at least to JJ Stevenson, *House Architecture* (London), 1877.

43. *The Small English House*, B Weinreb Architectural Books (London), 1977, is a catalogue with 29 pages of mainly early 20th-century books on domestic architecture.

44. Randal Phillips, *The Modern English House*, Country Life (London), 1927, p xiv.

45. Like many of his modernist contemporaries, Yorke had a liking for 'labour-saving devices' See, for example, *The Modern House*, pp 26, 39.

46. Hubert de Cronin Hastings, *Recent English Domestic Architecture*, The Architectural Press (London), 1929. This was based on a special edition of *The Architectural Review* on domestic architecture vol 64 December 1928. It includes articles by Michael Rosenauer and Le Corbusier. It was the first special edition on this topic for six years, but had been more or less annual before that.

47. Raymond MacGrath's *Twentieth Century Houses* Faber (London), 1934, was published shortly after *The Modern House*, and consequently had no effect on it. But that another publisher should be seeking to produce a book on an outwardly similar theme suggests its commercial viability.

48. Le Corbusier, trans Frederick Etchells, *Towards a New Architecture*, John Rodker (London), 1927. Bruno Taut, *Modern Architecture*, The Studio (London), 1929. Simultaneously published in Germany by Julius Hoffmann Verlag (Stuttgart), as *Die Neue Baukunst*.

49. Francis Yerbury, *Modern European Buildings*, (London), 1928.

50. Ibid, p 5.

51. Sir James Richards suggested this in discussion with Jeremy Melvin, 28 November 1991. No definitive evidence has come to light, but even if Hastings did not originate the idea, he must have known about it from an early stage. In the acknowledgements Yorke wrote 'Two years ago, when the project was originally contemplated . . .', so there was plenty of time for various views to contribute to the book's formation.

52. Nathaniel Lloyd, *A History of the English House*, The Architectural Press (London), 1931. It was based on material which had appeared in *The Architectural Review* intermittently over the previous three years.

53. Ibid, p v.

54. Ibid, p vi.

55. The title 'Scenario for a Human Drama' includes Yorke's preview of *The Modern House* in *The Architectural Review* vol 76, pp 9–16, to which Shand provided a foreword. The series continued with 'Immediate Background' August 1934, pp 39–42, 'Peter Behrens' September 1934, pp 83–9, 'van der Velde to Wagner' October 1934, pp 131–4, 'Glasgow interlude' vol 77, January 1935, pp 23–6 and 'Machine-à-Habiter to the house of character', March 1935, pp 61–4.

56. FRS Yorke, *The Modern House in England*, London The Architectural Press 1937. It was previewed in *The Architectural Review* of December 1936.

57. Foreword to "Scenario for a Human Drama", op cit.

58. Nikolaus Pevsner, *Pioneers of the Modern Movement*, Faber (London), 1936. In the foreword to the first edition, Pevsner acknowledges the similarity to Shand's work, but claims 'I did not know of P Morton Shand's excellent articles in *The Architectural Review*, of 1933, 1934, 1935 until I had almost finished my research. The fact that our conclusions coincide in so many ways is a gratifying confirmation of the views put forward in this book'.

59. Glasgow interlude in 'Scenario for a Human Drama', op cit, p 25.

60. *The Architectural Review* vol 70, December 1931, pp 171–8.

61. *The Modern House*, op cit, p 19.

62. Loc cit.

63. Ibid, p 25.

64. Steen Eiler Rasmussen, *London: The Unique City*, Jonathan Cape (London), 1934, and John Summerson, *John Nash* Allen & Unwin (London), 1935.

65. Albert Richardson and H Donaldson Eberlein, *The Smaller English House of the Later Renaissance 1660-1830*, Batsford (London), 1925.

66. JM Richards, 'The Regency Precedent', in *The Architects' Journal*, vol 78, 12 October 1933, p 455.

67. Erich Mendelsohn, in *The Architects' Journal*, vol 80, 12 July 1934, p 57.

68. *Country Life*, 18 August 1934, p 178–9.

69. *Design and Construction*, vol iv, no 12, October 1934, p 422.

70. Betjeman worked as assistant editor of *The Architectural Review*, from October 1930 until the end of 1933. See Bevis Hillier, *Young Betjeman*, John Murray (London), 1988, especially the chapter 'Archie Rev', pp 248–279, which portrays the Architectural Press at this time.

71. RIBA Journal, vol XLI, pp 929–30.

72. Carter quoted only half of Yorke's sentence. It can be found in its entirety on page 49 of *The Modern House*.

73. The letter is in the archives of the Aalto Foundation, Helsinki, Finland, York 55(1).

74. An obvious fruit of this boom in single family house design in America is the Case Study House programme, promoted by *Arts and Architecture* and its editor John Entenza. See Esther McCoy, *Blueprints for Modern Living*, MoCA (Los Angeles), 1990 for an overview of this programme.

75. See the foreword to *The Modern House*, 8th edition. Adrian Forty explains this view of the 'picturesque' approach to architectural criticism in 'Common sense and the Picturesque', Iain Borden and David Dunster, (eds) *Architecture and the Sites of History*, Butterworth Architecture (Oxford), 1995, pp 176–86.

Chapter 2

PREFABRICATION AND CONSTRUCTION

When *The Architects' Journal* designated Yorke as a 'technical expert', it identified one facet of his work which coloured his entire career.[1] It was the calling card he used to become involved with the Architectural Press in the first place, and if the company was shrewd enough to find numerous ways of turning his expertise to commercial advantage, its most direct applications brought Yorke the most tangible benefits. Editing the annual *Specification* provided much of his income in the late 1930s, though the association of construction technique with modern architecture ran much deeper.[2] The pattern of *The Modern House*, with its sections on 'Wall and Window', 'Roof' and especially 'Experimental and Prefabricated Houses', as well as its summary of materials used in each example, suggest that technical concerns structured his overall understanding of modernism. Not surprisingly, it was as a 'technical expert' that his old friend, colleague and erstwhile lodger Sir James Richards remembered him late in life.[3]

Despite this label Yorke never saw technology as an end in itself. 'The solution to the housing problem lies . . . in a reformed type of flat dwelling and controlled land development,'[4] he wrote, recognising that new techniques and materials were only one side of the equation. If political will were necessary for controlling land development, reforming dwellings at least, lay in the hands of architects, especially those who had technical expertise. From the outset of his career Yorke appreciated this asymmetrical balance in trying to achieve modern architecture's goals. One side came within the scope of architecture as he understood it. The other fell under the label of planning and, though equally essential, it was largely political; it needed more behind it than the MARS Group and the Architectural Press. Planning and construction technology were two vital constituents of modern architecture, but they followed different modalities and demanded different approaches. For Yorke, they were two faces of the same coin, but one, the understanding of which lay within his compass, he burnished brighter than the other.

In 1934 his sentiments about planning were conventionally modernist. 'We need new types of buildings, new plans fc. them and new plans for our towns,'[5] he wrote, knowing he was lamentably impotent to achieve the last part of this triad. 'There has been little actual development', he explained, of 'economic and convenient living quarters . . . partly because it is difficult to find finance for any scheme that makes a great break with normal procedure, but largely owing to difficulties of land ownership and the high prices of land.'[6] Meanwhile, 'the villa has had and will continue to have a great importance as the cheapest complete unit for examination and experiment,' to test the 'many new and untried materials.'[7] Neither the prestige of the Concrete Garden City of the Future, nor 'controlled land development' and major town planning opportunities becoming realistic prospects long before the end of World War II, could tempt him to shift the balance of his activities to the other side.[8]

By contrast Yorke's appreciation of materials, techniques and construction was rather deeper, more original and had greater consequences. It was essential to his career, his formulation of and contribution to modern architecture. Examining it involves untangling several strands whose weave

On the roof of this house, Shangri-La in Lee-on-Solent, on New Year's Day 1938, Randall Evans suggested that Yorke should not build any more concrete roofs because of the difficulties in making them watertight.

was contingent on each other, though the outcome was not predetermined. This necessarily starts with the complex and contradictory relationship between construction products and publishing which took shape during the apogee of the Arts and Crafts movement in the 1890s. A peculiar Englishness emerges in this aspect of Yorke's career. The Arts and Crafts movement originated in England, and the effects of the moral tone that it engendered spread broadly, not least to the evolution of socialism into a specifically British context.[9] Given the interdependence of the Arts and Crafts movement and an architectural publishing industry that was more extensive and influential than in other countries, Yorke's personal trajectory would have been impossible outside the UK.

The second strand concerns Yorke's contribution to an attempted reconciliation of this duality by actively promoting the role of mass-produced components in contemporary architecture. His 'Trade Notes' column in *The Architects' Journal*, published weekly almost without break between 22 March 1933 and 22 August 1935, charts his growing knowledge of and enthusiasm for new materials and construction techniques. In the American company General Houses he seemed to find a theoretical embodiment of the advantages of applying industrialisation to building construction, but growing practical experience of construction over the same period began to alter his views. If Randall Evans' comment 'No more concrete houses', uttered on top of the aptly named Shangri-La on New Year's Day 1938, brought to a head doubts which Yorke was already germinating, the shift became explicit and irreversible when Yorke expressed disillusionment with the efficacy of mechanisation to his friend J Homery Folks.[10]

A third thread in the fabric of Yorke's attitude to construction comes from the second: the gradual emergence of non-traditional construction systems finding some place for traditional materials, as evident in the brewery cottages at Stratford-upon-Avon, the experimental house at Codicote in Hertfordshire, the house at Luccombe on the Isle of Wight and even the Braithwaite House. Yorke's comment that the cladding of the supposedly factory-produced Braithwaite House could be brick or even fieldstone, as much as ribbed asbestos sheets, might be interpreted as a direct attack on the idea that technology should, in and of itself, determine appearance.[11]

In these projects Yorke came as close as ever to evolving a personal aesthetic. He was particularly proud of the brewery cottages. He wrote: 'It is a job of which I am personally rather fond, and it gives some ideas of the lines along which my work would have developed had it not been interrupted in 1939.'[12] The approaches they represent found outlets for his enthusiasm for innovative construction as well as his liking for traditional materials. At their best, he was able not just to reconcile these two urges, but to achieve efficiency of construction with satisfaction in use. Luccombe, for example, successfully combined an unambiguous modernity with the charm of a seaside cottage.

This particular balance did not last. Its most significant large-scale manifestation was the Barclay School at Stevenage, in Hertfordshire, where a Henry Moore *Madonna and Child* shines against a backdrop of carefully composed stone, brick and timber-framed windows. The sculpture was an unrepeatable *tour de force*, a one-off gesture of generosity from Moore to a new town close to his home; even if some Welfare State ideologues hoped to provide high-quality contemporary art as an adjunct to health care and education, economics intervened. Perhaps Yorke's particular aesthetic was ultimately unsuited to the realities of post-war building; in any case it was Breuer who developed the fieldstone aesthetic further just as he drew more solace from the Concrete Garden City.[13]

Yorke's interest in materials, techniques and construction derives in part from his paternal and pedagogic background in the Arts and Crafts movement. His father, FWB Yorke, was an architect who could swing easily between an Arts and Crafts idiom and gentle neo-classicism. His interest in craft extended to keeping a full set of tools, that his son saw fit to record in several artfully taken photographs.[14] Yorke's family home at 36 Calthorpe Road, Edgbaston, was in one of Birmingham's leafiest suburbs and his education in Chipping Camden further exposed him at least subliminally to an Arts and Crafts ethos. As a youth in architecture school, he cycled through northern France admiring its Gothic buildings with as much alacrity as any architectural student who had read Ruskin might have done, in the previous three-quarters of a century. His exploits from this trip would not seem out of place in a young architect's travel journal from thirty or forty years earlier.

'My sketching', he noted on 18 October 1927, showing that he was doing exactly as the ailing Ruskin had advised the young Detmar Blow shortly before he lapsed into his final insanity, 'seems to get worse – hell.'[15] Caudebec Cathedral, with its 'wonderful west front with beautiful carving', introduced him to French Gothic, and he found the town 'one of the few places which surpass expectation', with its 'almost touchingly half-timbered houses' and 'grey green slate'. Gothic, construction technique and material in the bag, he completed the Ruskinian cocktail with religion. 'Then we go to the church. It is dark and the lights inside invite us to enter. A service is in progress and we are handed hymn sheets. The priest has a fine deep voice and leads the hymns in a fascinating way . . . he seems to get very near to the people – seems to understand them and they him – would like to know him . . .'

Two days later, in Rouen, he expressed a wish that 'my life should be given to the care of the certain work of God rather than live to care for the uncertain work of man'. His subsequent career almost completely reversed these lofty aims. God, if he was in for the ride at all, was firmly in the back seat, as 'the uncertain work of man' – activities like living, learning, healing and flying, to say nothing of his extra-architectural pursuits – came to the fore.[16] Similarly, any contact his interest in materials and construction retained with its origins in Arts and Crafts sensibility was transformed almost beyond recognition.

One catalyst for this transformation came from the Architectural Press's extraordinary resolution of an old dilemma whose history stretched back to the company's foundation in the 1890s. In an amazing explosion of magazine publishing based on the exploitation of new printing techniques for a population with increasing literacy, leisure and disposable income,[17] that decade saw the foundation of several significant architectural periodicals. First came *The Studio* in 1891, *The Architectural Review* appeared in 1896 and the following year *Country Life* started publication.[18] All made use of new printing and reprographic techniques to make oversized cottages with their self-consciously stylised nooks and crannies – often with built-in or specially designed furniture – as appealing as possible. With these publications as well as innumerable books behind it, to say nothing of its origins in the literary endeavours of John Ruskin and William Morris, the Arts and Crafts movement might be redefined as a literary rather than a purely architectural phenomenon.[19]

Shortly after its foundation *The Architectural Review* fell under the sway of the Regan and Hastings families, who would own the Architectural Press until the 1980s. The journal's Arts and Crafts feel was indelible from the beginning. Henry Wilson, the first editor, continued the architectural practice of his mentor JD Sedding, one of the founding fathers of the Arts and Crafts movement.[20] The apparent message may have been Ruskinian out of William Morris, but ironically the architectural magazines relied on highly mechanised printing and distribution processes, as well as the willingness of building-component manufacturers to advertise their products to the architectural profession. So, in both production and business concept the success of these magazines depended on the division of labour, which those who followed the Arts and Crafts creed had sworn in their own blood to overcome.[21]

Whatever the rights and wrongs of this unlikely relationship, it endured almost unchanged for thirty years. Successive editors of *The Architectural Review* maintained a line that Wilson – and indeed Sedding – would have recognised, and it was external influence, rather than the weight of its own unwieldy contradictions, that brought about change. Christian Barman became editor of *The Architectural Review*: it was he who persuaded P Morton Shand to write about modern architecture, initiating his ascent as one of the most perceptive and important British critics. Once modernism, with its rhetoric of mechanisation, became acceptable editorial material, the uneasy balance between a pro-Arts and Crafts editorial line and advertising underwritten by the creeping commodification of the construction process became increasingly hard to hold.

Into this vacuum, in 1931, stepped FRS Yorke when he first worked for the Architectural Press. One interpretation of his work for that company is that it sought to reconcile the gulf between editorial and commercial priorities. Yorke, in the early part of his career before a mild disillusion set in, gamely tried to achieve such a reconciliation, though his attempts contributed admittedly, in a rather fragmentary and non-linear way, to new ways of considering architecture.

In the absence of any substantial building commissions and through the format of publishing, Yorke's 'Trade Notes' column charts his growing knowledge of materials and techniques in the early 1930s. This body of work gives some insight into the evolution of his ideas, from the recognisably Arts and Crafts-influenced agricultural workers' cottages at Webheath, Worcestershire, which he designed in 1928 to the nakedly modernist Torilla of 1934–5, his first solo commission, paid for by Christabel Burton.[23] Yorke's personal formation telescoped into a few years a process which took the Architectural Press several decades. A staging post is his first publication for the Architectural Press, a measured drawing of the Georgian Landor House in Warwick, found in the supplement to the *Architects' Journal* of 8 April 1931,[24] which takes his interest in construction into the medium of a publication.

For understandable reasons, studies of early modernist writings have tended to focus on manifestoes, and the manifesto-potential of a weekly column with little more intent than facilitating the relationship between product manufacturers and specifiers which underpinned the magazine's prosperity, is strictly limited. What Yorke did, however, was arguably more far-reaching than simple propaganda. He insinuated a view of modern architecture right into the heart of the architectural profession because, in its outward form of recommending building products, his column touched on the universal nexus of all professional architectural activity, whether traditionalist, modernist or futurist, of orchestrating components into a design. Under this umbrella, unsuspecting bald-headed architects on the back streets of Birmingham, if they read each of his columns, would not just have come across the names of Alvar Aalto, Mies van der Rohe and William Lescaze. They would also have read various suggestions for steel doorframes and numerous ways of making concrete waterproof, and been introduced to prefabricated houses of pressed steel and others from General Houses. They might have picked up *Lehre von neuen baukunst* (Lessons of new architecture) from EJ Siedler or instruction on acoustics from Emil Berliner. Of course, asbestos panels, cork and asphalt treatments for flat roofs do not in themselves generate modernist design, but it is impossible without such industrially produced materials. Through this compilation of aspirational exemplars and practical advice, modernist architecture might have seemed a less distant phenomenon than something practised by round-bespectacled, bow-tied continentals who had little better to do than swan around the Mediterranean on luxurious cruise liners. It might almost have seemed relevant to designing houses for the local rural district council.[25]

Yorke foreshadowed his gentle manifesto, if that is the right term, a few weeks before his column became a regular feature. On 15 February 1933 he reviewed the British Industries Fair, complaining about the lack of a connection between art and industry, in contrast to a recent fair in Brünn, in Czechoslovakia, where a trio of architects who would feature in *The Modern House*, Josef Gocar, Bohuslav Fuchs and Josef Havlicek, all participated. That might be read as a straight extrapolation of the Deutscher Werkbund's dream of uniting art and industry, but in Yorke's first column he argued that architects needed to nurture their taste in materials, and that giving the necessary data might help. Treating the architects' relationship to construction materials as one of 'taste', rather than active participation in their design and production, is a step away from the ideals of the Werkbund towards commercial publishing priorities. The following week he made this even more explicit, expressing a wish to bring the architect and manufacturer closer together. It was a sentiment made possible by the rise of modernist design as a cultural force; if it indicated that promoting the Arts and Crafts movement through publishing was to be an anachronism, it also indicated a primrose path for the Architectural Press's financial prospects.

In the agricultural workers' cottages Yorke strove for 'the completest possible standardisation of parts',[26] even though he did not yet know how, or perhaps want, to design in a modern idiom. When he designed Torilla he certainly wanted a modernist look, in achieving it he drew on products and techniques he had encountered in writing 'Trade Notes'. In the products he listed when he published Torilla there are several he had featured in his column, often ones which are essential to the aesthetic effect. They include pumice concrete partitions, cork insulation, asphalt roofing and the Lenscrete high-level window which helps to lend the living room its drama. Additionally, though he omitted to mention the metal windowsills of the house in the description, they are also an integral part of its design; he had written about them on 9 November 1933.

There were also many echoes between the houses he selected for *The Modern House* and the products he described in 'Trade Notes'. Lois Welzenbacher, Ladislav Zak, Otto Zollinger and Heinrich Lauterbach all used the Heraklith loosely compressed wood-wool board he had featured on the 16 November 1933.[27] Numerous architects faced the generic problem of making concrete waterproof, an issue Yorke addressed on many occasions and faced himself at Torilla. Several more, including Erich Mendelsohn, used copper roofing, a material of whose potential applications Yorke was well aware judging by the frequency of his reviews of Copper Development Association literature.

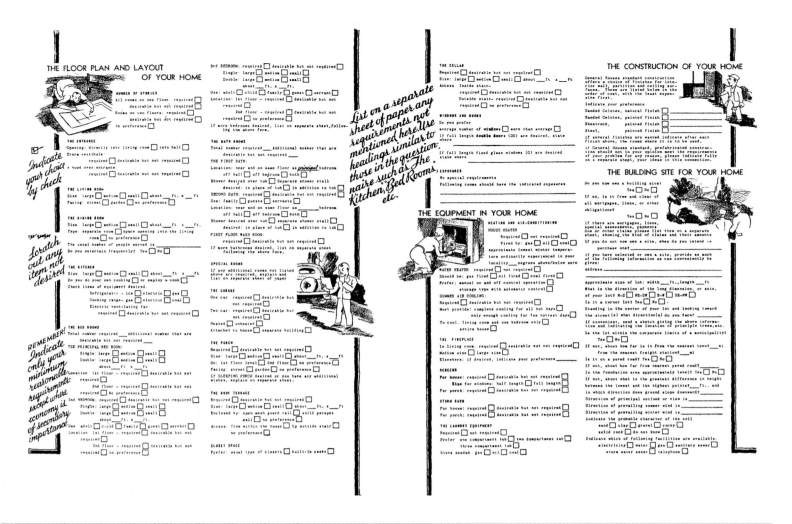

Clearly, in the mid-1930s there was significant common ground between Yorke's growing knowledge of materials, his work as a critic and advocate of the new architecture, and his own design intentions. But from this point the interests began to resolve themselves differently, according to the strictures of their medium. In publishing, his fascination with construction led logically to promoting prefabrication and in particular the Chicago-based company General Houses, while his own designs began to veer towards rationalised traditional construction rather than exploitation of industrial methods.

If houses were to be prefabricated, General Houses represented the apogee of house-building. Founded by the architect Howard T Fisher in 1932, it arrived on the scene at the Chicago Century of Progress Exhibition the following year alongside several other purveyors of prefabricated homes. By June 1933 it had reached the attention of *The Architects' Journal*, which published a picture of a General Houses project, significantly opposite 'Trade Notes'. It captured Yorke's attention to such an extent that he selected a drawing by Fisher for the dust jacket of *The Modern House* and in November 1934 he devoted most of one week's column to a 52-page booklet the company had produced. There he celebrated the fact that 'the American speculator who mass produces small houses in brick has at least one formidable rival now actively engaged in the production of prefabricated parts for the mass distribution of small houses built from standardised pressed steel components'.[28]

In choosing a name for his new company, HT Fisher obviously referred to General Motors. Even if he did not have Le Corbusier's plea 'We must have a house like a Ford motor car' ringing in his ears, he implicitly countered with, 'We will have houses like General Motors cars'.[29] This reflected a change in the balance between the world's two largest automobile producers, which in turn

Part of the questionnaire that General Houses used to design a customised house out of standardised components.

Courtesy of *The Architects' Journal*.

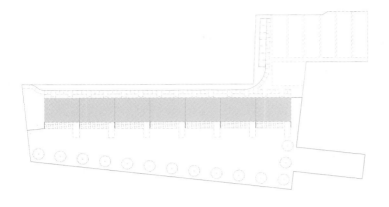

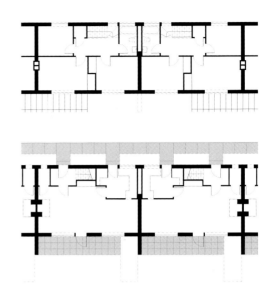

Plans and views of the seven brewery workers' cottages Yorke designed for the Flower's Brewery in Stratford-upon-Avon, of which he later professed to be especially proud.

Photos, courtesy of *The Architectural Review*.

indicated a shift in the potential and application of mass production. By the end of the 1920s General Motors, pursuing a strategy of diversification, variety and choice developed under the auspices of Alfred Sloan, jun, against Henry Ford's belief in the benefit of absolute standardisation, had usurped Ford's position as the biggest car manufacturer. Central to Sloan's business practice was a focus on flexibility so that customers could select a model tailored to their needs and budget. Scenting increasing affluence across society, he realised that the ability to upgrade incrementally from a basic Chevrolet through Buicks and Oldsmobiles to the luxurious Cadillac, would appeal to the broadest possible market and help to retain customer loyalty over a lifetime.

Sloan, an MIT-trained engineer, oversaw the introduction of a new management structure for General Motors in the early 1920s. General policy and certain functions, such as purchasing, research, public relations and advertising, were coordinated from the centre, giving an overall framework within which each division could operate with a degree of autonomy. Many years later Sloan remembered this period from the middle 1920s as 'the *mass-class* market, with increasing diversity . . . as the General Motors concept'.[30] Although Ford was eventually jolted out of his complacent belief that the Model T was the end of automobile evolution and introduced new lines, his company never made up the ground it had lost to General Motors.

Fisher, who was well connected – his father WL Fisher had been Secretary of the Interior under President Taft – and already had a reputation as a housing expert,[31] learned these lessons well. *Architectural Forum*, noting the formation of General Houses in its issue of April 1933, claimed that the company was 'the first commercial integration of prefabricating interests'.[32] Just as Sloan built a management system checked by financial controls to integrate the various tasks from research through procurement, to production and marketing, so Fisher had departments for sales, production, legal, financial and engineering, drafting and research. General Motors established a general purchasing committee in 1922 to overcome what Sloan recorded as 'the problem . . . as I saw it in 1922, was to get the advantages of volume . . . and at the same time to permit the divisions to have control over their own affairs'.[33] Conceding that it 'cannot be cited as an unqualified success,' Sloan nonetheless considered that the committee 'provided our first lesson in coordination . . . [and] our first experience of interdivisional activity'.[34]

Establishing a platform for procurement was as essential to Fisher's strategy as it was to Sloan's. However, with only twenty-seven staff he had nothing like the leverage of General Motors, whose sales had reached $1.5 billion in 1929, but he realised that developing relationships with very large suppliers such as Pullman and Inland Steel would give his fledgling enterprise the benefits of volume mass production. Variety was up to the design staff and their interpretation of clients' requirements, thus to facilitate this General Houses produced a questionnaire.[35] Broken into headings like 'The floor plan and layout of your home', equipment, site and buying, even giving potential purchasers an opportunity to sketch their own ideas, it allowed customers to take the lead, with the company's architectural staff merely interpreting their wishes.[36] It was some way from the visions of standardisation put forward by Ford or Le Corbusier, expressing instead the aspirations arising from 'the long-expanding American economy'.[37]

General Houses exemplified one aspect of the possibilities of industrialised construction. This was the standardised components, often made by vast corporations, which took advantage of volume mass production. Each house, though enjoying the benefits of the simplified process of erection which standard components offered, had the capacity for individuality, so the process of erection was not standardised to the same extent as it was in the construction of a Model T Ford. Yorke was clearly intrigued by the view of prefabricated housing which General Houses seemed to have brought to fruition from the outset, even here he was moving towards

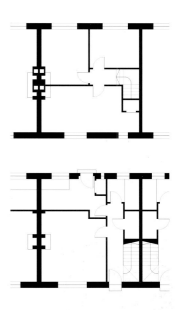

In *A Key to Modern Architecture*, Yorke and Colin Penn contrasted the rational, functional planning that went into the brewery workers' cottages with 'a typical cottage plan, as erected in thousands by local authorities . . .' Their typical example in fact came from eight semi-detached houses Yorke had designed in 1928, before he had begun to appreciate modernism.

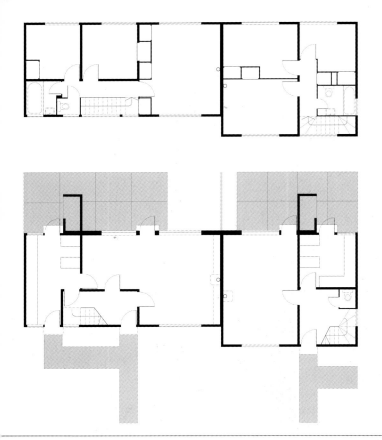

LEFT: Plans of the Braithwaite House. The wide-fronted version owed much to the plan Yorke devised for the brewery cottages, while the narrower fronted one was very close to the 'experimental house' Yorke designed in 1944 for Christabel Burton in Codicote.

OPPOSITE TOP: Despite its supposed prefabrication, the Braithwaite House was labour intensive, and Yorke deliberately left the choice of cladding material open.

OPPOSITE BOTTOM: The Braithwaite House as built. Only one pair was completed, on the London County Council's Watling Street estate, and it was badly damaged by a flying bomb.

Photo: G Street and Co.

rationalised construction rather than transforming the building site into a factory. He would have to wait ten years and for the extraordinary circumstances of wartime, to have an opportunity to design a prefabricated house himself. In the meantime several occurrences heightened his attraction to the idea of rationalised but traditional erection of standardised but largely familiar components. In the book *A Key to Modern Architecture* published in 1939, written by himself and Colin Penn, a fellow student from Birmingham School of Art, he claimed: 'Modern building methods demand the application of prefabrication and mass production to carefully considered and perfected components.'[38] This specifically avoided the issue of whether the construction assembly process itself, as opposed to the manufacture of components, might be susceptible to mass production techniques. Slightly later he wrote: 'My first experience . . . in 1940 when we tore up 800 acres of magnificent landscape,' made 'my feelings about the use of big machinery . . . very mixed'.[39]

Even though Yorke claimed to have achieved 'the completest possible standardisation of parts' in the cottages at Webheath, he was not able to develop the theme until he designed the seven brewery cottages at Stratford-upon-Avon in 1938. This commission came through his father who submitted the planning application on 2 August 1938, and its client was Flowers Brewery, then chaired by the redoubtable Sir Archibald Flower. However, the outcome seems to owe more to Yorke *fils*, who later claimed the design as one of his most satisfying,[40] and possibly Fordham Flower, Archibald's son, led the client's end of the project. The cottages are certainly more to Fordham's architectural taste than Archibald's, who favoured a more traditional architectural idiom.[41] Fordham commissioned the Yorkes for gently modern alterations to his house, Shottery Manor, shortly after the brewery cottages were completed. In 1946 he wrote to FRS Yorke enclosing a copy of a letter printed in a newspaper praising the cottages, a sentiment he obviously shared.[42]

With London stock brick walls, wooden pergolas and window frames on the south elevation of the brewery cottages, the visible materials at least can hardly have upset Sir Archibald. The design's hallmark is its fresh, clean use of those materials. The wooden windows are not sashes or casements, but slide sideways to emphasise the horizontal nature of the design. Due to the

Braithwaite House: porch and interior.

monopitch roof all rainwater pipes are on the north elevation, the roof oversails the south facade almost like a cornice, another way of stressing continuity above the individual units. Breaking the roofline by raising one of the end houses seems to be more a gesture to the collective aesthetic than to give the house status, while a firmly expressed stone flank wall at the other end gives a decisive conclusion to the composition, which might otherwise continue indefinitely.

In these cottages for a powerful and wealthy client Yorke managed to simulate the effect of 'controlled land development' which, as he explained in *The Modern House*, he saw as vital to modern architecture. As he saw it the benefit, apart from a construction cost of £462 for each cottage against about £350 for the local authority houses in Webheath, lay in the possibility for a different approach to land use. In *A Key to Modern Architecture* he illustrated plans which are very close to the Stratford cottages. He explained them as a modern, logical solution to the problem of 'typical cottage plans, as erected in thousands by local authorities during the last fifteen years', and they are uncannily close to the Webheath cottage plan! In essence the 'typical plan's' shortcomings were the poorly arranged bedrooms, and the bathroom being on the ground floor;[43] the Stratford plan overcame these by establishing the needs of the bedrooms and working out the first-floor plan to include a bathroom, and that set the template for the ground floor.

'Our planning', wrote Yorke and Penn, 'has resulted in each dwelling being rather wider than is normal', with the drawbacks of additional roads and services, as well as land usage.[44] While 'controlled land development' would offset the latter, they dismissed the other objections by claiming that, as at Stratford, there was no need for a road to each front door as modern central heating (from a communal plant) eliminated coal delivery. Under these idealised circumstances a knowledge of construction products and technique began to interweave to create a genuinely 'modern' architecture. No wonder Yorke was so proud of the Stratford project.

His pride in it can be detected in the Braithwaite House, the prefabricated system he designed under the auspices of the wartime housing programme.[45] Of the two basic plans he devised, one is wide-fronted and very close to the Stratford plan, although every dimension has to defer to the 3-foot 2-inch module.[46] The project's sponsor, Braithwaite and Co, was an engineering firm that produced a wide range of steel products in factories in the Midlands and South Wales. In 1924 it introduced the Telford steel-clad house of which between 200 and 300 were built for local authorities.[47] This differed from Yorke's house in using steel wall-panels as structure and on the roof. The structure in Yorke's house was lightweight welded cold-rolled steel units of 14 and 16 gauge which made, he claimed, 'site work . . . a simple matter of assembly. The system is like a meccano set, extended to include the finishes as well as the structural skeleton'.[48] Clearly one intention was to eliminate wet trades but Yorke's intimation that brick or even local stone might be used on the walls, which even the Burt Committee report tacitly acknowledged,[49] undermines this aim.

It is a project riddled with ambiguities and buried with a final irony. Here Yorke demonstrated sufficient mastery of industrial techniques and processes to devise a system that *could* be entirely produced in the factory, but chose to give it the option of traditional walling. The factory work involved a great deal of spot-welding, of the frame components to form units 3 feet 2 inches wide which would be bolted together on site, and of shaped plates to which the internal beams could be bolted. The narrow modular dimension and frequent horizontal members within each frame increased the thermal transmission of the structure, as the Burt Committee report anticipated.[50] The number of workmen in the trove of surviving construction photographs suggests that erection was not, after all, 'a simple matter of assembly . . . like a meccano set'. Finally, the pair of prototypes built in the London County Council's Watling Street estate at Burnt Oak were damaged by a flying bomb which landed sixty feet from the corner of the framework.[51] Given that 'the load-bearing structure was badly bent' when 'nearby brick houses . . . were completely demolished,' the Burt Committee 'safely assumed that the structure is capable of carrying any loads to which it will be subjected in normal circumstances.' But even though they lent their approval, it did not go into large-scale production. For reasons way beyond Yorke's control and outside the normal scope of architectural production, Yorke's most serious attempt at developing a prefabricated system failed – he was probably not overly disappointed. He might even have enjoyed the mischievous thought that, had the prototypes been clad in stone, their frames might not even have bent under the impact of the bomb blast. The combination of traditional and innovative constructive would have been irresistible.

The second plan-type Yorke devised for the Braithwaite system had a squarer, narrower fronted plan, but it still manages to contrive reasonably generous spaces in less than 1,000 square feet. It is also very similar to the 'experimental' house he built for Christabel Burton in Codicote towards the end of the war. One sheet of drawings survives in the Allford Yorke Archive dated 27 September 1944, showing that Mrs Burton had conceived the idea of building another house to accommodate members of her extended family some time before the war ended, although it was not built until 1945.[52] Within a more conventional width than the 'Stratford' plan-type of 21 feet, Yorke managed to conjure a reasonable entrance hall leading to a staircase with a stair well, a compact kitchen and a large living room. There was also a downstairs internal WC. Upstairs were a bathroom, two decently sized double bedrooms and a single room.

Two particular features of the planning permitted this accommodation within 950 square feet. The most dramatic was to project the first floor almost 5 feet over the line of the ground-floor entrance facade. Yorke's critique of the Webheath plans in *A Key to Modern Architecture* gives a clue to the thinking behind this device. 'The most obvious fault', wrote Yorke and Penn of this plan-type, was the 'barbaric practice' of placing the bathroom on the ground floor, 'in order to reduce the size of the floor above'.[53] Yorke's plan at Codicote is a neat and elegant rebuttal of that problem though, with no less external wall area and the same amount of first-floor structure, it cannot have been much cheaper than increasing the size of the ground floor. The second feature of the plan is that, without the bathroom placed directly over the kitchen, there is a need for two plumbing stacks, another potential increase in cost. In the Braithwaite version of this plan the position of the staircase and ground-floor WC is reversed, bringing the plumbing into one stack, but losing something in elegance and requiring artificial ventilation for the WC were the houses to be in a terrace.

For Mrs Burton, whose means were less limited than those of many a local authority, absolute cost was less of a difficulty than obtaining the materials. To overcome this she and Yorke had to ensure that the house could be seen as 'experimental', so when Yorke published it in the postwar editions of *The Modern House*, he produced a montage, showing a notional terrace of houses to extend a photograph of the one at Codicote. Compared with the Braithwaite House Codicote is hardly experimental, but it does represent a significant step in Yorke's thinking. Here he had a plan that was narrow enough to work in conventional site layouts and was built by adapting traditional constructional methods rather than appropriating industrial techniques. The roof, of concrete slab and bituminous felt, had a gently sloping double pitch. The flank or party walls were reinforced concrete, while the front and back walls were non-load-bearing infill, leaving the wall between the living room and hall as the only internal stuctural wall; it supports the staircase. The front wall was brick and the rear was pressed sawdust paper-pulp sandwiched between asbestos sheets, but conceptually they might just as well have been fieldstone.

Plans of the 'experimental house' in Codicote which Yorke designed in 1944 under wartime conditions.

To demonstrate its 'experimental' nature, Yorke extrapolated a photograph of the house into a drawing of a terrace.

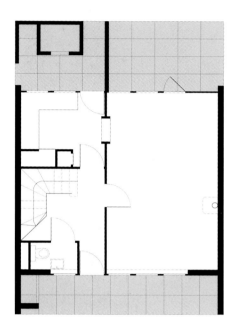

RIGHT: The New House at Luccombe, near Shanklin on the Isle of Wight, which Yorke built for his family – but they only owned it for one year. Using traditional construction such as masonry and carpentry proved simpler than the industrialisation of the Braithwaite House's production.

BELOW: The combination of traditional construction, in the form of fieldstone end walls and the innovative techniques of a monopitch roof and cantilevered concrete floor slab, was particular to Yorke at the time.

The house at Luccombe on the Isle of Wight, which Yorke built for himself and his family in 1947, gave him the opportunity to bring his experiences of housing design over the previous decade to personal fruition. It was with Marcel Breuer, on the Gane show house in Bristol in 1935, that Yorke first toyed with fieldstone in a domestic context; as a single elevated storey, the Luccombe house bears some similarity to Breuer's own weekend cottage, though this may also be a response to the site. Luccombe is in an area prone to land slippage, floating the floor slab on a sunken foundation at one end and an elevated footing at the other appears to have given it greater structural stability than its neighbours.[54] As at Stratford, a monopitch roof falls to the rear elevation, keeping the front visually clear and unimpeded for a veranda. Like Codicote, its long elevations are mainly non-load-bearing infill construction, though the house length necessitated intermediate cross walls between the flanks. Yorke neatly expressed this by returning the fieldstone on to the front elevation, one bay on one side and half a bay on the other, as if to show that two U-shapes at either end provided the main structure. Though Yorke and his wife Thelma only kept the house for one year, it embodied many of his architectural interests, even if it did not serve the purposes of his family.[55]

Through practical experience, some of it gained in the service of commercial publishing and another slice in wartime, Yorke acquired and demonstrated his status as a 'technical expert'. It also provided a framework which modified his early enthusiasm for industrialised production, initially towards factory manufacture of components and latterly to include space for traditional construction in rationalised form. When his technical expertise was combined with some form of 'controlled land development', as at Stratford, the results gave him enormous satisfaction, even the one-off 'experimental' houses at Luccombe and Codicote demonstrated conclusively that technical knowledge could conjure modern design from traditional materials. All have carefully produced plans which manage subtlety and flourishes within tight floor areas, achieving a clarity of expression which comes from confidence and knowledge in handling materials. In different ways they are considered in relation to their sites, particularly as part of potentially larger developments at Stratford and to take advantage of the views at Luccombe. Though recognisably modern and to some extent experimental, they are not overt manifestoes. Rather, they are summations of a series of themes which helped to shape Yorke's thinking into the 1940s, and provided a rich vein of inspiration for some of the early Yorke, Rosenberg and Mardall buildings, such as the Barclay School in Stevenage, and the housing at Bryn-mawr in Wales. However derivative it may have been, here was a version of modernism that had eased the British Establishment through its myriad crises of the 1930s and 1940s; it also acted as an outward manifestation of the negotiations between tradition and modernity which held those crises in check.

When David Allford and his fellow 'young Turks' engineered their revolution in the firm's office in the mid-1950s, Yorke's apparent support perhaps required more self-control than they realised.[56] It was more than just a generational upheaval, though it can be seen as a microcosm of the *coup de grâce* Team X administered to CIAM, or of the Corbusian formalists versus the Marxist realists at the London County Council.[57] Allford and his colleagues were challenging the essence of what Yorke had achieved in his first decade and half as a professional architect – a pragmatic approach to achieving modern design, through skilful adaptation of existing techniques.

By the time Yorke designed the **Barclay School in Stevenage in the late 1940s, he had evolved an undogmatic approach to modernist composition. The school's modernism depended on the use of components and the odd dramatic device, rather than drama.**

Photo: Philippa Lewis.

Notes

1. The rubric to the 'Trade Notes' column in *The Architects' Journal* of 22 March 1933 noted that it would be written by FRS Yorke from now on, as he was 'well-known as one of the most progressive younger architects [with] a unique knowledge of materials and is in close contact with the work of British manufacturers'. It was a phrase which might warm the hearts of advertisers. *The Architects' Journal*, vol 77 (January–June 1933), p 408.

2. The single period for which a full statement of Yorke's earnings from the Architectural Press exists is the tax year 1939–40. It shows his income for editing *Specification* was £505 5s. He received a further £50 4s in royalties. RIBA YoF/1/12.

3. Sir James Richards, in conversation with Jeremy Melvin, 28 November 1991.

4. FRS Yorke, *The Modern House*, Architectural Press (London), 1934, p 2.

5. Ibid, p 5.

6. Ibid, p 2.

7. Ibid, p 5.

8. Though largely Breuer's work, the Concrete Garden City of the Future brought Yorke international publicity, and occupied a prominent position in the MARS Exhibition of 1938. Controlled land development, of course, really did come about with the Town and Country Planning Act of 1947, on whose genesis Yorke's friend William Holford had been occupied since 1941/2. As early as 1941 Donald Gibson sounded Yorke out to work on Coventry on the advice of Geoffrey Jellicoe; within a few years several of Yorke's friends, Frederick Gibberd, Peter Shepheard and Jellicoe himself had become planners of new towns. There is no evidence that Yorke pursued such an appointment, though he must have known of their existence. See a letter from Gibson to Yorke dated 2 April 1941, in the RIBA YoF/1/ 12.

9. Mark Swenarton, *Artisans and Architects*, Heinemann (London), 1989.

10. Randall Evans remembered the episode on the roof late in life, repeating it to the present author and to Alan Powers, who recorded it in *In the Line of Development*, RIBA Heinz Gallery (London), 1992, p 18. For the comments to Folks, see letter dated 7 February 1944, in the RIBA YoF/1/8.

11. *Architects' Journal*, vol 92 (15 October 1944), pp 251–6. A caption (p 256) explains: 'Brick is a possible cladding material as well as local stone.' The cladding of the prototypes was actually asbestos-cement sheets.

12. A typescript headed 'Cottages at Stratford-upon-Avon, 1938/9', in the Allford Yorke Archive, Folder 16, pp 7–8. It was written to provide a committee with information, although the purpose of the committee is not clear.

13. Various speculative reasons might be offered. The US certainly offered Breuer more generous budgets, and fewer restrictions on materials and planning controls than Yorke had in postwar England. And where Yorke consciously decided to build a corporate practice around several partners, Breuer, after his split with Gropius in 1941, developed his firm in his own image. See Robert Gatje, *Marcel Breuer a memoir*, Monacelli (New York) 2000 for an anecdotal description of Breuer's office, by someone who eventually became his partner. Joachim Driller, the leading scholar of Breuer's domestic designs in *Breuer's Houses*, Phaidon (London), 2000 discusses the influence of the Gane Pavilion which Breuer designed while in partnership with Yorke on several post-war designs, notably the Clark House in Connecticut of 1949–51 (pp 34–6). Drawings for the Gane Pavilion survive in the RIBA Drawings Collection, PA 236/5.

14. Several photographs exist in the Allford Yorke Archive, Folder 12, pp 35–7. FWB Yorke also wrote a book called *Tools Used in the Building Trade*, 1907. See FWB Yorke's biography file at the RIBA.

15. See the diary Yorke kept of this cycling trip with his father to Normandy, now in the RIBA YoF/1/8. All quotes in this and the subsequent paragraph come from this source. See Tim Hilton, *John Ruskin: The Later Years*, Yale University Press (New Haven and London), 2000, pp 561–6 for an account of Ruskin's and Blow's relationship.

16. It might be noted that these activities are tied up with the nature of modernism, and not just in architecture. The first three were also hallmarks of the British Welfare State, while the fourth, especially in its manifestation

17. One of the most successful exploiters of this trend was Alfred Harmsworth, later Viscount Northcliffe, elder brother of Yorke's first significant client Christabel Burton. See Chapter Three.

18. To these might be added magazines with almost exclusively professional readerships: The *RIBA Journal* which began continuous publication as its third series in 1891, and the *Architects' Journal* whose ancestry can be traced to 1895.

19. Swenarton, op cit, puts Ruskin and Morris – writers rather than architects – firmly at the heart of the Arts and Crafts movement.

20. Margaret Richardson, *Architects of the Arts and Crafts Movement*, Trefoil Press (London), 1983, p 71. She wrote: '. . . the work of Sedding and his pupils . . . consistently and exactly realises the theories of the Arts and Crafts movement. It was the only office to do so.' Sedding's early death, aged 53, in 1891 was much lamented – at least in the memorial volume edited by Henry Wilson, *A Memorial to the Late JD Sedding*, 1892.

21. Investigating the Architectural Press's role in this process is beyond the scope of this study; but the establishment of *Specification* which Yorke edited from 1935, through to the creation of a system for cataloguing construction information, conducted in part by Michael Ventris in the mid-1950s, shows an awareness of it. Incidentally, Ventris lived for almost 20 years (and deciphered Linear B) in an apartment in Highpoint with interiors and furniture by Breuer and Yorke, itself three floors above the London residence of the present writer. As Ruskin himself wrote (admittedly in the not exactly related context of the last paragraph of his autobiography *Praeterita*) 'How things bind and blend themselves together'. Giedion might have intuited some sort of *geist*.

22. Le Corbusier, *Vers une architecture*, trans Frederick Etchells as *Towards a New Architecture*, John Rodker (London), 1928. The same year Evelyn Waugh, in his first novel, *Decline and Fall*, Chapman and Hall, 1928, has Arthur Potts and the hero Paul Pennyfeather dismiss Le Corbusier as old hat, 'pure 19th century Manchester School utilitarian' (p 122 of the Penguin edition).

23. The agricultural workers' cottages were designed before Yorke completed his studies at the Birmingham School of Architecture and joined the RIBA in 1930. See *Architects' Journal*, vol 78 (27 July 1933), p 114. In Yorke's nomination papers to become an Associate of the RIBA, held at the Institute and submitted on 26 August 1930, he admits to a period working 'full time in an office' between June 1927 and September 1928, presumably when he designed these dwellings. Although he does not specify which office, the location, architectural idiom of the houses and the very opportunity afforded to a 21-year-old, together with his reticence on the papers, strongly suggest it was his father's.

24. *Architects' Journal*, vol 73 (8 April 1931), supplement. The drawing was originally student work, preserved in the RIBA Drawings Collection, PA 237/9.

25. Yorke's father, though not bald and an habitué of the main rather than back streets of Birmingham, subsisted at least in part on such commissions. Yorke's writing seems to have appealed to architects like Fred Vaux of Bridlington (see note 11, Chapter 1) as well as more obvious soul mates such as Max Fry, who 'found it hard to over-estimate the value of the book [*The Modern House*]'. See Fry's appreciation of Yorke, *The Architectural Review*, vol 132 (October 1962) pp 279–80.

26. *The Architects' Journal*, vol 78 (27 July 1933), p 114.

27. *The Architects' Journal*, vol 78 (16 November 1933), p 644.

28. *The Architects' Journal*, vol 80 (15 November 1934), p 753.

29. With typically charming immodesty, Buckminster Fuller also claimed credit for General Houses. See his Grinch of Giants (www.bfi.org/grinch-_of_giants.htm). 'A group of prominent industrialists, led by one of my young fans, had incorporated "General Houses", and that was all it took to get *Fortune* excited,' he wrote, reflecting on an article on prefabrication in *Fortune*.

30. Alfred P Sloan Junior, *My Years with General Motors*, Pan (London), 1967, p 173.

31. HT Fisher had written on housing and had several of his own houses

featured in *Architectural Record*. See, for example, 'New Elements of House Design', *Architectural Record*, vol 66 (November 1929), pp 396–484, and 'The Country House', *Architectural Record*, vol 68 (September 1930), pp 199–204.

32. *Architectural Forum* (April 1933), p 330.
33. Sloan, op cit, p 126.
34. Ibid, p 127.
35. Yorke reproduced the questionnaire alongside his 'Trade Notes' column, *Architects' Journal*, vol 80 (15 November 1934), pp 753.
36. They even devised a coding system which shows something of the variety that could be achieved within the overall standardisation. The Allford Yorke Archive, Folder 8, has a loose leaf torn from a book – possibly the 52-page booklet mentioned by Yorke. On one side is the illustration, marked up with instructions to a printer, used on page 176 of *The Modern House*; the reverse side has a picture whose caption is headed K2H4O. The caption continues: 'K2H4O is an architectural, not a chemical formula. It represents upon the drafting boards of General Houses' architects, the prefabricated house shown above and on the facing page. "K" refers to the basic housing type: "2" indicates a subdivision of that type. "H" expresses entrance through a hall. "4" means that there is space for four beds in two bedrooms. "O" stands for an optional extra room.' All these specifications could be deduced from a completed questionnaire.
37. Sloan, op cit, p 173.
38. FRS Yorke and Colin Penn, *A Key to Modern Architecture*, Blackie (London and Glasgow), 1939, p 130.
39. Letter to J Homery Folkes, 7 February 1944, RIBA YoF/1/8.
40. See 'Cottages in Stratford-upon-Avon, 1938/9' in Allford Yorke Archive, Folder 16, p 7.
41. A drawing dating from 1933 and listing Archibald Flower as the client in the Shakespeare Centre, Stratford-upon-Avon, by John Knight (reg arch) for cottages on the Shottery estate shows them to be in a very traditional Cotswold style.
42. A letter from Fordham Flower to Yorke dated 14 June 1946 has the letter from MW Lee of 60 Ashburton Avenue, Addiscombe, printed in an unidentified newspaper, attached. It is preserved in the Allford Yorke Archive, Folder, 16, page 10. 'Dear Yorke', wrote Flower, 'I thought the attached might warm your heart. I have told the writer that you are the architect concerned. Hope you had a good holiday.' That Fordham and FRS were on friendly terms long after the completion of the cottages implies a compatibility between them and tends to support the theory that it was the two younger men, rather than their fathers, who implemented the project.
43. 'This barbaric practice ...' railed Yorke and Penn, op cit, p 111.
44. Ibid, p 118.
45. See Brian Finnimore, *Houses from the Factory*, Rivers Oram (London), 1989, for an overview of industrialised house-building in Britain. He has nothing explicitly on the Braithwaite House, which was clearly not one of the most successful of the various prefabricated systems developed at the same time.

46. See *Architects' Journal* vol 92 (15 October 1944), pp 251–6 for plans, illustrations and a description of the system. It is also noted approvingly in the 'Second Report on House Construction', HMSO, 1944, pp 4–8.
47. See the Building Research Establishment Report by E Grant on the Telford House, CI/SfB (99.71) H:h2 (A7), 1991, from which this information is taken. I am grateful to Stephen Mullin for drawing my attention to the Telford House, and providing information on it and the Braithwaite design.
48. See typescript description in the Allford Yorke Archive, Folder 13, p 18.
49. 'Second Report', op cit, p 4, notes: 'Alternative cladding materials [to asbestos cement sheets] can be used.' See also the picture caption in *Architects' Journal* (15 October 1944), p 256.
50. Second Report, op cit, p 5.
51. Ibid.
52. In *The Road Ahead*, Corgi (London), 1992, Christabel Bielenberg, one of Mrs Burton's daughters, recalls the house being under construction some time after she arrived in England after her wartime experiences in Germany. She also quips that its experimental qualities were unclear (p 69).
53. Yorke and Penn, op cit, p 111.
54. The house's owner, David Bottom, kindly showed me around on 7 September 2002. The information on land subsidence comes from him, though an inspection of the house showed that the floor slab has suffered slight cracking which is much more likely to come from thermal expansion due to the lack of expansion joints along its 65-foot length rather than subsidence.
55. Clues to the Yorke's reasons for selling come from two postcards from his wife Thelma to Yorke in the Allford Yorke Archive Folder 20, pp 19, 28, postmarked 8 and 28 May 1947. 'Do hope you have news of letting in June and July,' she wrote on the 8th, implying that the costs needed to be offset somehow. Her plea to hear 'all the fishing news' on the 28th suggests that Yorke, for whatever reason, did not spend all his free time on the Isle of Wight.
56. See Chapter 6.
57. Neither Yorke, nor Rosenberg or Mardall, however, were Marxists. During the 1950s they enjoyed increasing affluence, as the upgrade of motor-cars to Bentleys, Aston Martins and Alvises, listed in the partnership accounts, shows. Ironically, it was David Allford, who admitted to attending a meeting of the Stockholm Peace Appeal (which he came to consider as a front for Moscow-inspired activities) while a student at Sheffield University in the late 1940s, who had the most *gauchiste* tendencies at this stage, though his political views did modify somewhat. Indeed, an experience at that meeting sowed the seeds of his later discontent with socialism. He dared to make a joke, at which a young medical student, Dr Sammy Glatt, who later practised in London's East End, turned round and admonished him, 'You won't be laughing after the Revolution'. Allford later confessed that this implied to him that socialists lacked a sense of humour, and initiated a shift which saw him become an enthusiastic Conservative.

CHAPTER 3

NUDE SUNBATHERS OR ROYAL TUTORS?

Clients and patrons in the 1930s

BOTTOM: Much of the 1951 Festival of Britain was planned in the 'elephant room', an extension of a cottage Yorke modelled for the *News Chronicle* editor Gerald Barry in the late 1930s.

Photo: Cracknell.

One of the most obvious characteristics that distinguishes architecture from the other fine arts, at least when manifested in buildings, is its need for someone – a body or a person – to pick up an often substantial bill. Very rarely is that person the architect, and as architecture has evolved as an independent profession it has continuously struggled to define its role in terms that prove its 'usefulness' to bill payers, who we might term 'clients'.[1] Clients come in many shapes and sizes. Some 'view architectural production from a purely rational and instrumental perspective . . . [regarding] . . . buildings as capital assets, which should be managed like every other potential source of productivity, income and profit.'[2] Architects, though, often prefer clients with patience, far-sightedness and deep pockets, who might qualify for the accolade of 'patron'.[3]

In *The Modern House*, Yorke implied an empathy with both positions. Small-scale patrons were essential, he suggested, as their projects were laboratories where modern architecture could develop. They were a means to enabling architecture to achieve greater ends, such as 'the simplification of all communications, pipes and wires, and so on' and prefabricated dwellings built on communally controlled land – which could only be achieved through bodies who viewed buildings as capital assets.[4] In general terms World War II is a watershed which divides Yorke's clients into the two categories. Those before 1939 were largely small scale and private, while through Yorke, Rosenberg & Mardall he became one of the leading instruments in the vast expansion of state-funded building activity, designing schools, hospitals, housing and ultimately universities and airports.[5] This masks his experience in the 1930s of dealing with corporate bodies who did appoint him from a 'rational and instrumental perspective' because he convinced them his architecture would serve their particular needs. In its complexities, the story of the relationships between Yorke and his clients helps to explain how he was able to take advantage of the vastly increased, though very differently motivated, opportunities that occurred after 1945, and by extension offers a small contribution to understanding how this shift took place in more general terms.

Although scholars like Louise Campbell and Jeremy Gould have made significant advances in the historiography of modernist clients in the 1930s, the subject still lacks definitive study.[6] It is often understood in unfortunate stereotypes or half-truths. These are deeply ingrained. In 1971, no less distinguished a historian than Paul Thompson could write:

> Of the patrons of the houses built in Britain in the International Style up to 1939 and published in *The Architectural Review* . . . scholars and educationalists account for ten, architects and their relatives for six, other artists, designers and writers for six, other professionals and businessmen for eleven . . . There are no other significant groups and the old aristocracy is entirely unrepresented.[7]

By the late 1970s, an enduring stereotype of the 'modernist client of the 1930s', along the lines of a radical, nude-sunbathing solicitor living in Hampstead, had emerged.[8] Like all stereotypes this contains an element of truth, which might be distilled as someone with a certain degree of affluence, but probably outside the established systems of power and wealth, with a need or at least

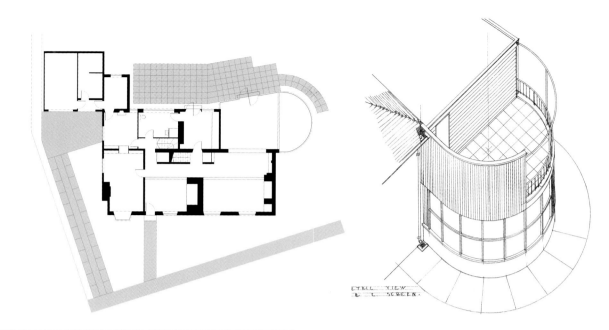

LEFT: Plan of the remodelled Forge Cottage.

RIGHT: Yorke's drawing of
the curved, glazed wall to
the 'elephant room'.

Courtesy of Richard Burton.

It was on the ski slopes of Berwang in the Tyrol in the winter of 1933–4 that the Yorke's met Christabel Burton (later Bielenberg), who remembered his enthusiasm about modern houses when she heard that her mother intended to build a home for her sister a few months later. Yorke selected the image for his 1934 Christmas card.

British Architectural Library, RIBA, London.

ABOVE: Mrs Christabel Burton, née Harmsworth, Yorke's redoubtable first client.

Courtesy of Richard Burton.

an urge to proclaim 'difference' from bourgeois conventions. More recently another generalisation has become part of the received wisdom, largely through its frequent repetition by Peter Cook: the seaside 'licenses' a certain freedom in behaviour which made it more receptive to modernist architecture.[9] The proliferation of variants of modernism in coastal resorts lends some credence to this argument. To these assumptions about the 'typical client' a third might be added: that there are connections with industry that make industrialised production a way of life. WJ Bassett-Lowke, client of CR Mackintosh and Peter Behrens, the Crittall family and Yorke's own clients, the Ganes, suggest some affinity between modernism and industry, especially when their products had some use in modernist design.[10]

Yorke's clients represent a much broader social spread than Thompson at least implies, and to some extent this prefigures the shift between pre-war and post-war patronage, making that shift seem less dramatic. It was an issue which Yorke considered either unimportant or too private to divulge; his books have hardly any reference to clients, and none to those for one-off houses. Several of his clients, however, seem to fit the typecasting. For example, Hugh Rose, for whom he designed a private swimming pool in Hampstead and Shangri-La, a house at Lee-on-Solent in Hampshire, and the bandleader James MacNabb who commissioned a house at Angmering-on-Sea in Sussex, here were two clients who could easily be slotted into both of the first two assumptions.[11] Gerald Barry, a radical intellectual, editor of the left-leaning *News Chronicle*, initiator of an important competition for school design and later the Festival of Britain, chose Yorke to design an extension to a Sussex cottage. The house, Forge Cottage in the village of Sutton, was one of Yorke's most subtle and successful pre-war designs. In converting two cottages into one house, Yorke reordered the plan, made a virtue of the existing structure and on the front added only a delicately minimal porch. For the rear he designed a far more dramatic addition, a curving, glass-fronted, double-height room, which conjured a series of grand and intimate spaces including a mezzanine and roof terrace that opened into the existing living room, encapsulating a union of old and new.[12] Another interesting client of the Yorke and Breuer partnership was Mrs Dorothy Ventris, a collector of contemporary art, for whom they, largely Breuer,[13] designed the interior of a flat at Highpoint, Tecton's residential masterpiece in Highgate, north London. It was in this flat that her son Michael decoded the Minoan Linear B script.[14]

Commissions from the furniture-making Gane family and the Concrete Garden City scheme for the Cement and Concrete Association fit nicely into the category of industrial concerns promoting their own products.[15] Three clients tell a different story: the Flower family, brewers, landowners and Shakespeare enthusiasts; the Burton family, who gave Yorke his first solo commission for Torilla, a house outside Hatfield, Hertfordshire; and Eton College, for which he designed a pair of houses for 'married non-housemasters'. On their own these clients suggest nothing especially unusual. It is when they are taken together that they begin to depict a different pattern in the reasons and motives for commissioning modern architecture in the 1930s.

The Flower family had established a brewery in Stratford-upon-Avon in 1832. By 1855 they were prosperous enough to buy a country estate, and twenty years later paid almost the entire cost of the first Shakespeare Memorial Theatre in the town, spurred by the tercentenary of his birth there in 1564. Their wealth came from a traditional industry, often associated with Conservative politics, and their cultural patronage was local and to some extent, given Shakespeare's status in British culture, nationalist.[16] Out of this background, though, one member of the family at least emerged as a significant supporter of contemporary arts. Sir Fordham Flower (1904–66) chaired the Coventry Cathedral rebuilding committee, established the Flowers (later Whitbread) Theatre awards and attracted testimonials from several avant-garde cultural figures; it was he who formed the closest relationship with Yorke.

The Burtons came from a different circle. Christabel Burton senior – one of her daughters was named Christabel – was a younger sister of the Harmsworth brothers, who between them revolutionised newspaper and periodical publishing between 1890 and the 1920s.[17] Her husband Percy had been secretary to one of the brothers, Cecil, and later established successful advertising businesses which expanded as magazines grew.[18] The family's wealth came from an industry transformed beyond all recognition by mass literacy, the growth of leisure time and new technology, and, in some members at least, greatly exceeded that of the Flowers. If the Establishment could easily assimilate the rise of yet another family of successful brewers, the emergence of such wealth through what was in effect a new industry was much more challenging. Eventually the growth of the media would totally alter the nature of power structures, by penetrating the Establishment the Harmsworths also changed its composition.[19] Through her husband's business success and perhaps outright gifts from her brothers, Christabel Burton paid for Yorke's first solo commission, the house Torilla, its extension, and a second house in Codicote, Hertfordshire.[20]

If the Flowers and Harmsworths both represented new money, Eton stood for stability.[21] Here Yorke encountered a major institution, governed by ancient statute and controlled by people who had achieved distinction in public life – though they often had more pressing concerns than the workings of their old school.[22] Many were aristocrats, including Lord Hugh Cecil, the provost after 1936, and Lord Halifax, erstwhile viceroy of India and later Foreign Secretary. Though Yorke's background was not aristocratic and he did not attend one of the major public schools, he had quite possibly encountered people in analogous positions.[23] In any case, this project gave him some experience of the frustrations and advantages of working with committees and the tactics which might be necessary to achieve his ends through them.

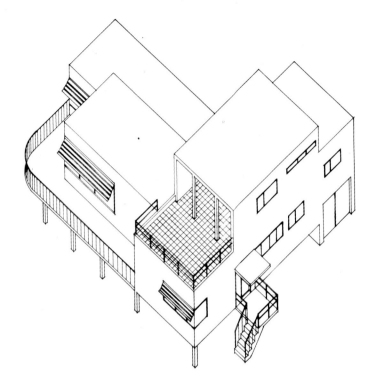

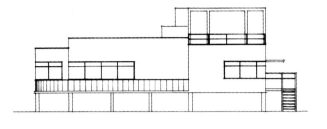

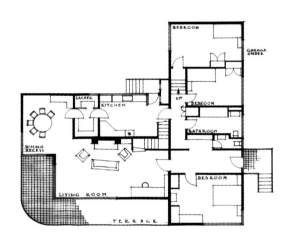

ABOVE : In an early design Torilla was to be raised on piloti, in a manner reminiscent of Heinrich Lauterbach's Haus Hasek (see p 24), an indication of the influence of Yorke's researches for *The Modern House* on his early design projects.

Each of these clients challenges the stereotypes in a particular way, but the first two, at least, partly fit them. This interweaving of stereotype and new material hints at something more: that large and traditional institutions were already aware of, and using, modern architecture in the 1930s, and their understanding of it was cast in terms that followed the claims made for its efficiency. Furthermore, Yorke was beginning to move in circles where he had to understand how such institutions came to decisions, triggering an engagement between modernism and the Establishment which he would help to bring to fruition after World War II. In short, explaining how Yorke's client base exposed him to these issues can help to illuminate why his firm became so successful after 1945, and offer some insights as to why the Establishment should have embraced this architectural idiom, notwithstanding its origins in radical thought, with such enthusiasm.

The story of Torilla, the first of Yorke's seminal commissions, starts on the ski slopes of Switzerland in the winter of 1933–4. Christabel Burton, who would marry the German lawyer Peter Bielenberg on 29 September 1934, met a slightly older English couple, FRS and Thelma Yorke. Yorke, it seems, spoke enthusiastically on the subject of *The Modern House*, which was published the following summer, and Christabel later confessed to being enchanted by his descriptions of modern houses.[24] Some months later her parents Percy and Christabel Burton expressed enthusiasm for building a house for her recently espoused younger sister Barbara,

ABOVE: Torilla's dramatic living room in 1935.
Conveniently planned, it also encapsulates a modernist
relationship between space, surface, form and light.

Photo: British Architectural Library, RIBA, London.

whose husband Charles MacDonald became an airline pilot. The house was to be in the grounds of her parents' magnificent Elizabethan manor house at Nast Hyde near Hatfield, just north of London. Barbara MacDonald remembers that, 'It couldn't be a copy of Nast Hyde or like the boring middle class houses down the road.'[25] Her sister Christabel recalled Yorke's monologues and wrote to him suggesting a meeting, which led to Yorke being commissioned in the summer of 1934. It was the first project he carried out entirely in his own name.[26]

Torilla is a magnificently assured project for an architect who was not yet 28. It uses unfamiliar forms of construction, such as flat roofs, cast *in situ* concrete walls and unusually large windows, and it is also exceedingly well planned. The kitchen is invisible from the dining room, but serves it easily. From the hall there is a discreet route to the kitchen for a maid to receive guests to the house, and the hall itself neatly tucks away coat-hanging space and a door to the lavatory while also offering a clearly visible route into the main living room, a sequence which starts under a cantilevered concrete canopy, leads into a recessed porch and then through a glazed door to the hall.[27] Not surprisingly, Yorke started by drawing on features he had published in *The Modern House*. Indeed, the design started off as a rather derivative version of the Haus Hasek designed by Heinrich Lauterbach in Gablonz (now Jablonec), Czechoslovakia, featured in *The Modern House*.[28] A preliminary proposal shows a main floor raised on stilts with an L-shaped balcony wrapping around two sides of the principal room. Later it lost the stilts and the balcony became a ground level terrace, but the essential T-shaped plan remained in the final scheme.

External details show that Yorke also had an appreciation of the technical problems which had to be overcome to ensure the modernist effect of white cubic forms.[29] Window sills for example, are slender, curved metal strips, which were extremely unusual in Britain at the time, minimising rain-staining and allowing the windows to appear as stark, punched holes in the homogenous walls. The parapet wall-tops slope slightly backwards to ensure that water falls into a gutter behind them, rather than streaking the outer face. Views from rooms, too, are well orientated so that the kitchen does not overlook the most public parts of the garden.

The most significant achievement in the house is the creation of two fine spaces: the living room and principal bedroom. The living room is L-shaped; within the angle of the L are the kitchen and a staircase wrapped around a large chimney stack. The layout is functional and elegant – the dining area is in the short arm of the L, where it can be served from the kitchen that is invisible from the rest of the room. A large dining table set for a dinner party would make a climax to the room, while a smaller table could be discreetly tucked away, and the large window open to the ground would suggest a continuation of the axis from the entrance into the garden.

The room's glory, though, is in the effect rather than the fact of its composition. Its volume is a complex interweaving of different spaces, varying in size and elevation: it could be three cuboids – the dining area, sitting area and balcony overlooking it from the top of the stairs – skewered together by the chimney, but they overlap in so many ways that defining it in these terms is bland. The sitting area is double height, with its upper level setting the top plane of the balcony while its floor is contiguous with that of the dining area. The ceiling of the single-height dining area is near enough the floor of the balcony, and so forth. Its composition is rich and dynamic, presenting a multiplicity of views and readings, suggesting a systemic relation between the traditional functions of a house. This is an effect that Yorke appreciated in the examples he included in *The Modern House*.

Different lighting effects are especially suggestive. At ground level are two large windows, one the height of the dining area, the other, south facing, nearly the full height of the sitting area. These admit direct light (with large external blinds to exclude unwanted summer sun), but there are also hidden light sources. A window on the balcony casts light onto the rear wall, its effect

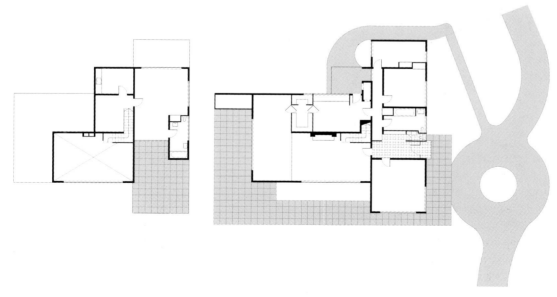

ABOVE: In its assembly of cuboid forms, Torilla recalls Czech Functionalism rather than Le Corbusier's Five Points of Architecture.

Courtesy of *The Architectural Review.*

LEFT: When built, the house lost its elevated main storey, but gained a double-height living room.

apparent but not its actuality. Above the height change between the sitting and dining areas is another high window: an ingenious construction of slender concrete glazing bars and obscured glass, its effect on light is similar to glass blocks, which were not available until some years later.

Some commentators have seen references to traditional English domestic architecture in this room, especially in the balcony and chimney.[30] Yorke was certainly familiar with such buildings.[31] In the other main space, the principal bedroom, the source is much more evident. With its sliding and folding glass wall to a terrace, it bears some resemblance to Lois Welzenbacher's house in Westphalia, which appeared in *The Modern House*.[32] As in the living room, architectural devices of light, volume and plane define zones for activities and establish possibilities that would have been impossible in traditional homes. Opening the windows creates a free flow of space from a low-walled roof-level terrace to a roofed zone, passing a bulge which houses the bathroom, into an entirely interior space with a window overlooking the entrance.

So far this demonstrates Yorke's ability as early as 1934 to bring together his knowledge of building craft and of modernist design to produce a convincing modernist house, whose sources are eclectic enough to justify an overall originality. The only fault Barbara MacDonald could remember sixty years later was that the coal bunker emptied into the kitchen. The house was satisfactorily tuned to comfortable middle-class life, making allowances for servants. The MacDonalds had no help initially (Barbara remembers doing much of the decoration), but there were six indoor servants at Nast Hyde, and Torilla proved popular with her parents when they moved in at the beginning of the war as call-ups and other obligations reduced their establishment. It also bore extension. In 1936 Yorke and Breuer added a nursery wing for the growing family.[33] By the time the MacDonalds left in 1939 they had three children.

Yorke's skill, however, was not Christabel Burton's prime motive in building such a house, nor does it explain why it should be a significant act of patronage for the modern movement. Certainly Barbara MacDonald's comment that the house should neither compete with Nast Hyde, nor resemble 'middle class houses', elucidates why her sister should have remembered Yorke's enthusiasm and her mother should have responded to them. It does not explain why they were building the house in the first place. Charles MacDonald was an Australian who came to England hoping to join the Royal Air Force. He became engaged to Barbara, but he was turned down by the RAF and returned to his father's sheep station in Queensland, where the pair married in 1933. Barbara remembers that he 'didn't quite know what to do'. When the couple were back in England in September 1933 her father Percy, inspired by the proximity of the De Havilland aircraft company to Nast Hyde, suggested Charles learn to fly. Charles replied that he would if he could afford it, to which her mother added that she would pay for his lessons. Christabel and Percy decided to build a house for the young couple.

By all accounts Mrs Christabel Burton was a formidable lady and she took the lead in appointing Yorke. Certainly, she was not the least remarkable member of her remarkable family. She was born in 1880 and the family's success was already established when she was a girl. As a young woman she saw this success come to fruition. She saw the family regularly, remaining close to several of her brothers and living opposite her mother in the London suburb of Totteridge until the move to Nast Hyde in 1927. Barbara MacDonald remembers frequent summonses to have lunch with her grandmother, heralded by a call from the butler: 'the heavies are arriving'.[34] Christabel shared much of the family forcefulness. Her grandson Richard Burton remembers her success in persuading the government of the day to introduce free school milk, whose value she learnt through running a canteen at Bedlam. She also sat on the financial committee of Queen Charlotte's Hospital. Other anecdotes abound. One of her committees, that included local worthies such as

The young Richard Burton on the terrace at Torilla. His grandmother paid for the house for his aunt and her family, and he was a frequent visitor to his cousins during the 1930s.

Courtesy of Richard Burton.

Lady Brocket and the wife of the largest magnate in the area, the Marchioness of Salisbury, was discussing the organisation of a fund-raising ball to buy a car for the district nurse, when Christabel interjected: 'Wouldn't it be much easier if we just wrote cheques now?' She did not share the aristocratic view that money should never be discussed at first hand, but took the direct initiative. Hectoring governments in pursuit of worthwhile causes was something of a family trait.

Torilla is a house paid for not just with new money, but money from a new industry. It was both an act of family generosity and the product of a forceful and determined client who had, remembers her daughter Barbara, 'ideas ahead of her time'. Barbara also remembers that Yorke was humorous, prepared to explain new techniques such as the manufacture of reinforced concrete and 'very firm about how it should be built – he was not to be pushed around'. Clearly she shared her sister's appreciation of his enthusiasm. Christabel Burton may have 'hoped it was all right' to use such an inexperienced architect, but his skill and explanations overcame her reservations. Clearly neither she nor Yorke was ready to compromise, and their going ahead successfully suggests a meeting of minds, even an affinity of approach, between a representative of one of the most remarkable and successful families of the early twentieth century and an architect already perceived to be one of the most progressive of the time.[35] What started in a chance meeting ended in Yorke proving his capabilities – and the capability of modern architecture to provide an elegant lifestyle.

Eton College represents a completely different milieu. While terms like 'progressive' and 'reactionary' are not very helpful when discussing traditional educational institutions, Eton is a complex organisation whose earliest governing charters and practices go back to the fifteenth century. A measure of its importance in providing a 'ruling elite' in the 1930s can be found in its roll of Members of Parliament – 106 in 1931 and 104 in 1935 – nearly one-sixth of the total. The school's pre-eminence in the House of Lords was at least equally strong. More than half its pupils went to Oxford or Cambridge, and another twenty per cent into the army.[36] This was also just after the era of the Eton Society of Arts, founded when the school educated novelists Anthony Powell and Henry Green (whose real name, by coincidence, was Yorke), writers Cyril Connolly, Harold Acton and George Orwell, and the travel writer and *The Architectural Review* contributor Robert Byron.[37] Not surprisingly for an institution of this diversity, its organisation is intricate. Few decisions can be made without being filtered by standing or specially composed committees, culminating in the council of the Provost and Fellows. Institutional thoroughness, with its latent tendencies to inertia and compromise between eccentricities, rather than individual dynamism drives the process. To survive the process unfolded here, the concept for Yorke's pair of houses must have been extremely robust.[38]

Presiding over Eton is the provost, appointed by the monarch. In 1935 the incumbent was Montague Rhodes James, now best known for his ghost stories, he was a thorough scholar of church art and architecture. He died in June 1936, eighteen years after his appointment, and six after being admitted to the Order of Merit. His successor was a combination of old aristocrat, politician and eccentric, Lord Hugh Cecil. The *Dictionary of National Biography* considered him 'unfitted for the discipline of [political] office', and he considered the school had a duty to educate the boys but not to provide them with air raid shelters. 'To aesthetic experience, however, he was immune', which may have helped or hindered Yorke but suggests he had no direct influence on the houses. His view on housing masters is not recorded for posterity.

The story of the pair of houses, known as Ainger and Benson, started in 1935 when two masters, more or less simultaneously, asked permission for building leases on college grounds.[39] Discussion of their requests is recorded in the minutes of the General Purposes Committee meeting of 22 March. The note runs: 'It was agreed not to sanction the erection of houses in Dutchman's [a meadow owned by the college, where one of the applicants suggested building a house] and that as regards the other sites [around Willowbrook Road], it would be preferable for the College to build the houses rather than grant building leases subject to an economic rent being obtainable.' The vice-provost and headmaster were asked to 'look into the question and suggest sites'.

When they reported on 5 July, they favoured the Willowbrook Road sites, with the caveat that the land had been gifted to the college in 1898 and that 'no building should be erected on [it] except for school purposes'. Whether accommodating masters and their families constituted school purposes apparently occasioned some discussion, but the meeting did decide to commission WD Hartley, 'a local architect . . . to look at the position, drainage and to produce sketch plans'.

What happened next was typical of Eton, and shows something of the complexity of its organisation. Already the recommendations of the General Purposes Committee required ratification from the full council of Provost and Fellows; now the headmaster appointed a committee of masters to study the issue of housing for junior married masters. The committee subsequently extended its reference to cover houses for non-housemasters. Housing was obviously an important issue to many masters: junior unmarried staff were accommodated in 'colonies' around Eton, while housemasters had accommodation within their boarding houses. The headmaster had a substantial home and an allowance for running it which included substantial provision for servants. Others presumably fended for themselves, or took on building leases.

On 1 November 1935, the headmaster Claude Elliott presented the masters' committee's report to the General Purposes Committee. Authorisation was granted to 'look into providing two houses on suitable sites for a total outlay yielding 4 per cent'. Just over a month later a preliminary report came before the General Purposes Committee. It estimated costs for two types of house at £3,000 and £2,600, and noted legal advice that the restrictions on usage did not extend to the proposed site and that Hartley should be paid for his sketch plans.

By the committee's next meeting, on 7 February 1936, the headmaster had already recommended that three houses – one larger and two smaller – be built, and even gone as far as commissioning three architects to prepare plans 'free of charge'. The committee decided to make 'small payments' to them. A meeting of the provost and fellows on 25 February 'approved one house in principle . . . with approximately the same accommodation as shown in Mr Yorke's plan, though perhaps some rooms might be rather smaller'. This is the first mention of Yorke's name in the records. Only at yet another meeting of the General Purposes Committee on 20 March – almost a year after the issue was first raised – does the committee decide to go ahead, with 'two houses of £2,500 each', and that 'Mr Yorke should be the architect'. As we shall see, Yorke had laid a few gin traps in the undergrowth.[40]

Nowhere in the records of this year-long debate about providing houses is there any direct indication as to why a particular architect should be chosen. I have been unable to trace the reports of the committee of masters, but this is not unusual.[41] According to Penny Hatfield, the college librarian in 1998, committees of masters are established for a specific purpose and then disbanded. Once their recommendations have been considered in higher, standing committees their records would generally be disposed of. All that is known of the deliberations of the committee of masters are the minutes of meetings where their proposals were raised. That WD Hartley was appointed for initial work is not surprising; he was a local architect and undertook numerous small works for the college. It also seems likely that he was one of the three considered for the full commission.[42] This does not explain, however, why Yorke was considered in the first place, nor who the third architect was.

There is no definitive answer to the latter, short of a chance discovery of documents probably disposed of long since, or records from the other architect containing sketch designs. The story of

One of the identical pair of houses Yorke designed for 'married non-housemasters' at Eton in 1936–7.

Photo: British Architectural Library, RIBA, London.

Eton's other building activities at the time and the individuals who appointed Yorke and oversaw his work, suggests some reasons for his appointment and the subsequent course of the project.

Construction work was a recurring subject in the deliberations of Eton's committees. The Provost and Fellows regularly had to approve expenditure for maintenance of the college's considerable estate.[43] During the 1930s too it seems that conditions in the boarding houses became marginally less spartan, with the installation of extra basins and WCs. Such improvements were not always straightforward, as the 'exercise of such powers [to force housemasters to undertake repairs] would have . . . required no small amount of bursarial courage'.[44] Maintenance was an ongoing process and to a certain extent it was provoked by the construction of a new boarding house, Mustians, where facilities were more up to date than in the older houses.

Eventually costing £40,000, Mustians was the most important single building project at Eton during the mid-1930s. Discussions started in 1934, about a year before the question of the masters' houses arose, but owing to its size it was finished around the same time. Its story helps to put the significance of Yorke's project into perspective. The commission was almost strangled at birth by complicated leases and landownerships but finally, at a meeting on 2 December 1934, three architects were considered. They were WG Newton, Hubert Worthington and RS Dodds. The first two are reasonably well known but Dodds is an obscure figure. The minutes record that he was based in Oxford and, like his competitors, he had laudatory testimonials from academic clients.[45]

Newton and Worthington, at least, are architects who might be expected to appeal to Eton. Their careers are curious reflections of each other's. Newton succeeded 'his friend Hubert Worthington as professor of architecture at the Royal College of Art in 1928'.[46] Both had numerous commissions at public schools – Newton at Marlborough, Radley, Bradfield and the new Merchant Taylors' buildings; Worthington at Sedbergh and Westminster. Newton's background may have appealed too: much is made of his educational credentials (Marlborough and Oriel, MA

Oxon); he became a lieutenant-colonel in 1918 and won a Military Cross the following year. Worthington came from a family of distinguished architects; his brother was Sir Percy Worthington and he would himself be knighted in 1949. Most importantly, perhaps, he 'pursued the classic way throughout his life'.[47] Mustians is indeed neoclassical, at least insofar as sash windows in brick walls are classical, but on a Y-shaped plan which derives more from the Arts and Crafts movement. Both architects were significantly older than Yorke: Newton was born in 1885 and Worthington the following year.

Worthington was appointed and his designs were first discussed at a General Purposes Committee meeting on 22 March 1935. This commission reveals several points about Yorke's appointment. Firstly, Yorke represented a significant break with tradition and generation. Although it cannot be proved, suspicion for this departure might fall on the committee of masters. It is the only identifiable piece of the institutional apparatus that did not participate in the selection of Worthington, before it was involved in the masters' houses the only architect mentioned was Hartley, nothing if not a safe choice. The school librarian confirms that the library held issues of the The Architectural Review during this period, and a diligent master who was researching housing could have consulted it; if so, Yorke's name would have figured prominently. Had this line of enquiry been followed and the RIBA or the Architectural Press been contacted, Yorke's name might well have been recommended. Therefore there are several possible ways which may have led to Yorke's inclusion on the shortlist of three.

A point which emerges in Worthington's project is controversy over materials and techniques. The General Purposes Committee minutes of a meeting of 10 May 1935 reported that, 'the use of ferro-concrete having been raised with a view to economy in the cost of construction, Mr Worthington submitted the results of his enquiries and also of his experience in this respect, when it was agreed that ordinary brick would be more economical and prove much more satisfactory.' Eton's decision-makers were aware of ferro-concrete, but considered it only as a cost-saving measure rather than for aesthetic reasons. That repairs to houses often ran into thousands was an incentive to focus their minds on reducing expenditure.

From the recorded deliberations about Mustians it is possible to infer several reasons behind Yorke's appointment. Firstly, the consideration of Dodds, Newton and Worthington depended on their credentials and testimonials on compatible projects. While Yorke had not then designed schools he had already established a reputation in domestic design, and by 1936 had several houses in his portfolio. Generically, the sort of accommodation a married non-housemaster at Eton might have needed did not differ greatly from that required by the niece of a clutch of peers, albeit of recent creation. Secondly, Yorke's reputation as an expert on new materials and construction might have appealed to Eton's wish to find cheaper forms of building. This point became explicit at a General Purposes Committee meeting of 8 May 1936, just over two months after Yorke's appointment was confirmed. The suggestion was made at this meeting that 'the college should explore the possibility of cheaper materials'. Possibly Yorke himself suggested it, in person or correspondence, possibly as a riposte to the wrangling over relatively small amounts of money – the headmaster's salary of £5,000 represented the projected cost of both houses together!.[48] In any case, the issue of cost reduction was a familiar one.

It seems that Yorke, however, had not laid all his cards on the table at the meeting of 20 March 1936. On 19 May 1936 the Provost and Fellows noted that a letter from Yorke '. . . proposed to build a flat roof . . .', as if that were unexpected. Perhaps Yorke dissembled his real intentions until he landed the job. The committee obviously felt it necessary to debate the issue and concluded that 'further investigation was needed of this type of roof', but they did agree to 'elasticity in

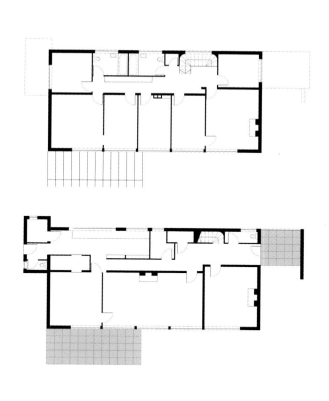

cost'.[49] Yorke 'submitted a plan for a modern building' on 3 July 1936. At this meeting were the Hon Jasper Ridley, the Provost of King's College Cambridge, Viscount (later the Earl of) Halifax and the scientist Lord Rayleigh.[50] The minutes book does not record the views of individuals, but it is clear that the flat roof – the most universal touchstone of modern architecture – was debated, and that these distinguished figures were aware of the arguments around such a design, and were prepared to treat it as an experiment.[51] Maybe, as it would be tucked away in Willowbrook out of sight of Windsor Castle and away from the eyes of distinguished parents and alumni, the provost and fellows were prepared to pay a little bit more to experiment with a new type of construction than they were for a boarding house. If so, it would bear out Yorke's argument that the villa is the best architectural forum for experiment. After exhibiting the design for masters' comments, and receiving none, the Provost and Fellows finally approved it on 20 July 1936. Thereafter it was to be Slough Council's duplicity over drainage – not provosts, fellows or masters – that caused the biggest problems.[52]

If, as mentioned above, the two provosts who spanned the period of Yorke's involvement at Eton were prevented by death or inclination to take a close interest in his work, the vice-provost seems to have taken a different line. He was Henry (later Sir Henry) Marten, and frequently chaired the General Purposes Committee which conducted the most thorough scrutiny of Yorke's work. An old Etonian who had returned to teach at the school and worked his way to the top (he succeeded Cecil as provost in 1944), he had a particular interest in the teaching of history. One of his pupils was the Princess Elizabeth (later Elizabeth II) whom he taught as a private tutor.[53] There is some evidence that Marten appreciated Yorke's design, or at least wanted to understand it. Yorke had to

LEFT: Plan of the masters houses at Eton, designed for their lifestyle.

RIGHT: Despite the simplicity of the design – and paucity of budgets for seven-bedroom houses, Yorke managed to make the Eton houses indelibly modern in feel.

Courtesy of The Architectural Review.

The brewery cottages in Stratford-upon-Avon, for workers at Flower's Brewery, the successful family business which provided the financial motor for the Shakespeare memorials in the town.

Courtesy of *The Architectural Review*.

ask the junior bursar, RW Corbett, to ask for the return of photographs Marten had borrowed, and the vice-provost probably did not borrow them to stick them on a wall and throw darts at them.[54] Even if he did not like them, it seems he tried to understand them.

The houses themselves are virtually identical. If not as dramatic as Torilla, they are important as buildings of which Yorke was proud, which seemed 'modern' to the fellows of Eton but were also acceptable to that body. Quite possibly these two houses represent the closest modernist architecture before 1939 came to penetrating the Establishment that found it perplexing, required reassurance, considered its efficacy in achieving their ends and ultimately accepted it. Each house is a large two-storey brick cuboid. Across the south front are three reception rooms: a dining room, study and large drawing room. Behind is a service zone with a narrow kitchen area – like Torilla – storage and an entrance corridor which is wide enough to be a hall. The staircase along the north wall is simple, but the stairwell also acts as a source of indirect light into the deepest part of the hall. Again this is a simplified form of the lighting effects achieved in Torilla. Above are seven rooms, five across the south and two small ones in the northern corners. These rooms are related to make a limited number of suites with dressing rooms, or adequate accommodation for a three-child family with a nanny and maid. They also enjoyed the luxury (for the 1930s) of two bathrooms. A carefully detailed porch offers another rare touch of architectural spirit; the roof and outer wall are clearly expressed as separate planes, the sort of detail that occurs in several later buildings. As at Torilla, the houses are neatly and tightly planned for comfortable, serviced life. Perhaps a closer analogy is with the Gane show house; which was an idealised expression of modernism, the others use practicality and the exigencies of bourgeois life to create a modern composition which managed to fulfil Eton's expectations.

In March 1937 the rents were fixed at £137 10s per year, 5.5 per cent of the cost originally envisaged. Rates were a further £88. PV Mackinnon, one of the two masters who had applied for a building lease two years previously, was one tenant. After some deliberation as to whether the houses should be reserved for married masters the Rev DL Graham moved into the second.

The last of our three clients to commission Yorke, the Flower family, represent yet another thread of engagement between modernism and the Establishment. Both projects Yorke undertook for them in the 1930s – a row of cottages for brewery workers and the remodelling of a small country house for Fordham Flower – were done with FWB Yorke, but the design work shows more affinities with FRS. Again these commissions show a spread of the client base beyond normal expectations. There was nothing unusual about a successful industrialist building a row of cottages for workers – Titus Salt had set a precedent as early as the 1850s at Saltaire in Yorkshire – but having a modernist design was. One of the few who did was the Crittall family, purveyors of windows to modernist architects. The Flower family's contribution to culture went beyond the material; they were instrumental in establishing the Shakespeare 'industry' in Stratford.

The Flower family has an interesting history, combining radicalism with that most conservative of industrial activities, brewing.[55] Their background lay in small farming. One branch of the family was among early settlers in Illinois. Another member, Benjamin (1755–1829), became a radical journalist during the French Revolution. His two daughters were similarly radical, Eliza becoming a composer and Sarah a poet. In the early nineteenth century intermarriage with the Fordhams, who owned a brewhouse as well as a farm, introduced the Flowers to brewing. A son from this marriage, Edward Fordham Flower (1805–83) established the brewery in Stratford in 1832. It prospered enough for him to build The Hill, – the seat with which the family is identified in *Burke's Landed Gentry* [56] – outside the town in 1855. In 1864 he was mayor of the town. That was the year of Shakespeare's tercentenary, and Edward used the opportunity to aggrandise Stratford, in part at least to record his self-earned status. Of his three sons, Charles Edward founded the Shakespeare Memorial Theatre with money from the family brewery and Edgar became chairman of Shakespeare's Birthplace Trustees. The third, William (later Sir William), having been a doctor in the Crimean War, he became professor of surgery at the Royal College of Surgeons and finally director of the Natural History Museum.

At the time when the memorial theatre was established the Flowers had yet to show any cultural interests. Charles Edward, for example, had left school at fifteen to work in the brewery. Not until the next generation did members of the family attend public school and university. It is perhaps the combination of growing wealth and uncertain social status that led the Flowers to do more to establish themselves than the mere token of buying a country estate.[57]

Edward Fordham Flower's grandson Archibald was chairman of the governors of the Shakespeare Memorial Theatre, chairman of the Shakespeare Birthplace Trust, chairman of the brewery and a noted Stratford citizen. He was six times mayor, the senior alderman, and knighted in 1930. He listed his hobbies in *Who's Who* as travel, hunting, fishing, golf and Shakespeare, as if in deliberate proclamation of his status as gentleman and cultural connoisseur. During the 1930s his annual income from the brewery of around £20,000 cannot have hindered him in his ambitions.[58]

Sir Archibald Flower was the head of the family when FRS Yorke first worked for them on the cottages in Birmingham Road, Stratford, in 1938.[59] Archibald had previously been deeply involved in one other major construction work: the new Shakespeare Memorial Theatre which opened in 1931.[60] His contribution was to ensure the highest level of expertise possible on the jury. 'Nothing but the best is good enough for Shakespeare,' he is quoted as saying.[61] But in general he 'preferred [to take decisions in] committees of two, where one member was unavailable'.[62] He was also something of a paternalist patrician, acquiring the estate just beyond the Hill to ensure the continued privacy of his home, and to give a park to the citizenry – and very possibly, to cement his social position. Archibald also tried persuading the local girls grammar school to take over its house, but it eventually became an hotel. He purchased the Shottery estate on the other side of the town, from the Trustees of the Marquess of Hertford in 1919, this did become the girls grammar school in 1951, after fifteen years as home to Archibald's son Fordham and his family.[63]

Archibald's own architectural tastes seem to have been traditional. Drawings in the Shakespeare Centre for alterations at The Hill and for cottages on the Shottery estate, both of the early 1930s, are essentially in an Arts and Crafts mode.[64] Yet the theatre is in an Art Deco *moderne* idiom, and the cottages in Birmingham Road, described in Chapter Two, display a restrained modernism – brick, but with monopitched roofs and expressions of planes not unlike the Eton house porches – a manner used extensively after 1945. If Archibald was keen to ensure expert advice for the theatre, despite his reputation as an autocrat he may have accepted that of a respected brewery architect and his much younger son who was already something of an expert on housing design.[65] It is not impossible, either, that FRS Yorke and Archibald's eldest son Fordham had some common cause. Fordham, born in 1904, was two years older than Yorke, and he developed a strong interest in contemporary art. He had been a director of the brewery since 1934.

At the beginning, though, the commission for the brewery cottages was primarily given to FWB Yorke who understood local circumstances. He had completed several projects in Stratford, including proposed cottage types for the local council during the World War I. It was FWB who submitted the planning application on 2 August 1938 and it was granted on 13 September.[66]

The second project for the Flower family was adding a new kitchen and nursery wing for Fordham Flower at Shottery Manor, a mile or so from the town centre. After school at Winchester, Fordham had gone on to Sandhurst and was commissioned into the 9th Queen's Royal Lancers in 1924. For the next ten years he had served in Egypt, Palestine and India before returning to Stratford and marrying Hersey Caroline Balfour. Their eldest child was born in 1936.

Two years later the remodelling of Shottery commenced. Again the commission probably went initially to FWB, who asked his son to join him.[67] Shottery was an ancient house, recorded as early as 790 in a charter of Offa of Mercia.[68] It is probably the original settlement in the area, Stratford having come later. The house has medieval traces and a magnificent first-floor room, once a chapel, with a hammer beam roof.[69] Its main front is a fifteenth-century Cotswold stone building centred on a generous, stone-floored entrance hall with a Tudor fireplace and clumsy though charming staircase. The east front saw numerous accretions. The Yorkes' task was to take them away and to add a new wing in the northeastern corner.

Externally their work is in a period style.[70] As the most overtly modern parts are limited to areas for servants and children, it would be easy to dismiss the Flowers' view of modernism as something that happened to 'other people'. However, there is one design feature that qualifies this. Around the eastern courtyard runs a balcony, admittedly in a period style, but it gives easy access between the parents' rooms and the nursery. Children were not entirely banished. The day nursery itself has some charming tiles of characters from *Alice in Wonderland*; but it is the cork-tiled floor and elegant metal-bannistered staircase that make it clearly modern.

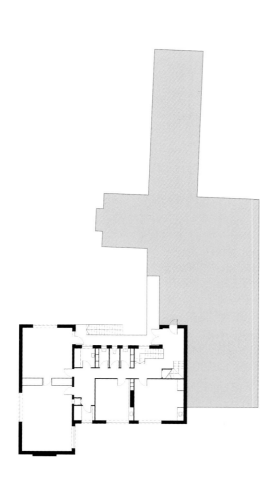

Fordham Flower's subsequent career also suggests that he had a serious interest in contemporary culture. It could be that his encounter with FRS Yorke was his first real, personal contact with it – ten years in a prestigious regiment in the Middle East and India would not readily have presented opportunities. Assuming the double mantle of beer and Shakespeare on his father's death in 1950, he made a name for himself as a patron of new ideas.

Levi Fox, director of the Shakespeare Centre from 1946, remembered Fordham Flower as 'a man with whom one could share a vision'.[71] This was borne out in a specifically architectural context by Basil Spence in comments about his rebuilding of Coventry Cathedral. Fordham Flower joined the Reconstruction Committee of Coventry Cathedral and became its chairman in 1954 on the death of EH Ford. Spence noted that 'as chairman of the Shakespeare Memorial Theatre, [Flower] understood artists and had a liberal and appreciative attitude to modern art'.[72] Flower joined with bishop and provost of Coventry, backing Jacob Epstein's appointment for the statue of St Michael at the cathedral against 'prejudice, fear and lack of understanding' from rest of the committee.[73] The theatre director Sir Peter Hall also praised Fordham Flower. Hall was artistic director of the memorial theatre when Flower died prematurely and quite unexpectedly in 1966.[74] Hall gave an address at the memorial service in July. 'He believed in', said Hall, 'and helped to create a forward-looking policy'.[75] These comments add a different perspective to Fordham Flower's achievements to a roll call of formal honours: Lt-Col (rtrd) late 9th Queen's Royal

Fordham Flower (right) kissing the hand of the American singer Barbra Streisand (left), while presenting her with a Flower's Theatre Award. A few days later he was dead.

Shakespeare Birthplace Trust Records **Office.**

Lancers, Knight Bachelor, OBE (mil) three times and chairman of the family brewery. They reveal someone whose experience of business has meshed with a genuine interest in cultural activities, perhaps more to the benefit of the latter than the former.

Fordham Flower brought his family to the peak of the cultural aristocracy, fulfilling the process his ancestors had started in the 1860s – at a time when cultural patronage was changing. In 1962 Flowers merged with Whitbread, ending 130 years of independence. It was a time of rationalisation in the brewing industry. The international success of the Shakespeare endeavours dwarfed the national success of the brewery.

FRS Yorke certainly played some role in Fordham's career. The work at Shottery is Fordham's first identifiable contact with modernism, and the two men remained on friendly terms.[76] Of course, Fordham may have craved such an opportunity, and counted on it becoming available at some stage in his life. Whatever the motive, the Shottery project initiated a line of support for the arts which reached through the constellation of Epstein, Spence, Sutherland and Piper, who worked on Coventry Cathedral, right up to Sir Peter Hall.[77] These are all people whose work has helped to build bridges between culture, the avant-garde and popular appreciation. Although Fordham's ancestors may have had similar radical ambitions, he was one of the first people to embrace modernism in his home rather than as an adjunct for others.

Each of these three clients shows a different aspect of an engagement between the power Establishment, that they all in varying degrees represent, and modernism, which Yorke certainly represents. Each party might have made compromises and learnt along the way. But by the end of the 1930s Yorke had had significant contact with a traditional institution, its committees and eccentricities; with a new and powerful family with an interest in new ideas and techniques which extended between building and business; and a slightly older and powerful family, who made an important contribution to national cultural life. Between them they gave Yorke experience of, and access to, trends which were to interwine with government policy, to radically alter social life and change the pattern of commissioning after the war.[78]

By 1939, Yorke had experience of dealing with a variety of clients, among them people who were rich, powerful and autocratic. He had found himself capable of impressing the Burton family, whose circle of acquaintances included some of the most charismatic figures of the twentieth century;[79] he had been able to manage committees at Eton, and to satisfy the Flower family. In doing so he had taken modernism right to the heart of the pre-war Establishment, partly by arguing for its potential to address pressing problems such as Eton's property maintenance bill, just as that Establishment was on the brink of a radical shake-up. Although the social structure, and in particular his client body, would represent different interests after 1945 Yorke had shown an ability to engage with sophisticated bodies and individuals and prove that modern architecture could work for them.

Notes

1. The literature on this subject is vast. See, for example, the RIBA's *Strategic Study of the Profession*, Phases 3 and 4, 1995, pp 9–66, which tries to define the needs and roles of clients; or the attempt by its Future Studies Group to define the role of the client, in a conference on 'The Role of the Client' held in the Millennium Dome in October 1999.

2. See Robert Gutman, *Architectural Practice: A Critical View*, Princeton Architectural Press (New York), 1988, p 50. Gutman has long been one of the shrewdest analysts of the architectural profession.

3. A raw example of this attitude can be found in a talk given by Alison Smithson at an RIBA private view of the exhibition on Edwin Lutyens, held at the Hayward Gallery on London's South Bank in November 1981. She argued that the only interesting point about Lutyens was the way he attracted 'patronage', and that the exhibition should have been 'a call to patronage . . . to create a microclimate favourable to patronage'. For our purposes the only interesting point in her talk is her appreciation of a typical Lutyen client as 'the modest patron . . . who wanted to show their ordinary things and their ordinary lives to best advantage'. In November 1998 this manuscript was the only document in the RIBA archive that responded to the search 'patronage'. RIBA/SPR/22.

4. FRS Yorke, *The Modern House*, Architectural Press (London), 1934, pp 1–2.

5. See *The Architecture of Yorke, Rosenberg, Mardall, 1944–1972*, Lund Humphries (London), 1972 for an overview of the work of the practice between these dates.

6. See also *Twentieth Century Architecture*, vol 2: guest editor Neil Bingham,'The Modern House Revisited', The Twentieth Century Society (London), 1996; Louise Campbell 'Patrons of Modern Architecture' pp 41–50; Jeremy Gould's 'Gazetteer of Modern Houses in the United Kingdom and the Republic of Ireland', pp 111–128; Gould's work is a massive expansion of a gazetteer published in his *Modern Houses in Britain*, Society of Architectural Historians (London), 1977. In the 1996 gazetteer (p 112) Gould explains: 'The most common characteristic of the Modern house was a flat roof.' However, there is no systematic analysis of the client base that might compare, say, with Richard Goldthwaite's study of the oligarchy in 15th-century Florence, *The Building of Renaissance Florence*, Johns Hopkins University Press (Baltimore and London), 1980, especially Part I, 'Demand: the patrons', pp 29–114.

7. Paul Thompson, *William Butterfield*, Routledge and Kegan Paul (London), 1971, p 378, fn 15.

8. Those responsible for this evolution include Maxwell Fry and Stephen Bayley. Lionel Esher included a letter from Fry as Appendix A, 'Early clients of Maxwell Fry' in *A Broken Wave*, Penguin (Harmondsworth), 1981, p 301, which states that the clients of the 1930s were 'a rum lot'. The letter, dated 28 May 1979, goes on to accuse the vicar of Chipperfield, site of another Fry house in the 1930s, of 'suspecting immorality at every move'. See also Stephen Bayley, 'Patrons of the modern movement', in 'Britain in the Thirties', *Architectural Design*, no 24, guest editor Gavin Stamp, pp 90–5. 'Frank Pick [the legendary creator of London Transport's design image] was not a nudist'; Bayley starts his article with this denial from the designer Milner Gray, and goes on to list leftish intellectual residents of Hampstead. Flat roofs, Gould's *sine qua non* of modern architecture, were often associated with nude sunbathing. Geoffrey Walford, client of Connell, Ward & Lucas for the house at 66 Frognal Hampstead, was a solicitor.

9. See, for example, Ian Latham's review of a lecture at the RIBA given by Cook and his partner Christine Hawley: 'Pete'n'Chris', *Building Design* (29 January 1988), p 2. Cook became professor of architecture at the Bartlett, UCL, in 1990 and Archigram, of which he was a member, won the Royal Gold Medal for Architecture in 2002.

10. The Crittalls made steel windows which became integral to modernism in the UK and on the European continent. Their development for factory workers and their family home in Essex, designed by Thomas Tait of Burnet, Tait & Lorne was a remarkably early (1927), if not the finest, example of modernist architecture. The Ganes made plywood. Yorke and Breuer remodelled a suburban home for one member of the family in Bristol (1935), and designed the famous show house (1936). This seems largely to have been Breuer's work and it is important in his development. See Isabelle Hyman, *Marcel Breuer, architect*, Abrams (New York), 2001; Joachim Driller, *Breuer Houses*, Phaidon (London), 2000. To these examples might be added extensive work by numerous architects for the Bata shoe company. See Jane Pavitt, 'The Bata Project; and Social and Industrial Experiment', *Twentieth Century Architecture*, vol 1 (1994), pp 31–44.

11. Drawings for both these houses exist in the RIBA Drawings Collection: PA 236/8 (1–6) for Shangri-La; PA 236/4 (1–11) for Sea Lane House, Angmering; and PA 238/5 for the swimming pool at 8 Ingram Avenue, Hampstead.

12. The house was published in *Architectural Review* vol 87,(June 1940), pp 122–5. Barry's stepson, the architect Richard Burton, remembers that the added room was known as the 'elephant room', and it was here that much of the Festival of Britain, an initiative of Barry's, was planned.

13. It is probably no more than a remarkable coincidence that two important cultural milestones of Britain in the 1950s, the Festival of Britain and the cracking of Linear B, were both conceived in interiors designed by Yorke or his partner.

14. IFor an account of Michael Ventris' extraordinary achievement, see Andrew Robinson, *The Man Who Decoded Linear B*, Thames and Hudson (London), 2002. It includes some information about life in Highpoint. Drawings for the flat exist in the RIBA Drawings Collection, PA/236/10, and it has been extensively published. See, for example, Christopher Wilk, *Marcel Breuer Furniture and Interiors*, Architectural Press (London), 1981, pp 142–5.

15. See Chapter 4 for discussion of the Concrete Garden City.

16. For information on the Flower family, see *Burkes Landed Gentry*; various family members are also listed in *Who's Who*. For information on the theatres in Stratford, see Marian Pringle, *The Theatres of Stratford-upon-Avon*, Stratford-upon-Avon Historical Society, 1993. She notes of the first theatre, designed by William Unsworth and Edward Dodgshun, that it 'had been virtually paid for by Charles Edward Flower', at a figure of £22,700 (p 19). Brewers were often Conservative, because the Liberal party, with a strong Nonconformist element, often flirted with temperance.

17. The eldest brother was Alfred, later Viscount Northcliffe; the second, Harold, became Viscount Rothermere; a third, Cecil, became Baron Harmsworth after sitting for years as a Conservative MP. Two other brothers, Leicester and Hildebrand, were made baronets. I have not been able to trace a similar instance of a family where five siblings were all given hereditary titles, and in one generation the Harmsworth family emerged if not to rival the Cecils, Howards or Russells, at least to give them a good run for their money. See *Debrett's Peerage and Baronetage*. They first achieved eminence by publishing popular magazines like *Answers* and *Comic Cuts*, but their real success came with the launch in 1896 of the *Daily Mail*, which is still controlled by the descendants of the first Viscount Rothermere. Northcliffe, whose outspoken criticism riled the coalition government during World War I, eventually acquired a controlling interest in *The Times*, placing him right at the heart of the Establishment. See J Lee Thompson, *Northcliffe, Press Baron in Politics 1865–1922*, John Murray (London), 2000 and SJ Taylor, *The Great Outsiders, Northcliffe, Rothermere and the Daily Mail* Weidenfeld and Nicholson (London), 1996, for further information on this remarkable family. Many of its members are also noted in the *Dictionary of National Biography*, and *Who's Who*.

18. Percy and Christabel Burton's daughter Barbara remembered that Cecil was 'by far the nicest' of the brothers. Interview with Jeremy Melvin, 20 November 1998. See Christabel Bielenberg, *The Past Is Myself*, Corgi (London), 1992, pp 127–30 for a telling anecdote about his character.

19. For a recent analysis of the influence of the media in moulding public life, see John Lloyd, 'Media Manifesto', *Prospect* (October 2002), pp 48–53. Lloyd argues that the media claims 'a right to rule' and that much of its criticism directed against public figures is motivated by perceived transgressions of this right. As Northcliffe orchestrated criticism of the government for its conduct of World War I, many members of the Cabinet

would have had sympathy with Lloyd's views.

20. J Lee Thompson, *Northcliffe, Press Baron in Politics 1865–1922*, (London), 2000, p 15. Thompson outlines 'arrangements for the education and security of the Harmsworth sisters', made by Alfred and Harold though footnote 25 only refers to a marriage portion given to the eldest, Geraldine. The Codicote house, described in Chapter Two, was published in later editions of *The Modern House*.

21. See Tim Land, *Eton Renewed*, John Murray (London) 1994 for information on Eton's history from 1860 to the 1990s, especially Chapter 8: 'Eton between the wars', pp 160–84.

22. The governing body of Eton College is the Provost and Fellows, drawn largely but not exclusively from Old Etonians. It oversees not just the school, but its considerable estates as well. Eton was established as a royal foundation in the 15th century, by Henry VI on 11 October 1440. See Land, op cit, p 1.

23. Yorke grew up in Edgbaston, the most exclusive suburb of England's second city, Birmingham. Its residents included Frys and Cadburys and its Member of Parliament from 1929 to 1940 was Neville Chamberlain, a member of Birmingham's most powerful family, and holder of various Cabinet posts culminating in that of prime minister (1937–40). See Douglas V Jones, *Edgbaston As It Was*, Westwood Press (Sutton Coldfield) nd and Martin Hampson, *Edgbaston*, Tempus Publishing (Stroud), 1999, for an impression of the area. See Iain Macleod, *Neville Chamberlain*, Muller (London), 1961 for details of Chamberlain's life. While not overtly interested in architecture, Chamberlain did institute important reforms in government spending on construction, including, as Minister of Health in 1924, the development of a part of Edgbaston for Birmingham's university hospital on land given by the Cadburys (p 41). Another fellow of Eton was the distinguished scientist Lord Rayleigh. By the end of the 1930s Yorke had become friendly with Patrick Blackett who, though somewhat younger than Rayleigh, was already a Fellow of the Royal Society and on a career curve that would see him win a Nobel Prize, appointment to the Order of Merit and a life peerage. Like Rayleigh, he had worked at the Cavendish Laboratories in Cambridge. If Yorke already knew him in 1936 Blackett might have had useful advice on how to deal with Rayleigh. See correspondence between Yorke and Blackett, RIBA YoF/1/12.

24. Letter in RIBA YoF/1/7. Christabel Bielenberg later wrote two best-selling books about her life in Germany under the Nazis and her subsequent experiences in post-war Britain and Ireland: *The Past is Myself*, Chatto and Windus (London), 1968; Corgi edition 1984; and *The Road Ahead*, Corgi (London), 1992.

25. Conversation with Jeremy Melvin, 20 November 1998. All quotes attributed to Mrs MacDonald below come from this interview.

26. 'As I remember talking to you on the subject of modern small houses, I thought I would let you know that my mother wants to build a bungalow for my married sister.' Letter from Christabel to Yorke, 20 July 1934. RIBA YoF/1/7.

27. I am grateful to the present owners, Alan and Lesley Charlton, for kindly showing me around, and to their architect, John Winter for comments.

28. Yorke, op cit, pp 83–5. Original drawings for Torilla survive in the RIBA Drawings Collection, PA 237/4; suffix 1 for the preliminary design, 2–6 for the design more or less as executed.

29. Further details about the construction of Torilla, including building products Yorke first wrote about in the *Architects' Journal* and used in the house, are in Chapter 2.

30. See, for example, Alan Powers, *A Continuity and a Theme*, RIBA Heinz Gallery (London), 1992, p 15, where he draws an analogy with the hall of Stokesay Castle.

31. See, for instance, measured drawings of late 16th-century almshouses and The Crown Hotel, Shipton-under-Wychwood, in the RIBA Drawings Collection, PA 237/10 and PA 237/5 respectively.

32. Yorke, op cit. pp 92–3.

33. See drawings in the RIBA Drawings Collection, PA 237/1, and contract in YoF/1/7

34. 'And they were heavy', Barbara MacDonald remembers, 'with their big

stomachs and their big Rolls-Royces . . .' Alfred was a godfather to Barbara, and in particular remained close to his mother. Among his reported last words were: 'Tell mother she was the only one.' He was then 57 years old, and left an estate worth £5 million. SJ Taylor, *The Great Outsiders, Northcliffe, Rothermere and the Daily Mail* (London) 1993, p 219.

35. This affinity is borne out in her decision immediately after the war to invite Yorke to design another house for her in Codicote, where she and her husband had taken refuge from the bombing during the war and where her family converged after it. See Christabel Bielenberg, *The Road Ahead*, Corgi (London), 1992, pp 58–69. See Chapter 2.

36. See Land, op cit, p 178.

37. Humphrey Carpenter, *The Brideshead Generation*, Faber (London), 1990, Part I: 'Eton Candle', pp 1–31.

38. That Eton managed to build modernist buildings at all is remarkable, given the tribulations of attempts to build modernism at Oxford and Cambridge. See Stephen Bayley, 'Patrons of the modern movement', in 'Britain in the Thirties', *Architectural Design*, no 24, guest editor Gavin Stamp, pp 93–4.

39. All quotes come from the minute books for the Standing General Purposes Committee, and the Provost and Fellows council (the ultimate governing body) held in the Eton College archive. The masters were PV Mackinnon, a mathematics teacher, and the linguist DA Haworth. Their salaries were £657 7s 9d and £918 13s 4d respectively. During the Michaelmas term, 1935, one Baron zu Franckenstein was paid £157 2s 3d for modern language instruction. The houses were named for former masters. AC Benson taught at Eton from 1885 to 1903 when he became master of Magdelene College, Cambridge. AC Ainger taught from 1864 to 1901. Both had attended the school as King's Scholars.

40. Drawings for these houses survive in the bursar's department at Eton, and in the RIBA Drawings Collection, PA 236/7 (1–5).

41. The minutes for the General Purposes Committee meeting of 20 March 1936 include a note of a report by the headmaster of a meeting with Mr Butterwick, of the masters' committee, the only named member of this committee in the record. According to Tim Land, JC Butterwick, who taught at the school from 1914 to 1945, was chiefly remembered for buying a first edition of John Milton's *Paradise Lost* for tuppence. Land, op cit, p 173n.

42. The college's accounts for 1936 record payments to architects for the masters' houses, but only as a total figure without any breakdown between them. The figure was £41 11s. In 1937 the figure rose to £106 17s, presumably all paid to Yorke.

43. For instance, the General Purposes Committee meeting of 20 March 1936 sanctioned the spending of £1,401 on maintenance of masters' residences.

44. Minutes of the General Purposes Committee meeting, 7 December 1934.

45. If Dodds was prominent, it escaped Pevsner who makes no mention of him in his volume *Oxfordshire*, in the Buildings of England series.

46. Obituary of Newton, Builder, vol 176 (21 January 1949), p 100.

47. Sir Edward Maufe, obituary of Worthington, *RIBA Journal vol 70* (October 1963), p 422.

48. This figure was fixed at a General Purposes Committee meeting of 12 May 1933, following the appointment of Claude Elliott to succeed Cyril Alington, the father-in-law of Alec Douglas-Home, who had been appointed dean of Durham. Elliott's salary included provision for staff and entertaining.

49. Both proved far-sighted. The construction sum was exceeded. See a memo from RW Corbett (the junior bursar) dated 29 November 1938. Almost inevitably the flat roof leaked. See Corbett's letter to Yorke of 6 April 1939, stating that 'serious defects are developing in the roofs of the two houses you built for us . . .'. After the war the roofs leaked again and Yorke arranged for the original contractor (Bowyer) and roofing subcontractor (Bitumen Industries) to repair them. See various correspondences between Corbett, Yorke and the contractors dating from early 1947, held in the files on these buildings at Eton.

50. It is worth noting that many of the fellows, though not Rayleigh, had ambiguous success. Lord Halifax, for example was 'uninterested [in his

first cabinet post] at the Board of Education ... unable as viceroy of India to deal with [the challenges of Gandhi's resistance] ... and found it unacceptable, as foreign minister, to condemn Hitler' (*Dictionary of National Biography*). By an odd coincidence, Christabel Bielenberg's husband Peter came London in the summer of 1939 to bring a personal warning about the Nazis and to alert Britain to its potential vulnerability should the British government lend support to the anti-Nazi resistance. Halifax felt it beneath him to negotiate with such a young lawyer, and in any case it was the grouse-shooting season. See Christabel Bielenberg, *The Past Is Myself*, Corgi (London), 1992, pp 46–8. Andrew Roberts, in *The Holy Fox, a Biography of Lord Halifax* Weidenfeld and Nicholson (London), 1991, gives a more sympathetic impression of this ambiguous figure.

51. See note 6 for an explanation of the importance of the flat roof in modern architecture.

52. Minutes of a General Purposes Committee meeting of 6 November 1936. Having accepted a septic tank earlier, Slough Urban District Council now wanted a sewerage lifting plant.

53. Marten was instrumental in establishing history as part of the curriculum in schools. See CHK Marten, *On the Teaching of History, and other Addresses*, Basil Blackwell (Oxford), 1938.

54. See letter from Yorke to Corbett, 1 May 1939, in the Eton archive. *Architect and Building News* photographed the houses in early 1939; see letter from Yorke to Corbett, 30 December 1938. The houses were featured in *The Architectural Review*, vol 85, (January 1939), pp 32–3.

55. See note 13 above. Documents on the family history can be found in the Shakespeare Centre, Stratford, DR227/218.

56. I have not been able to identify the date they were first included in *Burke's Landed Gentry*, but it cannot have been before 1855. Edward Fordham was not initially identified as a gentleman when he moved to Stratford; that designation came later in life.

57. There had been an architect in the family, though not one of great distinction. Arthur Smyth Flower FRIBA FSA (1860–1936) was a son of Sir William. The RIBA has little information on him but *Burke's Landed Gentry* gives biographical details, and archives in the Shakespeare Centre in Stratford show that he worked extensively for the brewery.

58. See the private family ledger in the Shakespeare Centre, Stratford.

59. The plans are published in later editions of *The Modern House*.

60. FRS Yorke contributed comments to the description of the theatre in *The Architectural Review* vol 71, (June 1932), p 260, which were broadly complimentary despite its dubious modernist credentials. Gropius and Pevsner certainly did not like it. See the descriptions of it and the National Theatre in London in Pevsner's *Buildings of England*. Yorke would certainly have known of Archibald Flower, and might have seen him as a potential client. In any case, FWB's connections with breweries through his expertise in pub architecture may not have been worth jeopardising at a time when FRS was still reliant on his father's support.

61. Marian Pringle, *The Theatres of Stratford-upon-Avon*, Stratford upon Avon Historical Society, 1993, p 31.

62. Ibid, p 25.

63. Ironically, somewhat later Shottery Manor, the house the Yorkes remodelled for Fordham Flower, became the girls' grammar school.

64. A Birmingham architect, LL Dussault, remodelled The Hill, and John H Knight 'Reg Arch' designed some cottages on the Shottery estate. See documents in the Shakespeare Centre: DR 430/128-9, DR 322/6.

65. FWB Yorke's reputation as an architect of public houses can be measured in his book *Planning and Equipment of Public Houses*, Architectural Press (London), 1949.

66. The documents are in the Shakespeare Centre, Stratford DR430/84.

67. The Flowers' private ledger shows payments to FWB Yorke from Fordham Flower in May 1938 and March 1939. Only in June 1939 does FRS Yorke's name appear. At the same time a substantial payment was made to Gordon Russell Ltd, who presumably made the fitted furniture. The ledger is housed in the Shakespeare Centre, Stratford. The project was published in *The Architectural Review* (January–June 1940), pp 111–12.

68. I am grateful to the Stratford Girls' Grammar School, who now occupy Shottery and allowed me to visit the house and see documents which contain this information.

69. Unsubstantiated legend has it that William Shakespeare and Ann Hathaway were betrothed in this room. Ann Hathaway's cottage is also in Shottery.

70. This contrasts with the 'elephant room' extension FRS Yorke did to Forge Cottage for Gerald Barry; but Forge Cottage was rather less grand, and Barry perhaps more prepared to show his modernist credentials than the scion of a Midlands brewery family who was only in his mid-30s.

71. Oral History interview transcript, August 1991, in the Shakespeare Centre, Stratford.

72. Sir Basil Spence, *Phoenix at Coventry*, Geoffrey Bles (London), 1962, p 69.

73. Ibid, p 70.

74. Sir Fordham died a day or two after he and Lady Flower returned from America where he had kissed the hand of Barbra Streisand to whom, with the impresario Bernard Delfont, he presented a theatrical award. A picture of this survives in the family picture album in the Shakespeare Centre, Stratford, DR227/219.

75. Copies of the order of service are held at the Shakespeare Centre, Stratford.

76. See, for instance, a letter in the Allford Yorke Archive, Folder 16, p 10.

77. It may be significant that Flower was educated at Winchester where the art connoisseur Kenneth Clark (Lord Clark of Saltwood) was a near contemporary. Clark certainly had a direct influence on businessmen like Sir Colin Anderson and Sir William Keswick, and championed John Piper and Graham Sutherland.

78. In very broad terms it could be said that the Burtons represent advertising and media – the affluent society; Eton, the institutional apparatus; and Flowers, the combination of populism and culture promoted by the Arts Council.

79 Quite apart from the other family members, Christabel Bielenberg was a member of the circle of courageous Germans who plotted to remove Adolf Hitler, culminating in the tragic events of 20 July 1944. See *The Past Is Myself*, Corgi (London), 1984.

CHAPTER 4

ENTHUSIASM, AMBIGUITY AND OPPORTUNITY
An individual approach to modernist planning

During the 1930s and 1940s town planning in Britain took the form of statutory regulation that it still largely bears.[1] Major Acts of Parliament reached the statute book in 1932 and 1947, almost coinciding with the period of Yorke's career with which this study is concerned, these fundamentally altered the conditions in which architecture was practised.[2] In particular, the second Act came close to achieving the 'controlled land development' which Yorke had claimed as an essential prerequisite to modern architecture in *The Modern House*.[3] Yorke's direct contribution to these hugely important legislative and social developments was insignificant, yet many of his friends, colleagues and contemporaries took instrumental parts in them. Paradoxically, as an overall, national planning strategy emerged which had at least something in common with the aims modernists stated in the 1930s, Yorke gradually altered his view towards instrumental planning.

The sentiments Yorke expressed about town planning in *The Modern House* may have been in accord with modernist convention of the time, but that convention had not yet evolved into a distinctive line of its own; it still owed much to the Garden City movement. From 1934 onwards, however, largely through CIAM's Charter of Athens and its aftermath – specifically, in Britain, the activities of the MARS (Modern Architecture Research) Group – modernists started to make claims that went beyond those of their Garden-City-designing predecessors.[4]

In parallel with MARS' attempts to reshape cities came a growing urge for more state intervention in physical planning. Provoked by the social deprivation of the early 1930s Depression, especially in areas of traditional industries compared to the relative success of new industries in the southeast, this trend led to the establishment of a Royal Commission on the Distribution of the Industrial Population in July 1937.[5] Known as the Barlow Commission after its chairman Sir Clement Montague Barlow, who had been a Minister for Labour in the early 1920s, it reported in January 1940, this would have been inauspicious except that it provided a recent blueprint for post-war reconstruction. The main report recommended creating a National Industrial Board to oversee development and help iron out the inconsistencies of the 1932 Act. A minority report written by Patrick Abercrombie, who was later to produce hugely influential plans for the development of London, argued for a new ministry.[6] A new ministry there would be. Under its first chief, Lord Reith, who had earlier created the BBC, it quickly absorbed the spirit of the Barlow Commission.[7] It began to replace piecemeal agglomeration of local government 'maps' and Ministry of Health regulations, which constituted the pre-war planning system, with supposedly rational, national policies. Rather than defining the minutiae of appearance, capriciously various according to different local authorities, it regulated the uses to which land could be put.

How the activities, motivations and ideas of the MARS Group and those of policy-making bodies like the Barlow Commission intersected is a fascinating and under-researched issue. On large issues such as controlling land use and smaller ones like measures for air-raid protection, both modernists and policy-makers recognised that planning was more than a question of appearance. But the methods of investigation and implementation were different. Where they

OPPOSITE TOP: Relief plan of the Concrete Garden City. The school is marked J; the curving glass-walled café N is in the bottom centre.

OPPOSITE BOTTOM: Model photograph. Breuer, whose design the Concrete Garden City was largely embodied in, recycled several previous schemes and anticipated others.

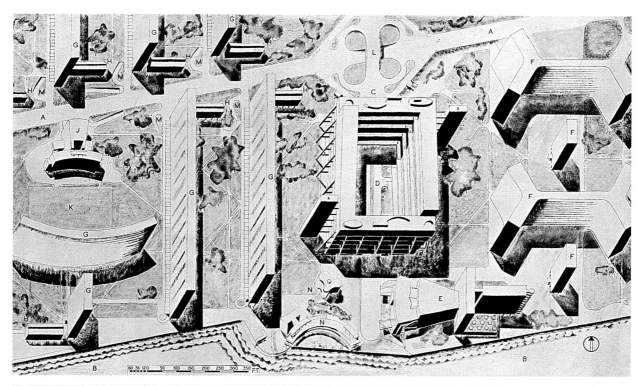

RIGHT Model photograph.

BELOW: Model perspective of the shopping centre, the largest and most thoroughly considered element of the design.

coincided most potently was in the belief that land had to be defined by use – what became the much-derided principle of zoning. For the policy-makers, it was the one handle that could be controlled from the centre; for the modernists, it was essential to their aesthetic vision. Irrespective of any further aims, however convergent or divergent, this might alone have been sufficient to splice modernism onto the priorities of government policy, and through the modernist architect, and Yorke's friend and colleague during the early war years, William (later Sir William and finally Lord) Holford they came into direct contact.[8]

It is a remarkable coincidence that so many of Yorke's circle had a specific influence in the evolution of planning. Arthur Korn, with whom he had a short-lived partnership, chaired the MARS town planning committee and was one of the progenitors of the MARS plan for London; after World War II he taught planning to generations of students at the Architectural Association.[9] Yorke's partnership with Marcel Breuer produced the Concrete Garden City of the Future which, when it appeared in 1936, was the most complete vision of a modernist urban utopia yet seen in Britain. Holford joined the newly established Ministry for Town and Country Planning in 1941, where he helped to develop the 1947 Act.[10] In 1944 Peter Shepheard, later to conceive Stevenage new town and Lancaster University, took time out from his work on the Abercrombie Plan to do some fastidious perspective renderings for Yorke of the Braithwaite House and a proposal for a roadside tea bar.[11] Geoffrey Jellicoe, who would create the subtle and sensitive water gardens in the centre of Hemel Hempstead and emerge as one of the most successful modernist landscape designers, had already suggested that Donald Gibson write to Yorke to sound him out about working on the reconstruction of Coventry. Finally, Yorke's closest friend in architecture, Frederick Gibberd, would plan Harlow new town. Yorke's circle of friends and acquaintances covered the gamut of post-war planning, from each of the educational, political and practical perspectives.

Proximity, of course, is no guarantee of active participation, and the basis of these relationships varies. While Marcel Breuer was almost certainly largely responsible for the outward form of the Concrete Garden City, he and Yorke were working at close quarters and it is unlikely that Yorke remained totally unaware of it.[12] As we shall see, what Yorke learnt from this project is more important and easier to define than what he contributed to it. Yorke's partnership with Arthur Korn was short-lived and produced one building, a block of flats in Camberwell, south London. It appears that they were not completely open with each other. When Ralph Tubbs telegraphed Yorke with an urgent request for the MARS town planning drawings on 4 March 1940, Yorke drafted a reply to his friend Colin Penn saying 'Please let Tubbs know Korn had the drawings', and suggested that Penn should 'try Rutter' – presumably if Korn or the drawings were untraceable.[13]

The relationship between Holford and Yorke is more complicated. It is relatively simple to exclude a direct influence from Yorke on Holford's work in planning, even though Yorke worked for Holford's firm during the early war years but thereafter geography intervened. Their correspondence suggests a warmer relationship than employer and employee, though Yorke yearned for more money and the pleasures of London. As an integral member of the Reconstruction Group which Reith formed within the ministry, Holford's role in forming policy was crucial.[14] Holford's biographer Gordon Cherry comments, 'The fundamental question which was begged by any talk of central authority was the relationship that Town and Country Planning was to have with whatever arrangements might emerge for national planning in the broader sense'.[15] Holford's presence near Reith ensured that modernism was represented whenever those talks took place.

Given Yorke's closeness to so influential a nexus, it is especially notable that he did not engage directly with the formulation of policy or after the war seek commissions that needed large-scale planning such as a new town. Suggesting that he deliberately eschewed such opportunities is tempting but speculative, though there are three aspects of his involvement with planning that lend this some credence. They are his gradual disillusionment with the activities of the MARS Group, three schemes of the 1930s which did raise implications for planning and comments on the drift of planning policy that can be identified as his.

Despite being a founder member and an active participant in the early meetings, the activities of the MARS Group, 'our unspeakable ex-racket', as Morton Shand was to call it in a private letter to Yorke,[16] eventually ceased to hold much interest for him. This change in attitude coincided with the time when MARS became bogged down in planning initiatives. Insights into the reasons for Yorke's change of heart can be found in the doings of the group itself between its foundation in 1933 and the end of the decade.[17] From the outset, MARS saw its destiny to be in planning as much as architectural aesthetics, which is difficult to understand as members of the group had conflicting views on the relationship between the ethics of planning and aesthetics that they were rarely prepared to, or indeed capable of, making explicit.[18]

Early on MARS decided to demonstrate how modern architecture might help with slum clearance, a goal of progressive architects and politicians since at least the 1890s, though early projects such as the London County Council's Millbank estate in Pimlico had set an Arts and Crafts precedent that persisted into the 1930s. The group set itself a task which, if successful, would conclusively prove the greater efficacy of modernism towards this end. Bethnal Green, that hub of social deprivation which since the late nineteenth century had been attracting philanthropists like Canon Barnett and Arnold Toynbee, would be the location of the study, as the MARS meeting of 14 February 1934 heard from the subcommittee formed to make the selection. Six days later, on 20 February, another meeting accepted the assumption of 'the existence of a State Planning Commission with sovereign powers over land in the borough', a sentiment close to Yorke's argument that modernism could not reach its full potential for social amelioration without 'controlled land development'.[19] So close was Yorke to the MARS mainstream at this point that he was delegated to procure a map of Bethnal Green at a scale of 25 inches to the mile, 'to show the main social and physical factors of the problem'.[20]

Bethnal Green though proved a rather tough problem for a bunch of young architects working in their spare time. Suggestions for exhibiting the fruits of their deliberations came and went,[21] and the MARS Group itself spent tedious hours debating its own constitution and other organisational matters.[22] There were numerous requests for more detailed statistical information, and almost as many regrets that demographic data was apparently so sparse. The subject expanded and, by 1938, six parts of London were under consideration. Contacts were made with the London County Council and that same year the idea of an exhibition finally bore fruit at the Grosvenor Gallery, with a foreword in the catalogue by George Bernard Shaw.[23] But by then Yorke had moved away from the MARS mainstream. The catalogue listed him as a member, but not as an active participant in arranging the exhibition, even though the model for the Concrete Garden City was in pride of place. As MARS' agenda grew, so Yorke's involvement with the group declined. By the time Ralph Tubbs wrote on the 14 May 1940, asking for his subscription of £2 2s, the weariness with which Yorke suggested Tubbs set it against the loan he had made to the group is palpable.[24]

Ennui does not alone account for Yorke bowing out of active participation in MARS. He was not generally prey to what his continental friends might have called Weltschmerz. But an examination of several planning projects with which he was involved, however loosely, in the 1930s indicates how his approach to architecture and planning evolved in the light of practical experience and exposure to opportunities. This puts his gradual drift away from the MARS Group into perspective.

The most important of these projects, despite Yorke's relatively small contribution, was the Concrete Garden City of the Future.[25] Undertaken during the first months of 1936, it was widely noted in architectural and other publications.[26] This was precisely the period when the MARS Group was floundering on two separate reefs – one the perceived need for more hard data before it could complete its 'plan', the other a growing concern with its own inner workings. Debates about the latter are unlikely to have been congenial to Yorke,[27] while Breuer's outburst of creative form-making at the other end of their office, perhaps leavened with the odd exchange of ideas, must have suggested that form, sometimes, could come before definition of need.

Of course, Breuer did not entirely reject the idea that social analysis played a part in new urban development. 'A new social science is emerging', he wrote, 'which represents a fresh angle of approach to civic planning. In former times town planning was almost exclusively governed by aesthetic considerations ... What I propose to call "positive" town planning, might be defined as the means of assimilating the design of towns to their several functions, is quite a recent development.'[28] Positive town planning, he continued, covered three separate fields: 'Investigation of the various administrative, social, hygienic, technical and legal conditions in the larger cities ...'; 'The planning of "Ideal towns" to demonstrate what our towns ought to be ...'; and 'The gradual reconstruction of existing cities.'[29] MARS aspired to the third and, mired in the first, more or less ignored the second.[30] Breuer placed each of these fields in relation to each other. Avoiding the first, at least in the context of this project, and confirming that the third 'is the most urgent and complicated question of all', his justification for concentrating on the second was that 'working out plans for "Ideal Cities" will gradually provide us with the essentials' for reconstructing existing cities.[31]

Part of the reason behind these priorities came from the particular dimensions and specified scale required for the model of the Concrete Garden City made to display the project at the Ideal Home Exhibition at Olympia in 1936. With its maximum dimensions of 9 feet 6 inches by 5 feet 6 inches, at 1/20 inch to 1 foot, the notional area would be about one-half by one-quarter of a mile. The only viable option was to make a demonstration city centre, 'a basis for amending present legislation' or an offering 'to local authorities as a skeleton programme'.[32] Given these limitations, and armed with the assumptions that the city ran east–west, with a river bank or lake shore setting the southern boundary and an east–west road a main armature, Breuer's imagination ran riot. A leisure quarter of cafés and theatre occupied much of the waterfront, and offices the eastern part. Residential areas formed the west, liberally interspersed with schools and enjoying plenty of open space with perhaps an overprovision of tennis courts.[33] As Breuer explained: 'The city of our model must be imagined as extending westwards, over further residential districts ... eastwards over an industrial area, towards the port; and northwards as being largely a repetition of the general planning disposition prevailing to the east and west.'[34] Much of this follows generic patterns of urban form, but the idea of a port to the east is perhaps a subliminal acknowledgement that the model, at whatever level of remove, was London.

Showing his affinity with Walter Gropius, Breuer aimed to give each block ample fresh air and sunlight.[35] This meant large areas of open space edged by relatively high blocks. 'A uniform height of twelve storeys was adopted', he explained, 'because calculations proved that this number of floors provides the most economical utilisation.'[36] Function times economy might have been his lodestar were it not for the ample evidence of formal invention in the service of defining new civic institutions or activities. Breuer's conception of a city balances different functions, each housed in a specific building type, with an architectural idiom devised to mark that function's institutional importance. It is almost, though its abstraction certainly gives it a degree of remove, an 'architecture' or 'cité parlante',[37] where the ground plane is a blank canvas for pedagogic expression.[38]

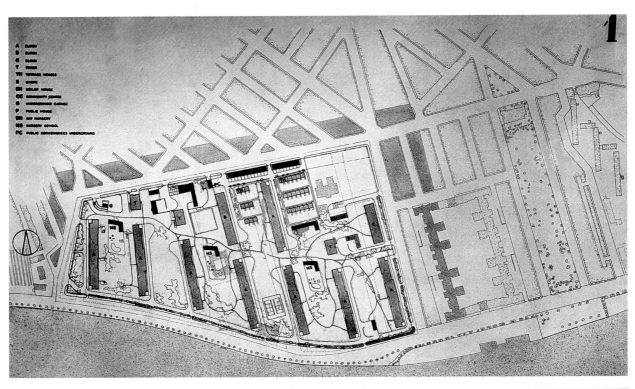

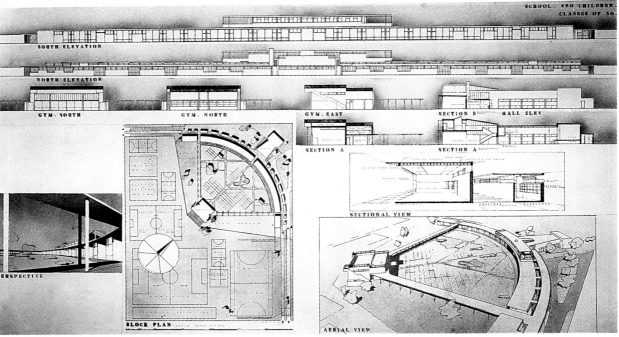

On the waterfront he recycled his unbuilt Kharkov Theatre project. The school has some resemblance to the entry he would make with Yorke to the *News Chronicle* school competition the following year, while the Y-shaped office blocks bear a striking similarity to the ones in which Breuer would, in the post World War II era, house UNESCO and an outpost of IBM.[39] Isabelle Hyman has some justification for her claim that: 'The model of Garden City of the Future (often called Civic Center after one of its sections) was probably the most significant formalist invention of Breuer's career, furnishing him with architectural capital to spend for the rest of his life.'[40]

Two formal developments merit special attention as both relate directly to the flaws and advantages of modernist town planning. Breuer gave special attention to traffic, incorporating an early if not entirely convincing clover leaf junction, 'a new solution of an urgent traffic problem which allows street intersections without periodic hold-ups by crossing traffic'.[41] It also has a shopping centre, derived from his 1929 scheme for a hospital at Elberfeld, Germany, providing for an activity that most modernist urban utopias overlooked. Breuer took special pleasure in it:

> The shopping centre forms a group of five double-storied premises facing the interior of a large public square. Its 'streets' which are partly covered over are a succession of terraces, set back one behind the other and connected by sloping ramps. Thanks to their all-glass fronts these shops enjoy a good natural lighting even at the back. Shoppers can move from shop-window to shop-window well protected from the elements, and without having to dodge wheeled traffic or being deafened by the roar of it. Compared with a big department store of the present day the principal difference evinced by the shopping centre is that it brings a number of independent and quite dissimilar shops into direct relation with one another . . . [42]

Both these features had some appeal for Yorke. He had expressed an interest in shop fronts in an early article for *The Architectural Review*, where he suggested that modern design could fulfil the promise of the Regency period, which had been lost under the Victorians.[43] More important, though, was the project's acknowledgement of so complex and vital an urban function as shopping, and the derivation or adaptation of a form to suit it. Throughout the Concrete Garden City there are demonstrations of such instrumental constructions. In his vicarious connection to the project, Yorke would have realised, were he not already aware, that modernism held a special place for devising new and sophisticated building types. Specifically in the shopping centre, Yorke would have seen how a modernist idiom could not just achieve the promise of Regency retail design, but might expand and enhance it on a massive scale. Even though Breuer had designed shops for the Wohnbedarf furniture retailer in Basle and Zurich, Yorke's interest in shop fronts suggests that his contribution to the Concrete Garden City might have been more than just a few comments from across the office.[44] Here, perhaps, is Randall Evans' 'ten per cent'.[45]

Breuer's ideas on road traffic found echoes in Yorke's subsequent work. Illustrating the Garden City in *A Key to Modern Architecture*, Yorke and Penn highlighted some of the features Breuer mentioned. 'Main traffic routes will be away from the building, which will be reached, in residential areas, through parkland by minor traffic lanes . . . Congestion on roads can be avoided by under-and-over 'clover leaf' crossings and intermediate subways, so that a driver need never leave the left-hand side of the road.'[46] Devising precisely the right form for the clover leaf clearly exercised Breuer – a drawing in the RIBA Drawings Collection shows studies for it at several levels.[47] Indeed, the sweeping though controlled and supposedly functional curves might have helped to generate another of the project's structures, the three-leafed clover-formed café. Another drawing at the RIBA, dated 24 February 1936, reveals the concept in more detail than the published drawings or model photographs. Three glass-walled storeys rise from a raised floor slab, resting on three piloti each roughly in the centre of its circular leaf form.[48] Free-form glass walls were, of course, a familiar modernist device, at least since Mies van der Rohe's second glass skyscaper design of 1922. Breuer's café building bears some similarities with Alvar Aalto's formal experiments of the same period, not least in its free-form glass perimeter, though in Aalto's case the form would manifest itself in vases while Breuer later built a four-leafed version of the design at the Ariston Club, Argentina, in 1948.[49]

More specifically, Breuer anticipated a planning principle Yorke would develop in the brewery cottages at Stratford-upon-Avon. 'This type of planning', he wrote of the concept of providing large open spaces, 'has a further advantage because it simplifies traffic conditions . . . There are fewer house doors, fewer streets, and above all, fewer street intersections.'[50] The potential to shorten streets and presumably reduce the number of junctions was Yorke's principal justification for the wide frontage of the Stratford cottages.

The Concrete Garden City indicates a critical moment in Yorke's personal development, over and above the credit and kudos he gained from the partnership with Marcel Breuer. As we have seen, when he wrote *The Modern House* in 1934 Yorke's ideas about town planning were unsophisticated, as was possible at a moment when the ethos of the Garden City movement towards controlled land development seemed to be the principal necessity for modern architecture. Many modernists, though, for various reasons agreed with Breuer that 'the gradual reconstruction of existing cities . . . is the most urgent and complicated question of all',[51] as the MARS Group's masochistic entrée into London's East End shows. The term 'garden city' in the title of the project clearly looked back to the legacy of the Garden City movement – to say nothing of suggesting that it came within a venerable British tradition – but its actual design would not have passed muster with Ebenezer Howard or his formidable successor Frederic Osborn. They disapproved of flats, which precluded the intimate connection with the land that they hoped garden cities promoted, and if neither had absolutely fixed views on architectural idiom, the massive scale of some of Breuer's buildings would have fitted ill with any existing Garden City. Looking one way in name but another in intention, the Concrete Garden City was a dichotomy with one part indicating a path that Yorke would follow: urban planning would become an extrapolation of building types, which would be new or radically overhauled according to modern needs. Having realised that the Garden City movement did not meet the needs of modernism, and dabbled in planning with the MARS Group, for him the Concrete Garden City marked a point where the possibility of a career based on devising functional building types came into focus.

Such a realisation did not occur in a flash, two planning initiatives to which Yorke devoted some effort between Breuer's departure for America and the outbreak of war in September 1939 show how these themes were taking root. Recalling the commercial interests behind the Concrete Garden City – sponsored by the Cement and Concrete Association – one initiative arose when the glass-maker Pilkington invited Yorke to join a 'Glass Age Town Planning Committee'. In an all-glass room on London's Piccadilly, as the *Edinburgh Evening Dispatch* noted, Yorke joined Grey Wornum, Howard Robertson, Robert Furneaux Jordan, Max Fry and Raymond McGrath, 'to help people to visualise familiar places as they could be if re-planned in this glass age', explained Geoffrey Pilkington.[52] Wornum and Robertson ensured it was not the most avant-garde committee possible; it would seem to be one which covered many different positions. This was understandable if the aim was to try to align glass with the broadest possible architectural trends.[53]

As they were unlikely to be built, the proposals did not require vast amounts of sociological information and were dramatically polemical. Max Fry, wrote the *Manchester Guardian*, offered a 'vision of the future Strand . . . in which the present (and growing) range of vast ferroconcrete blocks has been swept away and replaced by a series of glass skyscrapers spaced widely apart and separated by open spaces in which the inhabitants of these hives may find sunlight and fresh air'.[54] Almost certainly Fry had Le Corbusier's Plan Voisin in mind, another vision of isolated blocks striding along the river bank in an existing city centre. Like Fry, neither McGrath at Bournemouth nor Furneaux Jordan on Edinburgh's Prince's Street allowed any existing buildings to remain. Unsurprisingly, Grey Wornum took a different line. Reworking Liverpool's waterfront, he wanted 'to give a dignified approach from the river to the three important existing buildings – Liver Building, Cunard Building and the Port and Harbour Offices – that introduce the traveller to the city itself', as he told the *Manchester Evening News*.[55]

If one measure of the committee's success is the extent to which it anticipated future developments, Wornum's contribution is certainly successful. In the early 1990s, Allies & Morrison made improvements to the waterfront that were broadly compatible with Wornum's aims, even though, with the decline in passenger shipping, the Mersey river is no longer an introduction to the city.[56] Yorke's proposal for the precinct of Liverpool Street and Broad Street stations in London dwarfs Wornum's for far-sightedness. He realised that once the railway lines were electrified – a technical development commensurate with the 'Glass Age' – it would be possible to build over the stations, with reinforced concrete and steel frames, leaving the walls to be two-thirds glass. Building over London's major rail terminals was a fate that befell several stations in the 1980s, including Liverpool Street itself as the giant Broadgate development took shape.

As a member of Pilkington's 'Glass Age Town Planning Committee' in 1938, Yorke redesigned the precinct of Liverpool Street and Broad Street stations on the eastern fringe of the City of London.

Photo: British Architectural Library, RIBA, London.

Yorke's design for the buildings was prescient in another way. As he envisaged them, they were largely glass-walled, an augury for the post-war future when glass-walled, air-conditioned office blocks became standard fare in the City of London. Yorke, of course, was not the first to propose office buildings of this type and indeed, in the slightly chilling anonymity and recognition of the need to deal with large flows of traffic, his design has some resemblance to Mies van der Rohe's vision of 1929 of Berlin's Alexanderplatz. Like Mies' proposal, Yorke's was an attempt to bring calm and order to a hotchpotch of urban form. As he told the *Manchester Evening News*: 'Liverpool-street discharges a great volume of traffic into a maze of congested streets. My scheme for rebuilding Liverpool-street and Broad-street Stations embraces the replanning of both stations, to give an area, common to both, which will be free from main road traffic.'[57] Two years later he repeated the point, and stressed the need for comprehensive planning: 'An area like that which comprises [the two stations] . . . cannot be planned as an isolated unit without having regard to the streets and buildings beyond . . . A plan for Liverpool Street must be made in the light of the plan for London and the plan for London must take into account the planning of areas as far apart as Southend, Brighton, Slough and Birmingham.'[58] The repercussions of his design multiplied, rather as the MARS Group found that it could not replan Bethnal Green without reworking the whole of the city. Here were embodied some of the most common modernist views about replanning the metropolis, such as creating open space, rationalising buildings into fewer, larger blocks and separating pedestrians from traffic. Also, as in the Concrete Garden City, the ground plane is an empty screen. It would not have been a culture shock for Ludwig Hilberseimer.

The activities of the 'Glass Age Town Planning Committee' were nearly contemporaneous with Yorke's design work on the Stratford brewery cottages. Although outwardly different, and marking Yorke's growing interest in rationalised traditional construction rather than new materials, the cottages do share something with the Liverpool Street vision. Both use the design of individual buildings to set the pattern for much larger scale urban development, as if the buildings were single cells which could replicate across a theoretically unlimited and blank area to create an entire quarter or even a complete city, and both contain traces of determinism. At Liverpool Street that determinism comes from the need to use a particular material, a point which the *Manchester Evening News* underlined. The committee was convened, it reported, 'to examine the possibility of replanning London and other places in the light of knowledge of the manufacture of glass',[59] rather as the Cement and Concrete Association had sponsored the Concrete Garden City to promote the use of its products.

In *A Key to Modern Architecture*, Yorke and Colin Penn explain how cottages similar to those at Stratford might form a larger development.[60] As Yorke claimed that at Stratford 'the idea was to extend this principle to a village development'[61] it is fair to conclude that the book describes what Yorke would have done had the village come to fruition. The houses were devised, Yorke and Penn reveal, from initially considering the needs of a double bedroom and the first-floor layout. In essence the room must have space to move around a double bed, and room for a chair and dressing table, while the window should not cause a draught across the bed. That plan is then mirrored and the two rooms take the sunny side, while the third bedroom, staircase and bathroom lie behind. With the staircase fixed and the kitchen below the bathroom, the ground-floor plan is extrapolated from the first floor, and the single units then put together in rows. A communal heating plan eliminates the need for coal delivery to each front door, and its capacity governs the length of the rows, which can now be repeated in serried ranks across the site, rather as the steel-and-concrete-framed, glass-walled blocks stride out at Liverpool Street. Here too, the site is a neutral canvas.

In *A Key to Modern Architecture*, Yorke and Colin Penn used the brewery cottages in Stratford-upon-Avon to explain a functional plan. To show how the individual units might make a district plan, they extrapolated the idea of a terrace.

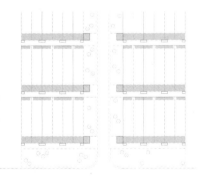

Where Liverpool Street is determined by its materials and construction – and anticipates the retro-chic anonymity of the modern office – Stratford derives from a formulation of function. Together they show that Yorke's most significant attempts to work in town planning on his own betray the normative tendencies of modernist convention. His originality did not extend to planning; rather he thought that single units, once established from their functional or constructional conditions, set the pattern for urban form on a large scale. According to this belief, the buildings themselves were inchoate, static agents with tightly specified purposes, rather like the window sills or wall finishes which they bore. Ironically, if the Stratford cottages were really derived from such monocular functionalism, it would preclude the possibility of any variety in their patterns of use which might lead to multiple, personal interpretations of them. It is easy to see how the weft and web of different activities which make up traditional urban life could be excluded in such visions as Yorke and Penn implied for their design.

The Garden City movement, to which Yorke at least paid lip service early in his career, suggested a way of overcoming social ills by reconfiguring space and form. The symptom and the cure were inextricably entwined. Although Ebenezer Howard did not prescribe an architectural idiom for garden cities, those built in Britain before World War II essentially followed some form of traditional design and the homespun Arts and Crafts image of buildings by architects such as Parker and Unwin became indelibly associated with the concept.

During World War II, however, the way policy developed made such piecemeal, homespun solutions seem anachronistic. Howard, with his Garden City movement, was only a pioneer for the new world inaugurated by the Barlow Report, and its successors by Lord Justice Scott and Mr Justice Uthwatt, as a little book called *Planning for Reconstruction*, of which Yorke was joint author put it.[62] Barlow, it helpfully explained, only examined towns and industry; Scott was 'a charter for countrymen and the countryside'; while Uthwatt was set up after one of Barlow's recommendations, to ensure 'the best use . . . of land with a view to economic efficiency for the community and well being for the individual.'[63] To all the well-rehearsed urban ills, 'THE SOLUTION LIES IN PLANNING,' emphasised Yorke and his fellow authors in capitals. Planning was no longer a series of discrete decisions, but a linked, interactive process that covered the entire land surface of the country so that it could contribute to one combined, national effort.[64] Instead, as the approving quote of Sir William (later Lord) Beveridge, the Welfare State's founding father, implies, planning had become an aspect of social policy: 'These, then, are the four stones which we must put in our sling before we set out to fight the giant Squalor: planned use of land, sane use of transport, right use of the right architects and the maximum of efficiency in the building industry.'[65]

Yorke would hardly have disagreed. However, where he did differ from the mainstream was in having an interest in agriculture alongside architecture, with which to conceptualise such far-reaching control of land use. He could regret the loss of prime farmland both in a letter to his friend Homery Folks and in *Planning for Reconstruction*.[66] His growing interest in farming and food production meant that land was not just a potential building site, while architecture meant the design of complex buildings, drawing on a knowledge of construction or an appreciation of functional planning.[67] As he anticipated in *Planning for Reconstruction*, the new-development regime would bring plenty of opportunities for designing buildings, without having to engage in planning itself.[68] Yorke was unusual because the new controlled planning helped to open another area of interest and enabled him to define architecture around his skills and interests; for many architects and politicians, planning and architecture became indissoluble because they had no other way of conceiving of physical planning.

Yorke owed much of this insight to the experience he gained while working with William Holford in the early years of World War II. It gave him the opportunity to work on far larger projects than he had done hitherto, with all the resources open to munitions production, and under centralised control with constrictions not just on the use of land but also the availability of construction materials.[69] Additionally, for the first time he was working for a large organisation. Holford's firm swelled to 200 people, and it was seconded to the giant engineering consultancy Sir Alexander Gibb and Partners.[70] In the engineering sector Gibb had pioneered the close relationship between publicly funded work and a private professional consultancy which accounted for the growth of Holford's organisation, and which Yorke would ultimately exploit at Yorke, Rosenberg & Mardall. Gibb, after a career in the civil service that culminated in his becoming an engineer to the Admiralty during World War I. This established his firm specifically to provide engineering services to government-sponsored initiatives. Projects undertaken included a bay barrage at Kuala Lumpur and, not surprisingly, a move towards the trend of government-backed industrial projects in Britain, such as the Team Valley Trading Estate outside Gateshead, in the late 1930s.[71] In this Keynesian programme of work-creation in an unemployment black spot, Holford was the architect, indicating that the relationship was well under way before war broke out in 1939. Once the new ministry was established, Holford and his colleagues in the Ministry for Town and Country Planning themselves. War intensified and focused the established drift of policy. Within the general and officially sanctioned enthusiasm for planning for post-war reconstruction, there was also scope for several extreme views, such as the diametrically opposed MARS and Royal Academy proposals for London.[72]

As we have seen, Yorke's planning method, such as it was, came from extrapolating function or construction technique. Town planning, in this conception at least, was subservient to the buildings themselves and his visions of new cities are not especially appealing. If his wartime work exposed him to the benefits of practising his profession as part of a large-scale private organisation with strong ties to government, it also led him to modify the approach to planning – 'controlled land development' – he had championed before the war. But a remodelled planning regime would intermesh with the Welfare State policies of providing many complex new building types which appealed to Yorke's strengths. Planning policy dictated that the new comprehensive schools built in response to the 1944 Education Act, and the hospitals built to serve the National Health Service once it was established in 1948 – both of which needed sophisticated, functionally based designs – would largely be on greenfield sites. Yorke's avoidance of the new political settlement in physical planning, therefore, is a close counterpart to his understanding of the opportunities the architectural profession offered, especially as it mutated into an agent of the Welfare State after 1945.[73] In his subsequent career he was free to concentrate on those more explicitly architectural skills of construction and functional planning, for which he had a particular aptitude, and developing political contacts. Large-scale physical planning he could leave to others.

Notes

1. There are useful accounts of this process in Jules Lubbock, *The Tyranny of Taste: The Politics of Architecture and Design in Britain 1550–1960*, Yale University Press and the Paul Mellon Centre for British Art (New Haven and London), 1995, especially Part VI, Chapter 3, 'Town Planning', pp 333–48; and John Gold, *The Experience of Modernity: Modern Architects and the Future City 1928-53*, Spon (London), 1997.

2. The effects of these Acts makes a parallel to the Architects' Registration Acts of the 1930s. While the detailed relationship between the two is not investigated here, and it is clear that they were not part of a coordinated programme, the fact that the title 'architect' was given legal protection probably made it easier for architects to fit into the increased statutory regulation of planning after 1947. The 1932 Act received considerable opprobrium, not least from the MARS Group, who disliked the lack of systematic national policies and strategies. See note 18.

3. FRS Yorke, *The Modern House*, Architectural Press (London), 1934, p 2. In private conversation in September 1994 Sir Peter Shepheard, who had worked with Sir Patrick Abercrombie on his plans for London in the 1940s, averred that one aim of the 1947 Act was to nationalise the right to develop land. In effect, it continued many of the wartime restrictions on building, caused by shortage of materials, into the post-war period by rationing land for particular uses. Lubbock, op cit, p 344, makes a similar point: 'The essence [of the 1947 Town and Country Planning Act] were to introduce national and regional planning for land use along the lines advocated by the Barlow Commission, Beveridge and others. The Act certainly imposed a tier of statute law over the common-law rights of property owners, which restricted the rights of use of any given piece of land.

4. What exposure to 'town planning' Yorke had in his education was in the Garden City tradition. A fourth-year town planning project, dated 18 June 1929, survives in the RIBA Drawings Collection, PA 237/3. Its blocks of four houses are arranged in a picturesque way to break up the street line with setbacks and slight alterations of angle, and at low density of eight houses to the acre.
   The most comprehensive study in English of CIAM is Eric Mumford, *The CIAM Discourse on Urbanism 1928–60*, MIT Press (Cambridge Mass), 2000, which sets the international context for Gold's studies of Britain.

5. Royal Commission on the Distribution of the Industrial Population, Cmd 6153, HMSO (London), January 1940. See Lubbock, op cit, pp 337–8 for a summary. Planning for Reconstruction, Architectural Press (Cheam) 1944, a little book of which Yorke, in his *Who's Who* entry, claimed joint authorship, summarised Barlow's recommendations as: creation of a central authority; redeveloping urban areas; decentralising industry; balancing areas of development across the country (p 40). Given Barlow's dates, it is fair to conclude that wartime conditions intensified these perceived needs, but did not create them.

6. Abercrombie's plans were *The County of London Plan* (1943) and the even more comprehensive *Greater London Plan*, HMSO (London), 1944.

7. See Ian McIntyre, *The Expense of Glory – a life of John Reith*, HarperCollins (London), 2000 for an account of Reith's life. The history of the ministry is complex. Reith was raised to the peerage and became Minister of Works and Buildings on 3 October 1940; see Winston S Churchill, *The Second World War, Volume II: Their Finest Hour*, Cassell (London), 1949, p 533. On 11 February 1942, this ministry absorbed responsibility for town and country planning from the Ministry of Health, and changed its name to the Ministry of Works and Planning. A mere 11 days later, in a reshuffle following the disaster of the fall of Singapore, Reith was sacked and replaced by Lord Portal. On 5 February 1943, a Ministry of Town and Country Planning was formed, under Herbert Morrison; Portal remained Minister of Works. (See Winston S Churchill, *The Second World War, Volume III: The Hinge of Fate*, Cassell (London), 1951, pp 866, 870.
   Churchill's own commitment, as Prime Minister, to reconstruction was not in doubt. 'I regard it as a definite part of the duty and responsibility of this National Government to here set about a vast and practical scheme to make sure that in the years immediately following the war

there will be food, work and homes for all.' Quoted on the final page of *Planning for Reconstruction*, Architectural Press (Cheam) 1944.

8. In *A Broken Wave*, Penguin (Harmondsworth), 1981 Viscount Esher gives a personal though lucid account of postwar British urban development which shows how closely architecture and planning were intertwined. For an author who, as the Hon Lionel Brett, was deeply involved from the late 1930s onwards it is remarkably free from prejudice or polemic.

9. Arthur Korn, *History Builds the Town*, Lund Humphries (London), 1955. His students included Peter Ahrends and Denise Scott Brown, both of whom have acknowledged his charismatic influence in private conversations.

10. See Gordon Cherry, *William Holford*, Mansell (London and New York), 1986 for an overview of Holford's career.

11. Copies of these are preserved in the Allford Yorke Archive, Folder 13, pp 27, 28, and Folder 16, p 21 respectively. Sir Patrick Abercombie was successively professor of planning at Liverpool University and University College London. His plansbecame the template for the redevelopment of London after World War II. See *Greater London Plan 1944* HMSO (London), 1945.

12. Breuer, rather than Yorke, was the partner who spoke about the Concrete Garden City in public. He accepted an invitation from George Checkley, honorary secretary of the Polytechnic Architectural Society, written on 31 July 1936, to give the talk on 2 December that year. Further correspondence shows that the project's sponsors, the Cement and Concrete Association, went to the expense of paying Morton Shand to translate Breuer's paper, entitled 'The Garden City of the Future' from German, and the typescript has phonetic markings on it, presumably to help Breuer with the correct pronunciation of a language with which he was not familiar. Breuer's awkwardness in English, and the cost of translation, suggest that it was absolutely essential for him, rather than Yorke, to give the talk. See documents in the RIBA YoF/2/2.
    Further evidence of Breuer's greater contribution comes from an examination of the design itself. As Isabelle Hyman writes in *Marcel Breuer Architect*, Harry N Abrams (New York), 2001, p 83: 'The model of Garden City of the Future (often called Civic Center after one of its sections) was probably the most significant formalist invention of Breuer's career, furnishing him with architectural capital to spend for the rest of his life'. As well as looking forward, the project also looked back over Breuer's career, with echoes of earlier designs such as the Kharkov Theatre.
    Finally, Randall Evans, who joined the Yorke and Breuer office shortly after the Concrete Garden City was produced, remembered many years later that it was '90 per cent Breuer'. (See note of the conversation between Evans and David Allford, in the Allford Yorke Archive.) A monograph on Yorke has to deal with the speculative 10 per cent, while recognising that it is only 10 per cent.

13. Both Tubbs' telegram and Yorke's draft reply, handwritten in pencil (a typical Yorke habit) are preserved in the RIBA YoF/1/12.

14. '. . . in but not of the Ministry' comments Cherry of this unit, op cit, p 81.

15. Ibid, p 94.

16. See letter from Shand to Yorke, dated 1 October 1940, YoF/1/12.

17. The formation of the MARS Group was announced in a communication of 25 April 1933, a copy of which is preserved in the Samuel (ie Godfrey Samuel) Papers in the RIBA, SaG/90/2. Yorke was the founding secretary. In *The Experience of Modernity* John Gold gives an overview of its activities, including how the programme it set itself expanded exponentially, leading to the delays in bringing their projects to fruition and the confusion of aims that scarred the group. MARS was formed at the suggestion of Sigfried Giedion, who was rather dismayed by the presence of Howard Robertson as an English delegate to CIAM, and appealed to architects in England who were more sympathetic to his view of modern architecture to create an English branch of CIAM.

18. For example, members expended much effort in pulling the 1932 Town and Country Planning Act to pieces, perhaps not without justification. See records in RIBA SaG/93/1, in particular a circular to all group members of 20 June 1938 from Samuel and Jim Cadbury Brown. It announced that at the 'meeting in January it was decided to take more active steps

19. See minutes of the meeting of 20 February 1934, RIBA SaG/90/2, and Yorke, op cit, p 2.

20. See minutes of the meeting of 20 February 1934, op cit.

21. For example, the minutes of the meeting of 20 February 1934 record an attempt to show something at the New Homes for Old exhibition at Olympia in June of that year, and the meeting of 5 December 1934 noted a proposal for a MARS exhibit at the Town Planning Congress at the RIBA on 11 April 1935. See RIBA Sag/90/2.

22. The constitution was debated on 5 December 1934

23. Exhibition Catalogue, MARS (London), 1938.

24. See letter in RIBA YoF/1/12. The MARS Exhibition of 1938 went some way over budget and members were asked to contribute. This probably accounts for Yorke's loan.

25. See note 12 for an explanation of this point.

26. See, for example, *Architectural Review*, vol 79 (April 1936), plate iii; *The Architects' Journal* vol 83 (26 March 1936), pp 48. See Chapter 5 for references to overseas publications.

27. No qualitative record of Yorke's attitude to MARS Group meetings exists, but Dick (Sir Richard) Sheppard, in his obituary of Yorke for the *RIBA Journal* vol 69 (August 1962), p 303 left this description of his behaviour while on the RIBA Council: 'He . . . was never really interested in Committee work, and sat in the RIBA Council Room, amused, benign and silent, voting for the right things but hardly bothering to speak for them.' Even if Yorke was initially enthusiastic about the MARS Group, by the last decade of his life he had developed an aversion to tedious committee work.

28. 'The Garden City of the Future'; typescript in the RIBA Yorke Archive, translated by Morton Shand and with phonetic markings which bear more relation to Hungarian than German, to assist Breuer with English pronunciation, in RIBA YoF/2/2, p 2.

29. Ibid, pp 3–4.

30. Korn, op cit, p 84. Arthur Korn's comments are interesting on this point, especially as his endeavours on the MARS Plan for London went in a quite different direction. He might have railed against the 'idealistic, unreal' utopianism of isolated visions such as the Concrete Garden City, but he also conceded the potential of such schemes to produce 'a new conception of the town and [to show] the way forward'. The MARS Plan was published in *The Architectural Review*, vol 91 (June 1942), pp 143–50, and 'explained' by Korn and the engineer Felix Samuely, who chaired one of the subcommittees. The main committee comprised, under Korn's chairmanship, Max Fry, William Tatton Brown, Arthur Ling and Christopher Tunnard.

31. 'The Garden City of the Future', op cit, p 4. Emphasising the importance of reconstruction, Breuer had opened his talk with an exhortation: 'Our towns are worn out organisms which can no longer adapt themselves either to the fresh possibilities offered by recent technical developments or the essential reforms we demand of them. Nor can it be said that they correspond to contemporary hygienic requirements. They are also wholly incapable of providing for the increasing tempo of modern life, or satisfying the normal expansion of vehicular traffic to anything like an adequate extent. Smoke and soot belch from them, and their growing din tortures our nerves.' And more in the same vein. Ibid, p 1.

32. Ibid, p 2.

33. Randall Evans in conversation with Jeremy Melvin, December 1991. Evans remembered that Breuer enjoyed playing tennis while he stayed in London. Yorke's outdoor pursuits did not include tennis, though the motif of tennis courts was repeated in the Yorke, Rosenberg & Mardall entry for the Pimlico housing scheme of 1945 which, won by Powell & Moya, became known as Churchill Gardens. Various drawings of the entry survive in the Allford Yorke Archive, so the Concrete Garden City had an influence on Yorke, Rosenberg & Mardall's drawing style, if nothing else! Allford Yorke Archive, Folder 13.

34. 'The Garden City of the Future', op cit, p 8.

35. Gropius had picked Breuer to run the furniture workshop at the Bauhaus, and the two were living in close proximity in the Isokon flats on Lawn Road, Hampstead. Gropius would later invite Breuer to join him at Harvard, and the two formed a partnership. In the 1920s Gropius had proposed the *zeilenbau* model of development – relatively tall blocks that gave space for light and air – as an antidote to crowded residential districts in existing cities. Breuer acknowledged this by using a slide of Gropius's design for the Haselhorst district of Berlin. See 'The Garden City of the Future', op cit, p14 for the list of illustrations used.

36. 'The Garden City of the Future', op cit, p 6.

37. On that score the Concrete Garden City might even bear comparison with Josef Plečnik's reworking of Ljubljana to mark its becoming the Slovenian capital, which continued through the 1920s and 1930s, as the city was not far from Breuer's *Mittel Europ* stomping ground.

38. I am grateful to David Dunster, Roscoe Professor of Architecture at the University of Liverpool, for this insight.

39. Illustrations of the unplaced entry to the *News Chronicle* schools competition survive in the Allford Yorke Archive, Folder 13.

40. Isabelle Hyman, *Marcel Breuer, Architect*, Harry N Abrams (New York), 2001, p 83.

41. 'The Garden City of the Future', op cit, p 13.

42. Ibid, p 11.

43. FRS Yorke, 'From order through disorder to order', *The Architectural Review*, vol 70, (November 1931), pp 171–8. While ignored by canonical modernism, shopping precincts would become one of the most notable features of post-war British architecture, for instance in Coventry and Harlow.

44. See Christopher Wilk, *Marcel Breuer Furniture and Interiors*, Architectural Press (London), 1981, pp 112–13 for some details on the design of the two stores.

45. See note 12 above. The shopping centre was an extraordinary proposal. A drawing in the RIBA Drawings Collection shows how the ramps worked within a dramatic structure, sloping on the long sides of the oblong shape and level on the shorter sides, so the whole circulation route is staggered within a series of giant trusses. PA 237/2/10.

46. FRS Yorke and Colin Penn, *A Key to Modern Architecture*, Blackie (London and Glasgow), 1939, pp 136–7.

47. RIBA PA 237/2/1.

48. RIBA PA 237/2.

49. Aalto and Breuer were among the two most fecund inventors of form in their generation, and the possibility of some overlap of influence cannot be totally dismissed, especially bearing in mind the curious interrelationship between their careers. They would have been aware of each other, at least from 1934, when the show flat at the Dolderthal apartments in Zurich was fitted out almost exclusively with furniture by one or the other. Two years later, in July 1936, the distributors of Aalto's furniture in Britain disputed a patent for Breuer's furniture on the grounds of similarity. See Wilk, op cit, p 115 and p 189, footnote 84. As a friend of both, Yorke might have been caught in the crossfire, though it would have been more in character for him to try to effect some form of resolution, and his hand might lie behind the dispute's reasonably amicable settlement. His possible role as midwife to some of modernism's most powerful forms would bear further investigation. For information on the Ariston Club, Mar del Plata, Argentina, see Hyman, op cit, p 279.

50. 'The Garden City of the Future', op cit, p 7.

51. Ibid, p 4.

52. Yorke preserved a cutting from the *Edinburgh Evening Dispatch* in a scrapbook containing records of his work in the 1930s, which entered the RIBA's archives from those of the firm YRM in 1997. Sadly, his diligence in preservation did not extend to recording the date, though a cutting from the *Manchester Evening News* on the same page with similar information is date-stamped 21 May 1938. It is from the second cutting that Pilkington's words are taken. For an account of the role of Pilkington as a patron of modern architecture, see Julian Holder, 'Reflecting Change: Pilkington as a Patron of Modern Architecture and Design', 'Industrial Architecture', *Twentieth Century Architecture*, no 1 (Summer 1994), the Twentieth Century Society, London, pp 65–76. Holder has

useful background on the company and its promotion of glass in modern architecture, but dismisses the 'Glass Age Town Planning Committee', calling it 'another of John Gloag's publicity stunts' (p 76). Gloag came from Pilkington's advertising agency, Pritchard and Partners.

53. Wornum designed the RIBA's – then new – headquarters in 1934, in a restrained Swedish-inspired neoclassical idiom. After World War II Robertson would design the elephantine Shell Centre on London's South Bank.

54. *Manchester Guardian*, 10 June 1938, cutting preserved in scrapbook.

55. *Manchester Evening News*, 21 May 1938.

56. A further competition was held in 2002 which resulted in a win for Will Alsop, who is probably not in sympathy with Grey Wornum.

57. *Manchester Evening News*, op cit

58. Typescript in the RIBA YoF/1/12; undated but explains that the scheme for Liverpool Street was 'made two years ago'. As the project can be dated to 1938, the paper must be 1940.

59. Ibid.

60. Yorke and Penn, op cit, pp 112–118.

61. See 'Cottages at Stratford-upon-Avon, 1938/9', Allford Yorke Archive, Folder 16, p 7. Yorke also made a similar claim on his nomination papers to become a Fellow of the RIBA, dated 14 November 1942 and held at the institute.

62. Scott reported in August 1942 (Cmd 6378, HMSO, London), and Uthwatt in September 1942 (Cmd 6386, HMSO, London); *Planning for Reconstruction*, Architectural Press (Cheam) 1944, pp 32ff. See note 5 for authorship.

63. *Planning for Reconstruction*, pp 44, 49.

64. Ibid, p16.

65. Ibid, p 97. Beveridge made these remarks at the opening of an exhibition 'Rebuilding Britain' at the RIBA.

66. See letter dated 7 February 1944 to J Homery Folks, in which Yorke expresses concern about his own involvement in ripping up 800 acres of countryside to build factories; RIBA YoF/1/8. See also *Planning for Reconstruction*, op cit, p 38 where he laments the 1932 Town and Country Planning Act as coming into force 'only after many thousands of acres of first class farming land had been lost forever'.

67. See Chapter 5 for more information on Yorke's agricultural ventures.

68. *Planning for Reconstruction*, op cit, p 15. Referring to existing cities the book says, 'The new community buildings: schools, hospitals, clubs, shops, churches and pubs, often provided as an afterthought, were inconveniently placed in the relation to the homes'. By implication new ones would be needed to overcome the 'inconvenience'.

69. See Chapter Five for more details of Yorke's work during World War II.

70. Planning for Reconstruction op cit.

71. Entry for Alexander Gibb, *Dictionary of National Biography*.

72. For the MARS Plan see *Architectural Review*, vol 91 (June 1942), pp 143–50.

73. Yorke was not alone if he believed that planning required skills outside the stable of architecture. In the 1960s Ahrends, Burton & Koralek, when engaged on a large housing scheme in Basildon new town in Essex, employed sociologists to help establish an understanding of the scope of the project.

CHAPTER 5

THE FRUITS OF PROFESSIONALISM

Architectural practice in Britain during the first third of the twentieth century was still shaped by the ethos of the generation that had come to prominence in the 1890s. Having made their names as Arts and Crafts architects, a few segued into classicism and several survived to be interviewed by Nikolaus Pevsner and canonised as 'pioneers of modern design' in his not wholly convincing attempt to establish a British ancestry for modern architecture.[1] Even if WR Lethaby died in 1931 before he could see FRS Yorke's attempt to cajole him into a similar role at the start of *The Modern House in England* and CFA Voysey resisted such blandishments, Sir Edwin Lutyens, Sir Herbert Baker and notably Sir Reginald Blomfield engaged in active resistance.[2] These three knights, born in 1869, 1862 and 1856 respectively, all survived into the 1940s, and, however progressive they may have been in their youth, by 1930 they represented the forces of undiluted reaction to the generation of modernists born in the first decade of the twentieth century.[3]

The pattern these prominent figures imprinted on the practice of architecture casts an even longer shadow than their presence as architectural figureheads.[4] Several, including Lethaby and Blomfield, had contributed to *Architecture: Profession or Art?*, the polemical bludgeon edited by TG Jackson and Norman Shaw in 1891, which was instrumental in defeating the RIBA's attempts, under its president J MacVicar Anderson, to bring about legal registration of the title 'architect'.[5] That triumph for the art party ensured that architectural practice would remain relatively loose and informal for a generation, and it was in this milieu that FRS Yorke's outlook was formed. His father, FWB Yorke, kept a prized set of craftsman's tools, sent his son to school in Chipping Camden and took him on a cycling tour, that essential rite of passage of the 1890s liberated middle classes. In dress he affected the air of a *fin-de-siècle*, Bohemian dandy.[6] FWB Yorke's work veered gently between Arts and Crafts and an undogmatic neoclassicism, not unlike FRS Yorke's surviving student work from his years after he entered Birmingham School of Art in 1924.[7]

Not surprisingly, for the first decade of his career after he became an associate of the RIBA in 1930, Yorke drew on the pattern of practice and network of contacts his father offered.[8] This enabled him to avoid full-time, paid employment and instead to develop a broad web of relationships in publishing and architecture, within the UK and abroad, which were essential in establishing his position among modernists in the 1930s. The model of practice fitted well with Yorke's lifestyle at the time, living a Bohemian life in the artists' quarter of Chelsea – and finding ingenious and not always entirely moral ways of stretching his insecure finances. As David Allford writes, even when Yorke was developing a large firm some of these characteristics remained with him.[9]

The 1930s was the decade when the professionalists took their revenge. An Act of Parliament in 1931 established a voluntary register of architects, and a second Act which came into force in 1938 made the step compulsory for anyone who wished to use the title 'architect'. During World War II, 'all private building work ceased', as Yorke put it, and architects, now a clearly and legally identifiable group, became agents of the state. Registration at least outwardly changed them from artists into a profession that could achieve measurable, mechanistic ends. Whether serving the

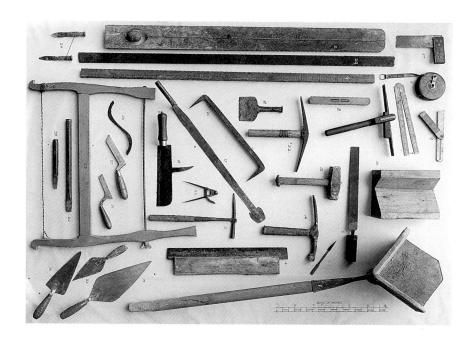

FWB Yorke's tools used in the building trade. He was steeped in the Arts and Crafts tradition.

war effort or building the peace in the post-war Welfare State, architects became conscious instruments of social and economic policy in a way that totally changed the profession.[10] The change in Yorke's own status was dramatic, but his experiences led him both to question assumptions he had taken for granted before the war, and to project a different future. Accepting these new circumstances meant totally changing his *modus operandi*, and his response was to establish a formal, long-lasting and ultimately extremely profitable partnership, while at the same time defining a clearer distinction between work and leisure pursuits than he had achieved hitherto. Of all the prominent pre-war modernists, Yorke was the most successful in exploiting these new opportunities and his innovative role in changing architectural practice was acknowledged as early as 1953, when he was asked to give a paper to a RIBA conference.[11] Having become a fellow of the RIBA in 1943 and founder partner of a successful practice a year later, Yorke's maturing as a professional is bound up with these changes. It is a reasonable hypothesis that a study of the first fifteen or so years of his career will help to throw them into relief.

Registration coloured another important development of the 1930s which contributed to an irreversible change in architectural practice: the influx of immigrants from continental Europe. Their presence posed some difficult questions for the new legislation, and indeed for a more general definition of a profession. In short, whether foreign qualifications were enough to satisfy the Architects Registration Council of the United Kingdom (ARCUK), the registrational bean-counters, and the weight a foreign reputation might carry became issues of debate. Perhaps most profound was the question whether a professional should understand the most modern ideas, whatever their national origin, or simply keep to narrow national norms.[12] Anyone who has laboured in the mire of the recent history of the architectural profession will know that these issues remain unresolved.

These questions highlighted another issue in the definition of the architectural profession: politics. As early as 1934 *The Architects' Journal* was uncommonly perceptive in identifying what later became an important question, throwing down the gauntlet to British Fascists to renounce the

RIGHT: FRS Yorke and his wife Thelma, née Austen Jones, on their wedding day, 13 August 1930. Thelma was a considerable beauty and modelled for several advertisements, including Craven A cigarettes.

BELOW: Havlicek & Honzik's Pensions Institute Building in Prague (1929–33), a large building by two architects who became friends of Yorke. At one time Honzik was to be co-author of *The Modern House*.

Nazis' views of modern architecture.[13] The status of architecture as a liberal profession came into focus several years later when refugees, almost all fleeing Nazism, started to request entry to Britain in appreciable numbers. It gained further credibility through the sterling work of the RIBA's Refugees Committee, and especially its secretary, the institute's librarian and *RIBA Journal* editor, EJ 'Bobby' Carter.

In the decade up to 1940 the architectural profession had changed more rapidly than at any time for perhaps as long as a century. Its skills became easier to define and measure, in theory at least, while a growing technocracy steered it away from the easy association with traditional societies and construction techniques – and national origins – that the Arts and Crafts movement implied. In numerous ways it became more politicised and on one level this process totally changed its relationship to its clients and users.[14] The roots of these developments did not lie entirely in the same place as those of modernist architecture, though its aesthetic became their outward symbol, especially after the influx of refugees brought direct knowledge of the forms, social aims and drawing techniques of modernism.[15]

This chapter explains how FRS Yorke was in the thick of these changes, and how the first part of his career gives some insight into his participation of them. In 1927 he was a callow twenty-year-old, suffering from adolescent *anxieties*, who wore plus fours on a cycling tour to look at traditional buildings with his father.[16] Less than two decades later he was senior partner of an ambitious and growing practice. *The Modern House* contained an early plea for rational use of land and building; if there was, as the *Economist* noted, a 'technological revolution', he was in its forefront. He cited his knowledge of building materials in his search for employment during the war.[17] His wartime work, on large factories for William Holford's firm and under secondment to Sir Alexander Gibb & Partners, a sizeable engineering consultancy, subjected him to the conditions of large organisations, which were carried forward into the post-war Yorke, Rosenberg & Mardall.[18] By 1953, his expertise in large architectural firms was sufficient to write a paper on their organisation for the *RIBA Journal*.[19] Yorke's career both symbolises, and was an active agent of, these general and widespread developments in the architectural profession.

In December 1930 Yorke reached his twenty-fourth birthday. It had been a momentous twelve months for him. Early in the year he left Birmingham School of Art. By high summer he was working in the office of Campbell-Jones, Son & Smithers in Dourgate Hill, EC. A mere thirteen days after his marriage to Thelma Austin Jones on 13 August 1930, he filled in his RIBA nomination form. Five days later, on 1 September, it was signed by his three sponsors – father FWB Yorke, employer Oliver Campbell-Jones and former teacher George Drysdale. Now he was a proper professional. His foreign tours distinguished him from his contemporaries, by placing him among British architects who felt it necessary to complete their intellectual formation on the continent.[20] A year later, still in what he later called his 'milk and buns period', Yorke took a small office in Wine Office Court, off Fleet Street, where he worked with his friend from Birmingham School of Art, Frederick Gibberd, who, legend has it, owned the office's sole sugar box.[21]

It was in 1931 that Yorke made his first visit to Prague, where he had his earliest encounter with modern architecture, beginning a series of continental trips that would make him the most knowledgeable British architect of his generation about developments on the European continent.[22] Previously his foreign trips, to places like Normandy and Belgium, seem to have had an emphasis on study of traditional architecture – not that there was much else to see. In the same year he made contact with the Architectural Press. That company's lore claims he was 'discovered' by an advertising manager, who took an avuncular interest in the young architect with a thirst for knowledge about building products.[23] Whatever the truth, by the end of 1931 he had published several articles in both *The Architectural Review* and the *The Architects' Journal*. In any case the combination of knowing about building materials, and international contacts, made him doubly valuable to the Architectual Press. The association was mutually beneficial. As we shall see, the income from the press was essential to Yorke throughout the 1930s. It was barely possible to scrape a living solely as a designer of modern buildings.[24]

Much more can be gleaned about Yorke's second visit to Prague in late 1932 than about his first the previous year.[25] A friendly letter to Yorke from the cartoonist and writer Adolf Hoffmeister offers the use of his Prague apartment to the young Englishman and his wife.[26] Clearly they were already acquainted and, judging by the tone of later correspondence, they developed a warm and enduring friendship. They could well have met on Yorke's previous visit and it is conceivable that some form of introduction was effected by P Morton Shand, a linguist and the Architectural Press's star critic in the early 1930s, who aided numerous international contacts between British architects and their continental counterparts.[27]

Most intriguingly, Hoffmeister's letter gives a clue to Yorke's most important professional contact in Prague at this period. This was the architect Karel Honzik, who collaborated with Yorke on the early stages of *The Modern House*. Hoffmeister advised that to gain access to his apartment: 'Will you kindly announce the day and time of your arrival to my friend Charles [sic] Honzik'. The tone of the letter suggests that Yorke and Honzik had not yet met. Furthermore, their relationship was facilitated by Hoffmeister, who was not himself an architect. In any case the relationship with Honzik blossomed. Honzik and his partner Josef Havlicek, who also became a friend, had recently completed the Pensions Institute, a large, Corbusian edifice, of which Yorke possessed numerous pictures. Eugene Rosenberg, whose arrival in England in 1939 would have such dramatic consequences for his and Yorke's subsequent careers, was working in their office at the time, although it seems that they did not meet on this occasion. Yorke later claimed he first met Rosenberg in 1938.[28]

Quite how Honzik and Yorke came to consider collaborating on *The Modern House* is not entirely clear. The most revealing letter between them, from Honzik to Yorke, is undated, and sets out Honzik's objections to the book as Yorke proposed it, showing that the letter was written at a fairly late date. Honzik's objections are essentially in opposition to the points which, I argue, can be traced to the exigencies of commercial publishing.[29] What can be concluded is far-reaching enough – that Yorke first saw modern architecture in Prague and considered working with a local architect to develop the book, suggesting that these continental jaunts, arranged with encouragement from the Architectural Press, were an important formative influence. Prague was certainly an important episode in Yorke's development into an expert on European modernism, and gave an extra boost to his value at the press, which the company then twisted to its own ends as it was moving from an eclectic mix to outright proselytising for modernist architecture.

Yorke's involvement with the Architectural Press went far beyond his relatively lowly official status as an assistant editor of *The Architects' Journal*. His house at 8, Old Church Street, Chelsea, seems to have been an outpost of the company's legendary headquarters, a short distance away at 9, Queen Anne's Gate, Westminster. Shortly after he leased the property Graham Hastings, son of the company's chairman Sir Percy, became a tenant, and in 1933 his place was taken by James Richards, who became editor of *The Architectural Review* in 1937 and remained in post until 1971.[30] At the time the Architectural Press showed uncanny prescience in giving breaks to young people who would later distinguish themselves in other fields, as well as supporting Yorke and Richards who would remain within the architectural fold. John Betjeman and Osbert Lancaster both had spells on *The Architectural Review*, and used their Oxford contacts to find new writers. Evelyn Waugh, Kenneth Clark, the novelist Bryan Guinness (later Lord Moyne) and most notably the travel writer Robert Byron all contributed to the journal during the 1930s, Byron landing the plum job of reviewing New Delhi on its opening in 1931.[31]

If the atmosphere at the company was convivial, something of this spilt over into its outpost in Old Church Street. Late in the evening of 9 November 1933, the ring of a telephone competed for attention with the noise of a party. Whoever answered it had a lapse of courtesy, with unfortunate consequences. At the other end of the line was Mrs Enid Holland who, as tenant of the ground floor, contributed a vital weekly £2 12s 6d in rent. The following day she wrote to Yorke to register 'a vehement protest at the uproar last night', and to her solicitors, who also sent an admonitory note.[32]

Yorke was within a month of his twenty-seventh birthday and might have had many reasons for throwing a rowdy party, but none of them explain why he let a flat to a distressed gentlewoman when the rent for the whole house was only £14 1s 8d per month. Despite his father's affluence, his wife's earnings as a model and his own status as a leading young architect, he found it hard to make ends meet. Landlords clamoured for their rent and tradesmen begged for their accounts to be settled, while one lady-shopkeeper, outraged by a long delay in settling her account, instructed her solicitors to effect an immediate recovery of the debt.[33] Yorke often found imaginative ways of living a lifestyle beyond his income. As a young man he had joined the Territorial Army, not out of political conviction or a wish to defend the realm, but because it enabled him to ride without the cost of keeping horses.[34] His residence in almost fashionable, decidedly Bohemian Chelsea, was made possible by a lucrative sublet – the rent on one floor paid nearly three-quarters of the rent he paid for the whole house – and by keeping tradesmen waiting. His habit of using colleagues from work to further subsidise his accommodation costs did not fade. A few years later his assistant Randall Evans, who became a partner in Yorke, Rosenberg & Mardall in 1958, asked for a pay rise which Yorke granted on the condition that he become a tenant in Yorke's house at 4 Tregunter Road, Kensington. Evans later remembered that the supposed benefit of his salary increase went straight back into Yorke's pocket! As David Allford writes, a vital factor in arranging premises for Yorke, Rosenberg & Mardall was ensuring that Yorke always had a flat 'over the shop'.[35]

It was not just in running his household that Yorke showed a creative attitude to money. It is evident also in the way in which he conducted his career. Here we have to take several factors into account. Yorke, in the early 1930s, was ambitious to be known as a 'modern architect', but few clients wanted 'modern architecture'. Those who did often faced almost insuperable difficulties in finding suitable sites.[36] The building contracts were hardly lucrative – the few that survive are for relatively small sums, and although they do not specify what percentage Yorke was paid as a fee it would have to have been enormous for it to represent a reasonable living. Apocryphally, too, Yorke claimed his practice left him 35 shillings a week out of pocket, a claim that his surviving accounts makes plausible.[37]

Yorke faced two choices in making up that deficit. Either he could take nonmodernist architectural commissions, or he could find nondesign work that satisfied his modernist cravings. In fact he did both. Here his father's connections, especially with the Flowers brewery in Stratford-upon-Avon, were very useful. Under FWB Yorke's name if necessary, Yorke undertook surveying work.[38] This drudgery eventually paid off. At the end of the decade two important projects emerged from this three-way relationship: the brewery cottages in Stratford and the remodelling of Shottery Manor for Fordham Flower.

Most important to Yorke in advancing this phase of his career, though, was his connection with the Architectural Press. It was both lucrative and indisputably modern. Some records survive of his earnings from the company at the end of the 1930s, when he edited the annual *Specification* and received royalties on his books, *The Modern House*, *The Modern House in England* and *The Modern Flat*. A letter from the Architectural Press to Yorke dated 16 April 1940 gives his income from the company in the tax year ending 5 April 1940. The total salary for editing *Specification* was £505 5s including a staff insurance premium of £20 1s 10d. On top of this he received another £50 4s in royalties, bringing his income from the Company to a healthy £555 9s, dwarfing his earnings from architecture at the same time.[39]

It is hard, though, to reconstruct fluctuations in his income over the whole decade. Even in the year covered, his salary as editor of *Specification* varied from month to month. For the first six months in the year ending April 1940 he was paid £44 19s 11d, for the next four it reduced to £40 8s 3d, the next month it dropped to £33 10s 9d while for the final month it collapsed to £19 19s 11d. This decline is likely to be attributable to World War II, which broke out a month before the first reduction, but it might also reflect the varying workload in producing an annual publication. Royalties for Yorke's books certainly tailed off early in the war. For the first six months of 1940 they totalled £19 18s 9d — only slightly less than the six-month average of £25 2s for the year ending April 1940. For the second six months they were less than £14.[40] During this period he would, too, have received some royalties on *A Key to Modern Architecture*, published by Blackie in 1939 and reprinted several times during the war.

By 1940 the books Yorke had published with the Architectural Press were past their first flush of sales. *The Modern House* was first published in 1934, and though the third, revised edition appeared in 1937 it must have reached sales maturity. In the six months covered by the royalties in 1934 it sold fifty-one copies at full price, with a further total of £29 18s 6d coming from copies sold on a discount of more than one-third. *The Modern House in England*, never so successful, it sold forty copies, while the more recent *The Modern Flat*, published in 1938, sold sixty-nine at full price and another single copy at a greater discount than 15 shillings. The royalty percentage was a generous 12.5 per cent on full price sales and 10 per cent on copies sold at substantial discounts. Immediately after publication, when *The Modern House* went quickly through several printings, the royalties must have made an appreciable contribution to Yorke's income.

Publishing books and articles about modern architecture, rather than practising it, brought Yorke three benefits. Economically it enabled him to survive; and it expanded his modernist credentials. It also facilitated his contacts with foreign practitioners. Many came through Morton Shand, and Yorke formed enduring friendships with Havlicek, Honzik and Alvar Aalto, probably closer than his relationship with Marcel Breuer.[41] Collaboration with Karel Honzik on *The Modern House*, ultimately failed because of their disagreement over the construction of a book on modernism, was the first;[42] later there were more successful ones in architectural practice with Marcel Breuer and Eugene Rosenberg. These contacts went far beyond simple professional and business relationships; they were the influences around which Yorke formed his appreciation of modern architecture.

The partnership with Breuer was formally established from Christmas 1935 by an agreement dated 20 November 1935.[43] It lasted for just over a year and a half before Breuer followed his master Walter Gropius's siren call to join him at Harvard.[44] Taking someone else into partnership is perhaps a surprising step for a young architect in FRS Yorke's position. It meant 'the income and expenses [were] to be shared in equal halves',[45] even though his income from architecture was hardly extensive. Yorke's practice and the demands of editing *Specification* were cited by *The Architects' Journal* as reasons why he gave up writing the weekly 'Trade Notes' column earlier in the year, but simple architectural assistance was not the prime motive for teaming up with Breuer. The agreement expressly states that 'For each work one of the partners shall be primarily responsible. He shall have the last word in questions concerning the particular work.'[46]

A far more plausible reason for the partnership was that Breuer was already a well-known international figure, and this association would benefit Yorke's reputation. There is certainly some evidence for this. In the RIBA Yorke Archive there are several requests for Breuer to lecture or write about modern architecture and design.[47] The invitations came from wide sources. From the emigré community came a request from Breuer's acquaintance Bruno Adler, a progressive educationalist and headmaster of the New Herrlingen School in Kent, to speak to the pupils. Leslie Martin invited him both to lecture to his students at Hull School of Architecture and to write an article about modern materials for *Circle*, the publication Martin edited with Ben Nicholson and the sculptor Naum Gabo; the Central School of Art and Design asked for 'a critical and comparative survey by a foreign designer' of English and continental furniture; and the Polytechnic (later called the Regent's Street Polytechnic) requested a lecture about the Concrete Garden City of the Future, probably the most significant project undertaken by the Yorke and Breuer partnership. Breuer's reluctance did not put off persistent would-be hosts — it took Martin nearly five months and repeated gentle chidings to cajole Breuer into writing for *Circle*, and almost a year to bring off the lecture.[48]

Breuer was clearly a reluctant public performer, and his frequent claims that 'my English is so bad' are just a little too shrill to suppress all suspicions that he found such engagements tiresome. But in demand he was, and from various communities: emigré, architectural and furniture design. By contrast, the earliest surviving similar invitations to Yorke date from the war years, some time after Breuer's departure for the United States.

Further evidence of Breuer's international reputation and its benefit to Yorke comes from correspondence with Lawrence Kocher, editor of the American journal the *Architectural Record*.

LEFT: Alvar Aalto's Paimio Sanatorium, completed in 1933, the year he and Yorke first met.

RIGHT: A short-lived partnership at the end of the 1930s between Yorke and Arthur Korn produced one building, a block of eight flats in Camberwell, south London. Korn had been a member of the avant-garde group The Ring in Berlin during the 1920s.

Yorke's name was already known to Kocher through *The Modern House*, but the partnership with Breuer evoked greater interest.[49] 'We would be very glad to represent Breuer or your partnership in the production of . . . furniture,' wrote Kocher, clearly a fan of Breuer's designs, to Yorke on 1 October 1936. Just over a month later in a letter to Breuer he suggested, 'We hope that you and Mr Yorke will send us any new work which you may have recently completed'.[50] At the end of the year Breuer's designs were included in a Museum of Modern Art catalogue. By association at least, Yorke had developed an international reputation: organisations as geographically dispersed as the Swedish magazine *Byggmastaren* and the Japanese Central Bureau for Foreign Cultures were aware of the Concrete Garden City of the Future.[51]

Breuer's departure, and the deteriorating international situation followed by the outbreak of war in 1939, prevented Yorke from capitalising on this cachet. The first clutch of partnerships between young British modernists and established foreign ones — Yorke and Breuer, Erich Mendelsohn and Serge Chermayeff, Maxwell Fry and Walter Gropius — enabled the foreigners to practise in Britain, and gave international credibility to the Britons. They were loose associations rather than tightly structured businesses and all ended before the close of the decade.

In the late 1930s the coincidence of the worsening conditions on the continent and the tightening of the rules on registration of architects, increased the obstacles to such arrangements.[52] The more recent arrivals were generally less eminent than their predecessors, while it became harder to convince the British authorities that they should be able to practise at all. This trend culminated in the wartime internment of several distinguished architects, who ironically had already suffered at the hands of the Nazis — Bruno Ahrends, Peter Moro and Eugene Rosenberg. Registration and questions of national identity probably contributed as much to the need for more rigid, formal partnerships after the war as did the new improved status that architects enjoyed under the Welfare State.

These difficulties did not deter Yorke from trying to form a new partnership with an *echt*-modern emigré after Breuer's departure. A short-lived arrangement with Arthur Korn resulted in one building, the apartment block at Cranston Court, Lettsom Street in Camberwell, south London, which became Yorke's London address for the early part of the war. Korn was an interesting choice. Born in 1891, he was half a generation older than Yorke and, of the German émigrés who stayed in Europe, he had the most direct experience of the heady days of the modernist crucible of Berlin in the early 1920s. He had been briefly in partnership with Erich Mendelsohn and a member of the radical modernist group, the Glass Chain. It was perhaps these credentials, and his interest in town planning, that attracted Yorke rather than a personal empathy. In any case the partnership did not last.[53]

Meanwhile, Eugene Rosenberg had escaped to England after the Nazi takeover of Czechoslovakia in 1939, foresaking his art collection and the small practice he had established in Prague. Yorke already knew him; they had first met in 1938.[54] When they decided to form a partnership is unclear, but they worked together on several projects including the Braithwaite House during the war, on either side of Rosenberg's internment between 1940 and 1942. Cyril Mardall, the third founder partner of Yorke, Rosenberg & Mardall, recalled that the first discussions were held in 1940, 'the year Hitler sent his tanks into France'. On being drafted into military intelligence at the start of the war, he asked Yorke, an acquaintance from the MARS Group, to look after his few small building projects. Yorke replied that he was intending to form a partnership with Rosenberg and suggested that the three of them have dinner in the Café Royal.[55]

No direct evidence to corroborate this version of the founding of YRM is available. Certainly the partnership was not formally established until 1944, and even then the accounts show that

Mardall did not become a partner until the following year. It is possible that some understanding predates that year, and nothing absolutely contradicts it. Circumstantially it is credible. Yorke was in an unsatisfactory partnership with Arthur Korn, his friend Rosenberg was in desperate need and Mardall had a few jobs where loose ends might have required attention. Furthermore, Yorke and Rosenberg were in contact for much of the war, while Mardall's absence makes it hard to see how he might have fitted into their developing relationship unless there was some prior agreement.

Even if the prehistory of the partnership of Yorke, Rosenberg & Mardall is not entirely clear, what is incontrovertible is that its formation marked a new point in the careers of the three partners. They drew on their experience of wartime organisations, the possibilities of huge architectural patronage offered by the state and their slightly varying commitments to modernism. Embedded in the new partnership were shards of their representative experience of architectural practice in the 1930s and early 1940s, hardened into a more effective and lucrative machine tuned to the conditions for architectural practice of the post-war period. What is also clear is that Yorke was both a driving force and a magnet. Rosenberg could hardly have initiated such an enterprise in a foreign country, and it was Mardall who approached Yorke because of his position, experience and reputation. Yorke was already in a strong position, but wartime conditions were to bring about new opportunities and circumstances that would augur and consolidate the future path of his career.

Exactly one month before World War II broke out FRS Yorke and his assistant Randall Evans let a new building contract. It was neither large nor glamorous — £120 10s for renovations to some almshouses in Hawkhurst, Kent — just one of those bread-and-butter jobs taken because 'staff must be kept productively employed for the whole of the year', as Yorke would write later in another context.[56] In concept it was very familiar to any small architectural practice, similar to the dreary surveying work Yorke had undertaken for his father, sometimes with Evans assistance.

One characteristic distinguished it from Yorke's surviving contracts of the mid-1930s: a clause setting out provisions to terminate the contract should war break out with any enemy powers specified in a separate appendix.[57] Germany, Japan and Italy were listed. Threat of war reached into the conditions of employment even for such a small job — which was complete before war was declared on 3 September 1939.

The storm clouds of war that had gathered in Czechoslovakia a year earlier, and in the Baltic republics and Poland at the declaration of the Ribbentrop–Molotov pact on 22 August 1939, now loomed over Yorke's personal life as well as his professional activities. In 1938 he bought the Mill Cottage at Wootton in Oxfordshire, a more secure haven than Tregunter Road for his family — twin daughters who were born shortly after he bought the cottage.[58] With his connections on the continent he had a heightened insight and emotional involvement with the deteriorating situation. Three days after the notorious treaty his old friend Adolf Hoffmeister wrote from Paris, in a tone which evokes all the sense of despair portrayed by Arthur Koestler in *The Scum of the Earth*. 'My dear and bloody Kay', he opened, 'As it usually is the case, in those days of bad humor and terrible mood, we write letters to good friends in bad english to say good bye and so long and I hope to see you on the front.'[59]

Yorke never reached the front. On 9 February 1940 he wrote to the War Office, mentioning that he had held 'commissioned rank from 1925–30', and informing them of his whereabouts for the first time since then. 'I would be prepared to take any appointment in which knowledge of building materials is required, and to go anywhere', he pleaded.[60] The reply was not promising, as no applications for officers submitted after November 1939 had been processed.[61] Architects found varied positions. Morton Shand hoped that 'Captain Maxwell Fry has been turfed out of the War House and made

An interior of one of the hostels for munitions workers at Swynnerton, which Yorke designed while working for William Holford, 1940–1. Despite the utilitarian construction (note the ceiling), Yorke managed to create a congenial environment for the young, single women who made up the bulk of the work force. It was also far larger than any single building he had completed before the war.

Courtesy of *The Architectural Review*.

to do some honest job of work on tank traps.' Valentine Harding died at Dunkirk. 'Rotten luck … one of the few really nice fellows in our unspeakable ex-racket,' lamented the unconscionable ex-critic.[62] The best Yorke could do was have his name placed on the central register of reserved employments so that he could be found suitable war work that would use his skills.

World War II offered perhaps more scope for architects to make a direct contribution to the war effort than any previous conflict. Even so, there was little coordinated deployment of architectural forces and no obvious or secure employment for architects where their skills could be deployed. Architecture was removed from the list of reserved professions – those whose members avoided the draft into the military – and at the same time 'all civil building work ceased', as Yorke wrote.[63] This meant architects were most likely to make themselves useful by joining private organisations that had already insinuated themselves into strong relationships with the government, something very few architectural firms had done.

One of the few that had was headed by Yorke's old friend William Holford, then a professor at Liverpool University; Yorke had worked with Holford, acting as a local executive architect, on a

house at Gidea Park in Essex in 1933.[64] In 1937 Holford had worked with the giant engineering consultancy Sir Alexander Gibb & Partners on the Team Valley Trading Estate outside Gateshead, a publicly subsidised Keynesian attempt to bring jobs to areas of high unemployment. Such relationships may have been unusual for architects at the time, but they were precisely the sort of opportunity Gibb's had been founded to exploit. Having been an engineer to the Admiralty during World War I, Gibb himself recognised that there would be a need for specialist consultants to tackle vast government-backed jobs throughout the British dominions, which he could obtain through his connections and understanding of the Civil Service. One of the largest commissions his firm undertook in its early years was a bay barrage at Kuala Lumpur. Not surprisingly, the association between Holford and Gibb's was renewed early in the war and, even as Holford's firm swelled to 200 people with the volume of wartime work, it was seconded to its larger associate. It was here that Yorke found his first wartime métier. In March 1940 he became an employee of Sir Alexander Gibb & Partners, agents to the Ministry of Supply, to work with William Holford on Factory No 7 at Kirkby, near Liverpool, for a salary of £540 per annum.[65] Through a personal contact, Yorke finally encountered corporate life.

Given the pattern of Yorke's practice up to then it is hard to avoid the conclusion that his time at Gibb's was 'dread inspiring', as one acquaintance suggested.[66] It was another crucial element in his transition from pre-war to post-war model. Here, for the first time, Yorke experienced the benefits and restrictions that a large organisation could bring. The benefits were obvious, and especially attractive to someone who had not been able to make ends meet in his chosen activity of designing modernist buildings. The buildings Yorke now constructed were far larger than anything he had been able to do on his own account, and the backing of government may have seemed a necessarily corollary to these achievements.

Viewed in all other lights, it was a position that held few attractions for Yorke. It meant submitting to an employer's discipline, which would severely curtail his scope for 'prowling round in the dark hours of the night'.[67] He had to leave Cranston Court, the building he designed with Arthur Korn, where he enjoyed the presence of his assistant Maryel Lloyd. He had few friends in the north of England. Even Patrick Blackett, a professor of physics at Manchester University, wrote 'How sad, when you go north we come south'.[68] Blackett, whose accolades in later life included a peerage, a Nobel Prize and appointment to the Order of Merit, had taken a job at the Royal Aircraft Research Establishment in Farnborough in Hampshire. He would be closely involved with the early British attempts to develop an atomic bomb, though his political sympathies were decidedly Fabian. Yorke's equanimity during this period was further disturbed by boring letters from Arthur Cobb of the Architectural Science Group, and by vacuous telegrams from Ralph Tubbs wanting the MARS town planning drawings and his subscription to the MARS Group.[69] To the former he replied curtly that Korn had the drawings and to the latter, contemptuously, that it should be set against his loan to the group.

Several letters early in 1941 indicate an intention to change jobs, and a few suggest that he was not entirely happy in his work in Liverpool. On the 7 January William Holford wrote a flattering reference for Yorke to TP Bennett, the brick controller at the Ministry of Works and Buildings.[70] The path to a new job in London was rugged. Twice later in the month Holford wrote to Yorke that he had heard nothing, although CD Spragg, the RIBA assistant secretary, thought Yorke was engaged with Bennett as early as the 2 January.[71] Holford's offer to help Yorke find a job indicates something of Yorke's eagerness to leave Liverpool.

The situation was further complicated because Holford wanted Yorke to stay in Liverpool. 'I said [in the reference for Bennett] you could only be spared Walsall for a more responsible job,' he wrote to Yorke on 23 January. He also offered to 'fix up something interesting and ask for an increased salary'.[72] A month later the situation was still unresolved. On the 26 February Yorke wrote to Michael Regan at the Architectural Press that he was 'still at Liverpool, but expect to move in about two weeks time, probably to the midlands' – possibly Holford's 'Walsall'.[73]

Yorke's plight seems to have been well known. Donald Gibson, the youthful chief architect for Coventry, wrote to him on the 2 April 1941 that Geoffrey Jellicoe had mentioned he was 'at a loose end'.[74] Coventry was almost totally destroyed in a Luftwaffe bombing raid on 14 November 1940. Gibson wondered whether Yorke would be interested in 'local government service . . . We hope to form a department which will show the way in which local authorities could produce good work'. The drawback was salary – £300 per annum, plus another £20 in cost of living allowance. It was hardly likely to tempt Yorke, who was earning £540 with the possibility of more. His handwritten draft reply on Gibson's letter says 'We are finding it difficult to get draughtsmen at less than £350', but he was keen to take up Gibson's offer to meet, to see, in Gibson's words, 'whether your views on planning and design would conform with mine'. Had Yorke chosen to apply the ideas of modernism he had advocated in the 1930s, somewhere within the growing appreciation of vast post-war reconstruction would lie opportunities that could not have been envisaged before.[75] Rather than enter direct public employment, the possibility of working on public projects as a private consultant was exemplified in his ultimate employer, Alexander Gibb and Partners.

Underneath the confused surface lay an irony. The rarefied conditions of wartime centralisation demanded the use of industrial production in building. Yorke had advocated such techniques in the early 1930s, but made very little headway. Only a massive change in the commissioning and operation of buildings, and not one which Yorke would have chosen, achieved this end. When achieved, it lost at least part of its attraction. 'My feelings about the use of big machinery are very mixed,' Yorke wrote to his friend J Homery Folks. 'My first experience was in 1940 when we tore up 800 acres of magnificent landscape. Perhaps we shall use them more sensibly in peacetime, but I doubt it.'[76] In this letter Yorke gave voice to an appreciation for countryside fruits and pursuits that had been germinating for several years – to the surprise of at least one friend.

For his Christmas card in 1940, Yorke sketched a simple line drawing of Bridge House at Wootton, the country cottage he had purchased in 1938. Three ducks swim contentedly in the millstream, watched over by a angrily protective goose. They are observed from the safety of the windows in the house by hordes of pigs, and from the two windows on the second floor, FRS and Thelma Yorke themselves. This card, rather less lavish than some of his photographic prints of foreign places he had used in earlier years, caught the eye of at least one recipient. Bertram Carter asked on 6 January 1941: 'Do the little pigs in your Christmas card signify: A) that you are farming? B) that you have evacuees with you?'.[77] Yorke had indeed started farming and to Bertram Carter, at least, it did not seem a logical step.

Farming had some social advantages. Miss VE Webb of the Architectural Press and Yorke's assistant on *Specification*, shared detailed correspondence with him in the early part of 1941. Producing the annual in wartime was hard, not least because the first print run was destroyed at the printers by a bomb, and the letters are full of reports of delays, followed by almost impossible requests to complete painstaking tasks quickly. Such adversity bred some camaraderie, and when Yorke requested three weeks for checking the proofs Miss Webb admitted that she should be nice to him. 'When those two pigs of yours are properly fattened up I must talk to you nicely,' she wrote.[78] Yorke's position as a source of unrationed meat facilitated his professional tasks and perhaps brought other pleasures too.

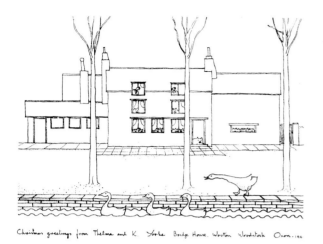

Christmas greetings from Thelma and K. Yorke Bridge House. Wootton Woodstock Oxon. 194

LEFT: Yorke's Christmas card for 1940 prompted one friend to ask whether the pigs in the lower windows signified that he had evacuees living with him, or if he had taken up farming. The latter was closer to his sentiments.

British Architectural Library, RIBA, London.

BELOW: Bridge House, a former mill in Wootton, Oxfordshire, which became Yorke's principal home in the late 1930s. The photograph dates from after his modifications in the early 1950s, and confirms his interest in working modernist details, such as the thin, metal-framed windows in the otherwise traditional fabric, which he had introduced at Forge Cottage and Shottery Manor in the late 1930s.

The earliest mention of agriculture in Yorke's surviving correspondence is in Morton Shand's letter dated 1 October 1940. He asked, 'Is Thelma still carrying on gamely at Wootton, pig-rearing and getting the very last out of the soil in the way of foodstuffs?'[79] Shand was an enthusiastic gardener – the same letter sang the praises of soft fruit and jam. A year earlier he had given Yorke numerous plants from his Ladbroke Grove garden for transfer to Wootton, as well as extensive instructions on how to keep them.[80] Shand, it would seem, introduced Yorke to a nascent interest in farming and food, rather as he had helped to introduce him to modern architecture. Just as Shand, at this time, was beginning to regret his championing of modernism, so Yorke was revising and expanding his enthusiasms. Yorke, trapped in Liverpool on £540 per annum with only Saturday afternoon and every other Sunday off, might otherwise have been enjoying 'un rêve virgilien', as Le Corbusier described the Arcadian life. At least retreat to the countryside offered an escape from corporate existence, and possibly the safety valve that made bearable the increased focus and concentration of running a large practice over his pre-war pattern of working.

Yorke initially addressed his waxing interest in farming in much the same way as he had approached his fascination for modern architecture a decade earlier. He proposed to write a book about it. On 26 February 1941 he mentioned to the RIBA librarian EJ 'Bobby' Carter: 'I had an idea that, in view of the poor state of farm buildings at present in this country, and the fact that some thing must be done about agriculture, it would be a good thing to assemble all the information . . . It would interest me very much to do the work, and I am beginning to need something of the sort'.[81] Carter helped Yorke prepare a bibliography, and the book progressed some way before dying at the stake of Architectural Press business sense. A few days earlier, on 21 February 1941, Yorke had mentioned the book in a letter to 'AED' of the Architectural Press's books department, only to receive a reply, dated 25 February: 'I doubt whether the book would catch . . . '[82]

The book on farm buildings may not have caught, but Yorke's interest in agriculture stuck fast. When his first response to a new enthusiasm drew a blank, he found another outlet for it. He bought a farm and, after the war, became a successful cattle breeder.[83] This outlet has two notable characteristics: firstly, it was made possible by increased affluence; and secondly, it was an activity almost totally removed from architecture. One obituarist, Richard Sheppard, noted the increasing variety in Yorke's life: 'He was also a farmer, fisherman, traveller and sportsman.'[84] Apocryphally, too, Yorke spent less time in the office of Yorke, Rosenberg & Mardall during the 1950s and made long trips such as a journey to Czechoslovakia, Russia and China in 1958.[85] As Yorke's architectural activities became more profitable, architecture became less all-absorbing.[86]

He never lost contact with architecture altogether. Sheppard went on to note that, 'Despite all these extramural activities he was first and always an architect'. In the 1930s architecture was at the centre of most of Yorke's work, whether writing about it, surveying it or designing it. By the 1950s the successful partnership he had co-founded was able to absorb much of the drudgery, leaving Yorke to pursue other interests. In the 1930s he had been keen to stress the essential compatibility between modernist buildings wherever they were in the world. After the war the sheer volume of work for which modernism was acceptable, even desirable, in Britain, inevitably played down the international implications as Yorke and his contemporaries gave modernism a specifically national character.[87] These major changes in his conduct of his practice were underwritten by a widespread change in the nature of architectural practice itself.

Yorke's comments on management of large practices are especially important in the light of his wartime experiences that changed his perception of architecture as a business. 'While there have been very great changes . . . in architectural design and technique', he noted, 'there seems to have been little change in the machinery for the control and administration of the private

OPPOSITE TOP: Middlefield Farm near Witney in Oxfordshire, which Yorke bought in the 1950s as his earnings from Yorke, Rosenberg & Mardall began to multiply.

OPPOSITE BOTTOM: Yorke listed breeding Guernsey cattle as one of his hobbies in his *Who's Who* entry. Rearing animals on his farm provided an outlet which architecture could not.

architect's office.'[88] He identified three main reasons for the need for change: the increased difficulty in starting up a practice; continuity of a small firm; and the near impossibility for an architect 'to save sufficient money to allow him to retire from his practice at a reasonable age and hand it on to a younger and more energetic man'. In short, Yorke was grappling with the problem of how to make an architect's office profitable for its principals and efficient for its clients – how to fit practice to the demands and opportunities of the time.

Much of 'The Private Architect's Problem', the paper where Yorke made these points, is devoted to the implications for office organisation of designing large schools, 'costing around £200,000' at 1953 prices – the sort of project that became far more common after the war than before and enabled the growth of many large architectural practices including Yorke, Rosenberg & Mardall. Essentially, Yorke saw the problem to be matching resources to time scale and income. Projects of this size have peaks and troughs in demand and fee income, although 'the staff must be kept productively employed for the whole of the year'. Although Yorke himself would not have recognised the term, in a clear perception of asset specificity he realised: 'If one is to maintain a high standard of work there can be no question of taking on people for a particular job and dismissing them when the rush is over.' Ensuring a steady inflow of work was vital for stability.

Yorke suggested that a company rather than partnership structure would help to overcome the difficulties. He listed five main advantages: 'the company structure, being less dependent on personalities, is more likely to achieve continuity'; it might also be financially stronger, 'to carry the firm over slack periods, and so to achieve continuity'; security for clients would benefit from financial strength; administrative specialists could undertake administration, leaving the architect 'to devote himself to architecture and better building'; and finally, the 'possibility of retirement through ... a pension scheme'. Yorke was well aware that RIBA rules forbade architectural firms from being companies. He considered these rules outmoded because they failed to take account of both the needs and the opportunities offered by the changing pattern of post-war practice.

He identified and expressed some of the most pressing problems faced by architectural practice because of changing circumstances, and proposed a way of dealing with them. Nothing could better illustrate how his career and the evolution of architectural practice were interwined. No longer, for him, the vagaries of loose partnerships, uncertain workloads and the need to find other ways of making an income. Rather, he sought the continuity and security of a major professional firm where he could pursue extramural interests free of hassle from unpaid tradespeople, and, unusually, he was prepared to consider how it might best outlast its initial partners.

Between 1940 and 1950 Yorke managed to negotiate a profound change in the nature of his practice, and one which typified more general changes across the architectural profession. He also managed to come to terms with his own evolving interests and circumstances, recognising early that the simple modernist formulae he had advocated in the 1930s were no more suitable than the pattern of practice which he had adopted at the time. In some senses, as his architectural practice grew more intense, he used its profits to develop completely different interests. He saw that private consultants could effectively deliver large-scale building programmes, during the war and, by extension, after it too, perhaps more efficiently than public employees. The idea of a large-scale corporate architectural practices did not exist in Britain before 1945. To fill this gap Yorke took a model that had its origins in Alexander Gibb's vision of a private engineering practice delivering state policy. As wartime demonstrated the efficacy of this vision for construction in general, Yorke began to adapt it to his conception of modern architecture, showing how a large private firm could be compatible with a modernist architecture geared towards social ends and the prosperity of its proprietors.

Yorke gave his paper on 'The Private Architect's Problem' at the RIBA conference of 1953, the same time as Yorke, Rosenberg & Mardall were designing a large school in Tulse Hill, south London.

Photo: G Hana.

Notes

1. Nikolaus Pevsner, *Pioneers of Modern the Modern Movement*, Faber (London), 1936

2. FRS Yorke, *The Modern House in England*, Architectural Press (London), 1937. The book opens with a long quotation from Lethaby.

3. Each of the three knights completed major projects in the 1920s or 1930s, such as the Bank of England (Baker), New Delhi (Lutyens and Baker) and remodelling the south end of Regent's Street, London (Blomfield). For an indication of Blomfield's views of modernism, see his *Modernismus*, Macmillan (London) 1934, and his debate with the young MARS Group star Amyas Connell, broadcast by the BBC and published in the *Builder* (30 November 1934), p 930. Blomfield was an outspoken critic of modernism.

4. An indication of the stasis in architectural practice over this period can be found in 'Architectural Practice', a paper read to the Guildford District Chapter of the South-Eastern Society of Architects by Sydney Tatchell FRIBA on 9 January 1935. He found it necessary to give advice such as 'Correspondence should be carefully kept . . . A filing system should be used . . . A drawing register should be kept', implying that such attributes of sound practice management were not common, even in the mid-1930s. Although Tatchell claims practice had changed since the beginning of his career '30 or 40 years ago', the differences he cites are largely to do with technology – typewriters, telephones and photography – and not with the organisation of architectural firms. The paper was published in the *RIBA Journal*, vol XLII (September 1935) pp 1103–5.

5. TG Jackson and Norman Shaw (eds), *Architecture: Profession or Art*, Murray (London), 1892. It contained several essays, often by well-known architects, in favour of architecture as art. Their views were in opposition to those of J MacVicar Anderson, president of the RIBA, who favoured the idea of architecture as a profession.

6. See Yorke's diary of a cycling tour to Normandy, 15–28 October 1927. RIBA YoF/1/ 8.

7. Several examples survive in the RIBA Drawings Collection, see for example PA 237.

8. While there is no evidence that FWB Yorke paid his son an allowance, he certainly offered him opportunities. They worked together on a competition-winning design for civic offices in Romsey, Hampshire, in 1934 (see *The Architects' Journal*, vol 80 6 December 1934, p 848 for an illustration of this project) and on various projects for Flowers brewery throughout the decade. It is also possible that FWB introduced FRS to the Architectural Press, as his work was occasionally published in its magazines.

9. See Chapter 6, especially on the subject of Yorke's accommodation combined with the office.

10. This phenomenon is so well known that it almost requires no explanation. One objective noting of it can be found in 'The Architect's Dilemma', *Economist* (25 July 1953): 'The social changes which have taken place since 1939 have overset the traditional order of things for the architectural as well as for the medical profession; moreover, architects are struggling to come to terms with the technological revolution that is slowly overtaking building.' Prescient words, as will be seen in relation to the career of FRS Yorke. This was reprinted in the *RIBA Journal*, April 1954, vol 61, pp 226–7. Yorke's quote comes from 'Glass Buildings of the Future', a paper preserved in the RIBA YoF/1/12.

11. FRS Yorke, 'The Private Architect's Problem', *RIBA Journal* (June 1953), vol 60, pp 325–7. Yorke started by going through the organisational problems arising from a large school commission, the sort of job that became far more common after the Education Act of 1944, and which comprised a significant part of the early oeuvre of Yorke, Rosenberg & Mardall. See *The Architecture of Yorke, Rosenberg, Mardall 1944–1972*, Lund Humphries (London), 1972. That Yorke chose a publicly funded commission to illustrate his theme suggests that the problems of large practices were tied up with the management of public work. He continued by discussing the problems of practice in general, ending with the prescient suggestion that architectural firms might be better off as companies rather than partnerships, a move that was then against the RIBA's Code of Conduct. See Raglan Squire, *Portrait of an Architect*, Smythe (Gerrards Cross, 1984, pp 179–80 for a cheerful though not verifiably accurate account of the conference.

12. Pembroke Wicks, registrar of the Architects Registration Council of the United Kingdom, wrote to Sir Ian MacAlister, secretary of the RIBA, on 17 July 1939, expressing concern about 'passages [in the RIBA Refugees Committee Report] calculated to lead foreign refugees to believe that if they are admitted to this country they will be able to practise as architects'. But, 'in consequence of the Architects Registration Act, 1938, such persons will only be entitled to carry on business under the style of title of Architect until August 1940.' The letter is among the papers of the RIBA Refugees Committee, and the report mentioned was published in *RIBA Journal* vol 46 (June 1939), pp 830–1. Wicks had cut his teeth in public life as secretary to Sir Edward Carson, the Ulster Unionist politician and prosecuting counsel at Oscar Wilde's trial.

13. See the editorial 'A Question to Sir Oswald Mosley', *The Architects' Journal* vol 79 (22 February 1934) p269 and the answers, in the *The Architects' Journal* vol 79 (19 April 1934), p 566. Mosley was the leader of the British Union of Fascists.

14. See Chapter 3, and Adrian Forty, *Words and Buildings*, Thames and Hudson (London), 2000, pp 312–17 for an analysis of how the meaning of the word 'user' has evolved.

15. Drawing technique was one of the most significant innovations the emigrés brought. Most British drawings of the time, certainly when done for presentation, were watercolour washes on cartridge paper. Yorke himself gained a proficiency in this technique as shown by his surviving student work and a few later drawings in the RIBA Drawings Collection. In the Allford Yorke Archive Folder are several drawings submitted for *The Modern House*. These, in particular ones from Czechoslovakia, are precise, ink-drawn and extremely accurate, totally different in character to those from Britain.

16. See Yorke's diary of a cycling tour to Normandy, 15–28 October 1927. RIBA YoF/1/8. At one point he mentions that his plus fours were dry after being soaked in a storm.

17. See, for example, Yorke's letter to the War Office dated 9 February 1940, claiming 'a somewhat unusually wide knowledge of building materials'. RIBA YoF/1/12. In this letter he proposed that his skills might be serviceable to the war effort, and the reply suggested looking for a civilian position, tacitly acknowledging that the new status architects enjoyed as a registered profession put them on something like a par with the military.

18. Yorke had, for example, to sign the Official Secrets Act and to succumb to the long hours and disciplinary rigours of wartime employment. Given his behavioural patterns of the 1930s, this probably did not come naturally. See letters of 12 and 13 March 1940, from Sir Alexander Gibb & Partners to Yorke, and 'General Circular 5' on working hours – 9am – 6.15pm on weekdays, 9am – 12.30pm Saturdays and two Sundays a month. RIBA YoF/1/2.

19. Yorke, The Private Architect's Problem', op cit.

20. Yorke's nomination papers, dated 26 August 1930 for an associateship and 14 November 1942 for a fellowship, both held at the RIBA.

21. Culled from office lore, as cited by Alan Powers, *In the Line of Development*, RIBA Heinz Gallery (London), 1992, p 12 and 'Astragal' in *The Architects' Journal* vol 135 (20 June 1962) p1364.

22. Yorke claims this date in a paper, as far as I can tell unpublished, but sharing something with the introduction to *The Modern House in England*, and which can be dated to 1937. RIBA YoF/1/12.

23. By the arcane and not always reliable standards of that company's mythology, this is fairly credible. Advertising managers love to find writers who are interested in what their customers advertise.

24. This point is starkly made in Yorke's accounts, which survive almost unbroken in a stash of material turned over to the RIBA by YRM (as Yorke, Rosenberg & Mardall had become known) in 1997. These show that Yorke's annual drawings from his architectural practice in the 1930s never exceeded £230 and were frequently between £150 and £200, a fraction of his earnings as a writer, dropping, for instance, from £228 4s 5d in 1936 to £161 3s 0d in 1937. Of course, after 1945, and especially from the mid-1950s, it was a different story.

25. See a paper in the RIBA YoF/1/12.

26. Letter dated 30 November 1932 in the RIBA YoF/1/12.

27. Shand was an old Etonian and graduated in French and German from

King's College, Cambridge. Socially and often intellectually he was in a different class to most British architects of the period. He first wrote about architecture at the request of his friend Christian Barman, then editor of *the Architectural Review*, in 1928 when he was living in France. As well as acting as a roving critic he translated several important texts, including Walter Gropius's *The New Architecture and the Bauhaus*. He helped immigrants with English and was the first secretary of the MARS Group, the British arm of CIAM, where his linguistic skills were needed to bring the Giedion/ Le Corbusier line to their rapt English disciples.

28. Yorke claimed this on Rosenberg's nomination paper to become a fellow of the RIBA, dated 28 August 1950. He was one of his sponsors. The paper is held at the RIBA.

29. The letter, in the RIBA YoF/1/12, is undated, but must have been written shortly before a letter dated 23 April 1934 which just preceded publication of *The Modern House* in the summer of 1934. See notes 42 and 43.

30. Yorke took a lease on 8 Church Street from 1 July 1931 from Fraser & Ellis, 'General Ironfounders', whose address was 10 Church Street. He continued to lease the house until the end of January 1936, after he had moved to 4 Tregunter Road, Kensington, in January 1935. Correspondence which establishes these dates and figures with Fraser & Ellis, various tenants at Church Street and Walter Cave, surveyor to the Gunter Estate who were landlords at Tregunter Road, can be found in the RIBA YoF/2 /1. Correspondence between Yorke and Sir Percy Hastings in the same folder suggests that Hastings *fils* was not an ideal tenant – Yorke had to ask his father to make up a shortfall in rent.
Sir James Richards, in conversation with Jeremy Melvin on 28 November 1991, recalled living in the house, and mentioned it in his autobiography, *Memoirs of an Unjust Fella*, Weidenfeld and Nicholson (London), 1980. Pages 91–2 give some reminiscence of the house. With access to only one outside lavatory, it was spartan.

31. Bevis Hillier, *Young Betjeman*, John Murray (London), 1988, pp 271–2. Hillier mentions numerous writers who contributed to *The Architectural Review* during and after Betjeman's time on the journal between 1930 and 1933.

32. See letters to Yorke in the RIBA YoF/2/1, from Mrs Enid Holland dated 10 November 1933, and from Speechly, Mumford & Craig dated 11 November 1933.

33. In November 1934 Yorke wrote to the landlords of 8 Church Street, asking them to reduce the rent. They did so, but only to £13 per month which was a smaller reduction than he requested. See letter from Yorke to Fraser & Ellis dated 9 November 1934 in the RIBA YoF/2/1. Further evidence of Yorke's penury, or meanness, can be seen in a letter to Mrs Yorke from CL Hacking Ltd, 'builders, decorators, sanitary and electrical engineers', dated 27 November 1934, asking for payment of £1 14s 6d, outstanding since December 1933. RIBA YoF/2/1.
The same folder has considerable correspondence from Sewell, Edwards & Nevill, solicitors to Miss Clements, requesting payment of a small bill for furnishings. Yorke seems to have stalled, offering to return the goods or to pay by instalments, but the implacable Miss Clements did not yield. This correspondence dates from October and November 1931. It is not clear whether this Miss Clements is the same as AA Clements, who was a tenant at Church Street in 1930. A letter from AA Clements dated 18 November 1930, about arrangements for paying rent, survives in the same folder.
Further intimations of Yorke's parsimony come in a letter from Adolf Hoffmeister, dated 25 May 1939: 'I take the liberty to mention – humbly, modestly and politely, that it is usual to stamp letters from England [to Paris] with a 2$\frac{1}{2}$ pence stamp at least.' YoF/1/12

35. Yorke 'held commissioned rank from 1925–30 in the 48th SM divisional Train' and his transfer to the Territorial Army was gazetted in June 1930. See letters, from Yorke to the War Office dated 9 February 1940, and from E Langridge to Yorke dated 30 June 1930, in the RIBA YoF/1/12 and YoF/2/1 respectively.
It was an adjutant's habit of calling Yorke 'Yor-kay' that, picked up by Thelma, gave Yorke the soubriquet 'K' by which many of his friends knew him.

35. See Chapter 6.

36. Typical of clients at this period was Mrs Marjorie Palin, who wanted a house of the 'small, white modern type' for between £1,200 and £1,300. Correspondence in the RIBA Yorke Archive shows what difficulty the

Palins had in finding a site, before eventually locating one in Iver, Buckinghamshire. See letters in the RIBA YoF/1/6. Less typical was Mrs Christabel Burton, who is described in more detail in Chapter 3.
The largest sum in any of the surviving contracts is for £2,800 for the London Theatre Studio in Islington, north London. See the contract dated 20 July 1936 in the RIBA YoF/1/5. Contrast these sums with the $250,000 Breuer had to play with in 1940 for a house, in Pittsburgh, for a partner in the Kaufmann department store business, whose president, Edgar J Kaufmann, paid a mere $145,000 for Frank Lloyd Wright's *Fallingwater*, though that was a weekend house. See a letter from Marcel Breuer to Yorke dated 9 February 1940 in the RIBA YoF/1/12, and Edgar J Kaufmann Jnr, *Fallingwater*, Architectural Press (London), 1986, p 45.

37. See Astragal, *The Architects' Journal* vol 135 (20 June 1962), p1364 and accounts fn 24.

38. The RIBA Drawings Collection holds survey drawings of the Crown Hotel at Shipton-under-Wychwood, dated March and April 1931 when Yorke had his office at Wine Office Court, off Fleet Street, London EC4. Evidence of collaboration lies in the signature, FWB Yorke overwritten as FRS Yorke. PA 237/5

39. This letter is preserved in the RIBA YoF/1/12; Yorke's accounts, discovered by Jeremy Melvin among 31 boxes of randomly collated material which entered the RIBA's collection in 1997, had not been given a full reference at the time of writing.

40. See a statement of royalties from the Architectural Press, dated July 1940, in the RIBA YoF/1/12.

41. A letter from Aalto thanking Yorke for his hospitality in London survives in the archives of the Aalto Foundation in Helsinki, Finland, but would seem to be written after their first meeting. This was through Morton Shand, who had met Aalto in 1933 at the famous CIAM conference which produced the Charter of Athens, and arranged an exhibition at Fortnum and Mason in London, November of that year. Numerous letters followed, including, most poignantly, a telegram sent after Yorke's death, sending 'our deepest sympathy . . . [for] a sweet and good friend and a great architect'. It is dated 22 June 1962 Ref Yorke62.

42. Honzik's undated letter (see note 29 above) admitted that he had not really appreciated that the point of *The Modern House* was to examine modern houses, rather than modernism in general. Consequently he can hardly have accepted Yorke's premise that the villa, while not the end of modern architecture, was an essential laboratory to its progress. See FRS Yorke, *The Modern House*, Architectural Press (London), 1934, p 1.
In a letter discussing how he should be credited in *The Modern House*, Honzik mentions, 'I wouldn't like to give reasons for any complications or troubles'. Although he and Yorke remained on amicable terms, clearly the collaboration had not worked out as planned. The letter is dated 23 April 1934 and is held in the RIBA YoF/1/12.

43. A signed copy of the agreement survives in the RIBA YoF/1/10. It is pretty sparse, though its notable points are that partners would work separately on projects and that split any architectural fees would be split equally after expenses, but significantly Yorke's income from writing and journalism and Breuer's from furniture design are excluded from the split. The signed agreement stipulates that the order of names in the partnership would vary according to which partner had been responsible for the design of the project in question.

44. The painter Ben Nicholson wrote to Breuer on 15 July 1937, as Breuer was leaving for a trip to the US: 'I expect you will stay there . . . I am sorry if you leave us so soon.' RIBA YoF/2/2.

45. Partnership agreement, op cit.

46. Ibid.

47. See RIBA YoF/2/2, 'Breuer's Personal File'.

48. Persuading Breuer to give a lecture required considerable persistence. Adler first wrote to him on 18 November 1936, and eventually got a positive reply on 4 February 1937. George Checkley of the Polytechnic school of architecture in Regents Street, London, had an easier ride, writing on 31 July 1936 and receiving an acceptance on 4 August 1936, perhaps speeded up because of the involvement of the client, the Cement and Concrete Association. Correspondence with Phillip Gooding of the Cement and Concrete Association during November 1936, though, suggests that Shand, who had been commissioned to translate Breuer's paper from German, was kept on tenterhooks for the manuscript. This is

dwarfed by the response to an invitation from Leslie Martin, first issued on 21 November 1936 and not accepted until 26 May 1937. Breuer also took from 22 July 1936 until early January 1937 to finish an article for *Circle*, the publication Martin edited with Ben Nicholson and the sculptor Naum Gabo. By December Martin's apprehension was becoming tangible in numerous letters. HG Murphy, principal of the Central School of Art and Design, had less difficulty, issuing an invitation on 12 November 1936 and getting a refusal the following day. All these letters are in the RIBA YoF/2/2.

49. In a letter to Yorke dated 28 February 1941, Michael Regan of the Architectural Press mentioned that *Architectural Record* was the only effective American publisher of modern architecture, but that even they had not done much with Architectural Press books, except for *The Modern House*. The letter is a reply to Yorke who had set out Breuer's proposal for a book. Regan wrote that an American publisher would have to take 500 to 1,000 copies for it to be worth considering. It has not been possible to locate Breuer's proposal. RIBA YoF/1/12.

50. See letters dated 1 October and 6 November 1941. RIBA YoF/1/12.

51. Letters from both organisations survive, from S Koike of Kaigai Bunka Tyuo Kyoku (Central Bureau for Foreign Cultures) to Breuer, dated 10 July 1936, and from Sune Lindstrom of *Byggmasteren* to Yorke, dated 21 September 1937. RIBA YoF/1/12.

52. There were relatively few architect refugees in Britain. A letter dated 23 February 1939 in the RIBA Refugees Committee papers from MG Russell of the Home Office identifies 24, less than one per cent of the profession, which then numbered about 12,000. The report submitted to the RIBA Council later in the year stated that up to 18 per cent of the architectural profession in Sweden was made up of refugees.

53. Rumour has it that Yorke was angry when Korn arranged for headed stationery to be printed, implying that he did not see the partnership as a long-term arrangement. At this stage Yorke was either still looking for a network of loose partnerships or, if he had already realised the advantages of a stable partnership, did not think Korn a suitable candidate.

54. Although Rosenberg worked in Havlicek and Honzik's office in Prague in the early 1930s, it seems Yorke did not meet him until 1938, the date he gives on Rosenberg's RIBA fellowship application, dated 28 August 1950 and preserved at the RIBA.

55. Cyril Mardall suggested this in a conversation with Jeremy Melvin in November 1991.

56. The contract, dated 3 August 1939, is preserved in the RIBA YoF/1/2. The other context is Yorke's 1953 paper on the organisation of architects' offices, Yorke, 'The Private Architect's Problem', op cit.

57. Several other contracts surviving from the late 1930s include similar provisions, although earlier ones do not. A sample can be found in the RIBA YoF/1/2/4/5/7.

58. An insurance policy for Wootton with the Eagle Star, dated 14 July 1938, is preserved in the RIBA YoF/2/1.

59. This extraordinary letter is preserved in the RIBA YoF/1/12. Hoffmeister was unsure about going to the PEN Club conference in Sweden scheduled for 1 September, the day the Germans marched into Poland. Another quotation gives an impression of Hoffmeister's state of mind: 'I am very glad you got the picture at least, and I remember often the days we have spend together in different parts of the continent. I think I being to be a little sentimental too. Never mind you bloody bastard, all will be better once. Today I got a letter from my mother. She asks if you will not come to see her in Strancice, but I answered all ready you will not.'

60. RIBA YoF/1/12.

61. Ibid. Letter from the War Office to Yorke, dated 14 February 1940.

62. Ibid. Shand's splenetic comments are in a letter dated 1 October 1940, one of several he wrote to Yorke between the summer of 1940 and spring of 1941 while working for the Admiralty in Bath. As well as giving Yorke plants from his garden and enquiring as to their well-being in Wootton, Shand invited Yorke to stay and gave him the benefit of his characterisations of mutual acquaintances. More priceless comments relate to the two owning families of the Architectural Press: 'I hope to God the brothers Regan are married already, and that Master Hubert [de Cronin Hastings] has been cured of his chronic neurasthenia by something dropping rather close to him, but not too close to rob him of his childlike charm.'

63. FRS Yorke, 'Glass Buildings of the Future', typescript in the RIBA YoF/1/12.

64. For details of Holford's career, see Gordon Cherry, *William Holford*, Mansell (London and New York), 1986.

65. RIBA YoF/1/12. See correspondence from Gibb dated 12 and 13 March 1940.

66. Ibid. The phrase 'dread inspiring' about this job was actually used in a letter dated 11 March 1940 from the Architectural Press's Michael Regan to Yorke.

67. Ibid. Randall Evans' friend from New Zealand, John Brewster, wrote to Yorke on 23 August 1940 asking whether 'you still occasionally prowl around in the dark hours of the night', and suggested meeting if he did so. See also note 18 for Yorke's restrictive working hours.

68. Ibid. See a letter from Blackett to Yorke, dated 2 July 1940.

69. Ibid. Cobb's letter is dated 9 September 1940, Tubbs' 14 May of the same year.

70. Ibid. Holford described the reference in a letter dated 7 January 1941 to Yorke.

71. Ibid. Letter from Spragg to Yorke, dated 2 January 1941.

72. Ibid. Letter from Holford to Yorke, dated 23 January 1941.

73. Ibid. Letter from Yorke to Regan, dated 26 February 1941.

74. Ibid. Letter from Gibson to Yorke, dated 2 April 1941.

75. Yorke would also have been aware of these opportunities from Holford's move into the Ministry of Town and Country Planning which was established in 1941 precisely to plan for and manage post-war reconstruction. Hugh Beaver, the driving force of Gibb's, also worked in the ministry, whose first minister was Sir John (later Lord) Reith, who had achieved public fame as the creator of the BBC. See the *Dictionary of National Biography* for details of Beaver's career. The architect Clough Williams-Ellis, no modernist, welcomed Reith's appointment: 'If Sir John's immediate function is no more than to act as a sort of burly commissionaire, restraining the queue of property owners from pushing past him to set about rebuilding incontinently on their shattered sites, that is a very necessary task that will need all his relentless strength of purpose.' Ian McIntyre, *The Expense of Glory – a life of John Reith*, HarperCollins (London), 2000, p 259, from the *Spectator*.

76. Folks was a friend from Yorke's student days in Birmingham. He made a transcript of Yorke's cycling holiday diary to Normandy and donated it to the RIBA, along with the original manuscript and several of Yorke's Christmas cards. The letter, dated 7 February 1944, is preserved with the diary in the RIBA YoF/1/8. The Christmas cards are in YoF/2/3.

77. RIBA YoF/1/12.

78. Ibid. Letter from Miss Webb to Yorke, dated 17 February 1941.

79. See note 59.

80. RIBA YoF/1/12. Letter from Shand to Yorke, dated 13 November 1940.

81. Ibid. Letter from Yorke to Carter, dated 26 February 1941. Carter, then the RIBA librarian, replied with a helpful bibliography.

82. RIBA YoF/1/12. Letter from 'AED' to Yorke, dated 25 February 1941.

83. This was Middlefield Farm, near Witney, Oxfordshire. Photographs survive in the Allford Yorke Archive, Folder 14.

84. See Richard Sheppard's obituary in the *RIBA Journal* vol 69 (August 1962), p 303. Sheppard's typescript is preserved in the RIBA's Biography file on Yorke and differs slightly from the published version.

85. Penelope Whiting kindly gave Jeremy Melvin and David Allford a copy of letters written to her during this trip.

86. Yorke's surviving accounts (see note 24) show significant increases in his income almost year on year in the 1950s. Just before his death his annual income reached £18,000, and he had enjoyed the trappings of wealth, such as owning land, art and a Bentley motorcar.

87. Most of the work of Yorke, Rosenberg & Mardall until Yorke's death in 1962 was located in Britain. Yorke even seems to have shunned one possible opportunity to develop an international practice. In *Portrait of an Architect*, Smythe (Gerrards Cross), 1984, p 180, the garrulous Raglan Squire recalled suggesting that his firm and Yorke's might merge, saying, 'With my overseas connections and yours at home we would be a pretty powerful combination'. 'Yes, that's an idea,' Yorke reportedly replied – but did nothing.

88. See Yorke, 'The Private Architect's Problem', op cit, for this and following quotes.

CHAPTER 6

FRS YORKE – A MEMOIR 1952–62

'If you don't like what you're doing, don't do it'

David Allford

FRS Yorke's *The Modern House* was the first book I had ever seen on modern architecture. In 1943 Mr Furse, my art teacher in the fifth form at High Storrs Grammar School, had been to the Sheffield city library on my behalf and said this was the book I should get. Mr Furse was new to the school and had introduced the history of architecture as part of the Art Higher School Certificate.

This was fortunate, as for the previous couple of years I had thought I would like to be an architect without knowing, formally, anything of the subject. Yorke's book was an introduction to – rather, a revelation of – a brand-new other world: the white architecture, in black-and-white photographs, with Gill Sans black-and-white printing on art paper. The text, too, was clear, the analysis convincing – the old order was intolerable, a new one was in preparation, its ideas clearly available for takeover.

New names – Le Corbusier, Gropius, Forbat, Rading – were introduced to me. In the middle of most destructive war in history, those European drawing rooms in the photographs, with huge windows, radiators and chrome tube furniture, seemed so optimistic. The fact (if it occurred to me at all) that they were all in enemy-occupied territory and being bombed by the RAF seemed irrelevant.

These were the built examples of the idealist propositions for the future rethinking of Europe. I wrote to Yorke care of the Architectural Press in 1943 asking for clarification on some technical point about structure in one of the examples – I've forgotten which. I received a charming and clear answer from him on Ministry of Works (or Ministry of Supply) notepaper, explaining the point and adding that steel structure was likely to be used for post-war prefabricated houses in the way his answer to my question implied. He was, I realised much later, referring to the Braithwaite House he was working on at the time.[1]

Other books, of course, came to me after *The Modern House* over the next few years when I was a student of architecture and during nearly three years in the RAF, including Yorke's later works *The Modern Flat* and *The Modern House in England*. Yorke's first and best book, *The Modern House*, has always remained my first and strongest influence. Looking at it today, and handling the first edition (1934), one senses beneath the methodology of description ('walls, floors, roof...') the controlled excitement of discovery.

Yorke was under thirty, very English, travelling all over the continent, corresponding with and meeting young architects who were building in a way that had few, if any, comparable examples in England. He must have been amazed, thrilled, even on occasion shocked. Yet, having got to know him twenty years later, I can imagine him controlling his enthusiasm under the kind of English reserve that foreigners, at least in those days, expected. The fact that he could drink any of them under the table must have delighted them.

Not studying or living in London, I heard neither stories nor gossip about London architects, so they were simply names attached to publications of work in the magazines. I worked for Maxwell Fry and Jane Drew as a student in the summer of 1950 and inevitably learnt something,

not only of my employers but of other architects. I heard two things about Yorke, both from Jock Todd, for whom I worked at Fry Drew. First, he was a 'wizard at human relations' and second, that he could be 'charmingly bloody-minded'. Jock introduced me to his great friend and drinking companion, Kitch (CA Kitchen), who worked for Yorke, Rosenberg & Mardall.

When I graduated from the University of Sheffield in 1952, it was Kitch who got me an interview at Yorke, Rosenberg & Mardall after I had had two or three other interviews, all unsuccessful. I was lucky to get it and, indeed, to get a job at £9 a week starting 18 August 1952.

The interview was memorable. It was the first time I had met Yorke, which was unexpecting, as the interview was undertaken by Randall Evans, Yorke's associate at Yorke, Rosenberg & Mardall and chief assistant to Yorke and Breuer before the war. I showed my school work to Randall who with his friendly New Zealand informality, put me very much at ease in his small office off a half-landing in 2 Hyde Park Place, London W2. I never found out whether Yorke's entry, also very informal, after about half an hour was staged or not. Anyway, it seemed very natural, as did the man himself. I warmed to him at once, though I was unprepared for his somewhat casual, if not dishevelled (crumpled), appearance. You must remember that 'modern architects' were associated with well-cut suits and bow ties (think of Gropius, the artist Max Bill, Corb) yet here was 'one of them' in greenish-grey thornproof trousers (part of a two-piece suit) held up with a leather belt (more like a strap) without belt loops and the material scooped together at the waist. Then a greenish shirt open at the neck. Attached to the neck, so to speak, was a good-shaped head with darkish (chestnut) dishevelled hair. He was the face was ruddy, the eyes (grey/blue) and mouth smiling. Between slightly stained teeth was a pipe, which he removed before shaking hands. The very picture of the English countryman, completely unphoney, instantly

FRS Yorke on the steps of 2 Hyde Park Place, the offices where David Allford had a memorable interview in June 1952, flanked by Cyril Mardall (left) and Eugene Rosenberg (right).

Photo: Sam Lambert, courtesy of The Architectural Review.

friendly, quietly perceptive. Yet somehow, and this was additionally attractive, 'not quite a gentleman'. This was the sobriquet of a great old comedian still around in the dying days of the music hall of the 1950s – Billy Bennett, red face, beery with a deep rasping voice. He always appeared on the variety bill as Billy Bennett 'almost a gentleman', and Yorke loved him.

Randall, having introduced me, briefly described a couple of my small projects and Yorke picked them up the better to get the sidelight in a slightly gloomy room, chewed on his pipe and said absolutely nothing. Randall said, just to help me I'm sure, things like 'Don't you think that's not bad Kay?' Kay was Yorke's familiar name – he told me once it derived from roll call (perhaps in the Territorial Army) when his name was called out Yor-kay as distinct from Yorke.

I think Yorke, in the friendliest possible way, just grunted through his pipe-retaining teeth, 'Yuuus'. He also said something like, 'Do you know you can't park in London and I have a hell of a job'. Randall then made some pleasantry, Yorke laughed attractively, shook hands again and said he had to go – and went! I describe this interview (non-interview!) in some detail as everything that happened, the little that was said, the manner of all the nuances and implications were, it turned out, absolutely typical. The character and personality of the man that I gained instinctively from those first impressions were a clear and true picture of what he was in essence – open, friendly, without 'side' or pomp, unsnobbish, completely trustworthy and humorous.

Of course, I learned much more later of the complexities and contradictions of his character, his uncertainties and disappointments, and his occasional bloody-mindedness; but the essence was in the first meeting. I was delighted to be engaged to work with such a person and with his colleague Randall Evans, who shared many similarities of character, especially openness and lack of pomposity.

I don't think I saw Yorke again for about two months. I was assigned to work as an assistant to Kitch, who was the job architect on a very large technical college, Leeds City Colleges, for Leeds City Corporation, the first stage of which was to go to tender in about a year.[2] The scheme consisted of low buildings of some three storeys with a long 15-storey teaching block above. It bore some resemblance to one of the same period for Sheffield Polytechnic by Gollins, Melvin & Ward. It was one of the largest (potentially, depending on the government finance for the stages) jobs in the office. Its derivatives were rooted in modernist suburban buildings like Le Corbusier's *Armée de Salut* as well as the Berne technical school and the large London comprehensive schools (also contemporaneous). It bore, too, certain resemblance to American (particularly SOM) office buildings such as Lever House, New York, the latter influence particularly evident on all the glass cladding systems. The office was just completing another large technical college in Merthyr Tydfil, Wales.

In those days the office was simply divided into three sections, respectively under Yorke, Rosenberg and Mardall, each with an associate working under the partners – John Penoyre under Rosenberg and Ian B Wilson for Mardall. Each section worked in separate parts (floors) of the office. Assistants occasionally moved to other sections depending on workload or compatibility, but the distinctiveness between sections was very clear. Relations within sections and between sections were generally informal, but Yorke's section was where there was laughter and the most discussion. The linkage and solidarity between the partners was obvious in that it worked as a partnership, but the style of the office was clearly derived from the style and personality of three different (very different) partners and the style of architecture varied accordingly. It was very quickly clear to me that I was fortunate to be working for Yorke and Randall Evans. Kitch was a delight to work for in my first years, as I started to learn the difficult trade of being an architect.[3]

In Yorke's group the work at that time consisted of the Leeds colleges, several schools for county councils, principally in Worcestershire, a comprehensive school at Tulse Hill in south

London for the London County Council and a Methodist teacher training college in Wimbledon. There was also the odd conversion and some small house extensions (including some personal work for Yorke himself on his house at Wootton in Oxfordshire, and later his farm at Witney, also in Oxfordshire). Yorke edited *Specification* as well, and revised some of his books. Penelope Whiting, whom Yorke had met at the Ministry of Works in the war, was assisting him on all these literary and editing matters as well as producing a book herself – *The New Small House*.[4] The office at 2 Hyde Park Place, W2, on the Bayswater Road in Marble Arch, was a handsome early Victorian building with a basement, three floors of offices and Yorke's flat and office on the fourth-floor attic storey. Yorke had always lived 'over the shop' since the Yorke and Breuer office in Tregunter Road, SW10. In his own words he did not like paying rent! His office was a large, low-ceilinged room with a large mahogany early Victorian conference table, a large desk and a fireplace. Adjoining the office was a bedroom/meeting room with bathroom attached and there was a small kitchen off the landing. When I joined it was being fitted out with new cupboards, etc by Reggie Dobson, a young student studying externally at the Regent Street Polytechnic night school. He was Yorke's only ever 'articled pupil' – a form then very much out of date, but which I believe Yorke had done as a favour to Reggie's father.[5]

Rosenberg had the ground floor and second floor and Yorke the first floor – two interconnecting piano nobile rooms with large sash windows overlooking Hyde Park. In the basement was a library (of sorts!) and at the rear of the building a canteen/bar. The canteen was presided over by the caretaker, Mr Dawkins, whose wife acted as housekeeper for Yorke. They both carried coal to Yorke's flat from the basement. The bar was run informally on a 'slate' system, with beer and cider ordered weekly in barrels from a supplier called Unwins; Kitch did the ordering. Occasionally a barber (from Simpson's) came to do Yorke's hair and, if the timing was right, anyone else's. The barbering took place in the bar among the drinkers. Mrs Dawkins also did meals, pre-ordered, at lunchtime. The bar, in a way, helped relationships informally between staff and partners and worked well until it ran out of steam (or perhaps drink) in about 1957. Christmas parties always finished up there and were riotous on occasion.

Yorke's office bore the imprint of a strong and clearly fascinating character. It was probably the room which reflected personality, whims and preoccupations more than any I have ever seen. The immediate impression (especially when there was a large fire burning – illegally!) was of a cross between a gentleman's club and a university don with wide and esoteric interests. The large mahogany desk was loaded with papers, letters from all over the world, a rack of pipes, rosettes from Yorke's prize-winning cows and fishing flies; a friend from the Architectural Press used to come and tie his special ones for Yorke, a keen fisherman. In addition, there were various items of memorabilia and samples of materials from current jobs. The office was tidy, despite the amount and variable nature of the clutter, but the casual arrangement indicated a wide range of interests in addition to architecture. It was very much a man's room, and it felt good to be in it, especially if Yorke offered you a drink after hours. On the walls were contemporary paintings by Ivon Hitchens, Kenneth Rowntree (I believe a Richard Hamilton in the lobby) and a sketch by Le Corbusier that I believe Yorke 'obtained' during a party at Wells Coates' house when the master was too inebriated to care.

Every so often Yorke would visit the drawing boards. The timing depended on his wish to see the work, though was more often prompted by Randall after the team requested to see Yorke in order to clear a particular stage or resolve a problem, even a disagreement about design. Yorke would appear at the drawing board, usually with Randall and usually smoking a pipe or cigarette, or a cigar if it was after lunch (usually what we called 'garlic lunches'); he would greet one with a smile (charming, or 'charmingly bloody-minded') and lean on the board or accept a seat if offered. Depending on the weight of what was under discussion, the pattern of the conversation was always consistent: first, explanation by oneself, the job architect or Randall (or all three) with Yorke listening intently, slowly and pensively pipe-puffing. Then Randall (who had married Pegi, a sister of Yorke's wife Thelma) would look quizzically at him and say something like, 'Don't you think that's all right, Kay?' (gentle New Zealand accent, sentences ending always on a rising note). Yorke would remove his (large) pipe or slide it to the side of his mouth and say 'Yuuus' or 'Didn't we do something like that at so and so', mentioning some comparable job. He rarely said much more but somehow, when you got the code, you knew whether he was pleased, satisfied or not quite so, or really in disagreement.

He rarely, if ever, gave praise or expressed his approval. The most he would say if pleased was 'Yes, very nice'; if critical, 'Shouldn't we look at the detail again?' He would then leave for the next board (or meeting or lunch!) and Randall would turn and say, 'I think he liked that, don't you?' (New Zealand understatement for 'He likes it'), or 'I think we'll have to look at that again.'

Even on the most serious issue Yorke would hardly ever directly engage the particular assistant involved. Word would come down from Randall to the effect that 'Yorke's bloody angry about … he says he made it clear he wasn't going to have it' ('it' in New Zealandish). Randall was thus the courtier/messenger closest to the throne but because he was an honest and modest man, you believed that his messages either of praise or criticism were handed down truthfully and without distortion. This is a rare gift. Courtiers so often, for their own purposes (or for pure ego), distort the messages they learn from on high. We all, without discussion amongst ourselves, knew this and trusted 'the word'. Without such trust it would not have worked and morale, consequently, was high in Yorke's group.

Kitch (CA Kitchen), from Hunslet, Leeds, was about ten years older than myself. He was unqualified and an exceptional designer, mad about architecture and, like all autodidacts, open-minded and widely read: he got on very well with Randall (most people did) and Yorke. He could drink as much as Yorke, but not eat as much. There were stories of drinking occasions, usually spontaneous, when much was drunk and many home truths, particularly from Kitch (blunt, Yorkshire), were exchanged. To the credit of both, neither took advantage of any possible indiscretion *in vino veritas*. It is a tribute to Yorke's quality that whatever was said in the pub the night before, encounters in the office the next day were always businesslike, however informal. Only Randall, apart from the partners, called Yorke 'Kay'.

Although I was a partner for four years before Yorke's death in 1962, even then I mostly left out the address rather than call him 'Kay'. On reflection this is strange considering how approachable and friendly he normally was. The casual use of the first name, derived undoubtedly from America, was not in general use between employee and employer before the 1960s. Indeed, in more formal organisations, architectural or otherwise, it was not always common between colleagues. The reason for making the point about the formal address towards Yorke is perhaps the clue it gives to his personality and character.

It is true Yorke hated pomp and formality, was never himself arrogant or gratuitously cruel or humiliating to those beneath him; it is true that he was famously even-handed in the way he spoke to those on his level or above or below – his manners were good towards all; it is also true that one could be critical to Yorke in an architectural discussion without causing offence. Yet one knew there was a limit somewhere to his obvious tolerance and openness (charmingly bloody-minded). Born in 1906 into a professional middle-class family, his upbringing in a public school (Chipping Camden) would indicate a polite, formal, well-mannered household of the period. Sir Frederick

Gibberd, before he died in 1984, kindly took me to lunch to tell me about Yorke in the early days. They were long-term friends, who first met in the Birmingham School of Art. Gibberd, who came from a 'relatively humble' background (his words), was amazed when he went to Yorke's family house which, to him, spoke of luxury, culture (in the Arts and Crafts school) and affluence (there were servants). Yorke's background, though probably considered liberated for the time, was formal and upper middle class compared with the manners of postwar England.

This family background, combined with boarding at a public school (1919–24), imprinted a certain convention on Yorke which was typical of the period, though after World War I had started to undergo an enormous change. His accent and manner of speech, though derived from the 'received pronunciation' of the English public school, was, someone in the office (himself from public school) once said to me, 'slightly phoney'. It was a clever observation. On reflection I could speculate, and it is only speculation, that here was a highly intelligent man and a very attractive personality whose manners and upbringing derived from a professional middle-class Edwardian background, but whose sensitivity to change in society (education in the 1920s), and whose obvious sympathy for the 'underdog' (he always supported the Labour Party, though he was not very political) led him to modify his behaviour – possibly even his accent – to avoid the pitfalls of arrogance that his background, however 'liberal' at home, could have inclined him towards. The ultimate authority was always there and was exercised, to his credit, with a light touch, mostly only when necessary. Even so, there was always, as Randall once said, 'a streak of madness in the family', in that Yorke could on rare occasions assume a terrifying anger, often about quite small matters. He was, at such points, impossible to reason with and best left alone to smoulder having just exploded. Having met both his mother and father briefly on the stairs of 2 Hyde Park Place some time in the early 1950s, I gained an instant impression that his father was a benign and gentle character. His mother, whom Yorke resembled in features, seemed to have a determination of eye and set of mouth that I had observed in Yorke himself. My impression was confirmed by Randall, and by Miss Kent, the partnership secretary and factotum of the office, who worked for Cyril Mardall in United Nations Refugees Relief Agency towards the end of the war, and was a 'founder member' of the office in 1944.

I was intrigued by Yorke's approach to architecture, closely observing the image I had of him as a seminal figure of the pioneering days of the establishment of modernism in England, and his performance and attitudes in practice in the 1950s. His analysis was always remarkably penetrating, and it took a very short time for him to understand and penetrate the ideas presented to him. His views, as I have said, were implied, though quite clear, rather than stated directly. With his rich and very English sense of humour, they were often amusing as well as pertinent. Any counterargument or defence was absorbed by him quietly and usually without further comment. Once I said something to the effect that I was sure he'd like it better the way we had done it, and he replied that people who said that they were sure usually weren't!

He was totally untheoretical and very suspicious of 'systems', though sensitive and receptive to matters of taste. He was pragmatic in a very English way and all this is what gave his buildings humanity. Nevertheless, I was sometimes amazed, even appalled, by the lack of consistency in the work around me. I had left university with a passion for modern architecture – a passion touched off first by Yorke himself (*The Modern House*). I arrived in London full of Le Corbusier's *Oeuvre Complète* and the growing stature of Mies van de Rohe in the USA. My good fortune was meeting and working for Kitch who shared these passions in a way hardly anyone else in the office did. Randall, born in 1908, shared a pragmatic view of architecture very similar to Yorke's.

Randall was also a good critic, particularly of functional requirements and of practical building – in this latter regard perhaps the best all-rounder in the office. His great qualitys were tolerance

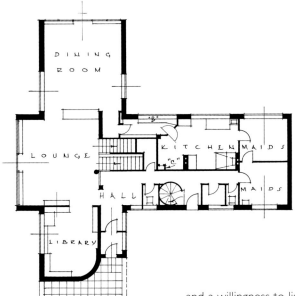

DINING ROOM

KITCHEN MAIDS

LOUNGE

MAIDS

HALL

LIBRARY

LEFT AND OPPOSITE: Plan of the Gocar's house at Dvur Kralove.

OPPOSITE BOTTOM: The elegant suite of reception rooms, looking along a 70-foot vista from a library through a saloon to the dining room in the house by Josef Gocar: the sort of image in *The Modern House* that caught Allford's attention in 1943, without worrying him that it was in Nazi-occupied territory.

and a willingness to listen to ideas, provided they made basic sense, without any tendency whatsoever to stifle them because they were inconvenient, challenging or threatening to his own position. He had predilection, but little prejudice. He had worked with Yorke and Breuer since 1936 and had joined Yorke, Rosenberg & Mardell in 1944 on demobilisation, after five years in the Royal Engineers where he held the rank of major. He had that easy-going, antihierarchical manner of management and, relations that are the trademark of so many antipodeans. They can spot phoneyness, insincerity and pomposity like a hound smells a fox. If Randall can be faulted it is that he was too tolerant, but of course this was to the advantage of Kitch, myself and others about us who generally wanted to affect and improve the work being done in the office.

We eagerly awaited the new work coming from Le Corbusier and Mies, and were staggered by the technology, panache and sheer professionalism of people like SOM in America. Nearer home, the work of rival and comparable offices like Richard Sheppard ('an old pal of Yorke's'), Powell & Moya, Lyons, Israel & Ellis and, more recently, Alison and Peter Smithson were studied eagerly and with varying scales of admiration. The Smithsons' school at Hunstanton (1949–54) was a revelation and several of us borrowed a car one weekend and went to see it. There is no doubt that this remarkable work, their first large one and the result of an open competition, recharged our will to change the course of work over which we had influence in the office. It was not in any sense a calculated 'putsch', and it was not conspiratorially achieved, to the extent that it was successful. It absolutely required the understanding and backing of the two chief personalities, first FRS Yorke and second Randall Evans. They were bubbling and exciting times. Kitch, totally loyal to the office which he had joined from the architects department of the 'miners welfare', had nevertheless said to me early on that the office was producing 'potboilers'.

This was all too evident in such statements by Yorke or Randall as 'Why not do it like the workshop block or teaching block at so-and-so?'. One learns from one's own history, and while an office cannot reinvent everything on every new job, the attitude struck us as one that was lazy rather than anything else.

It must have been irritating for Yorke to have these challenges tossed to him on every occasion, especially as in my case I had not been out of school for more than a few minutes. To his great credit he never showed it; rather, and this was his great quality, he showed minor irritation at our effrontery whilst backing us by mostly accepting our arguments. Randall was the catalyst who made the change one that was acceptable and worked reasonably, at least in practice. When necessary, Yorke's humour helped him to counter the assault. An example was at the drawing board when showing the details we were proposing for the plant room on the roof of the workshop block at Leeds Central Colleges, and backing up the proposals with examples of Mies' steel

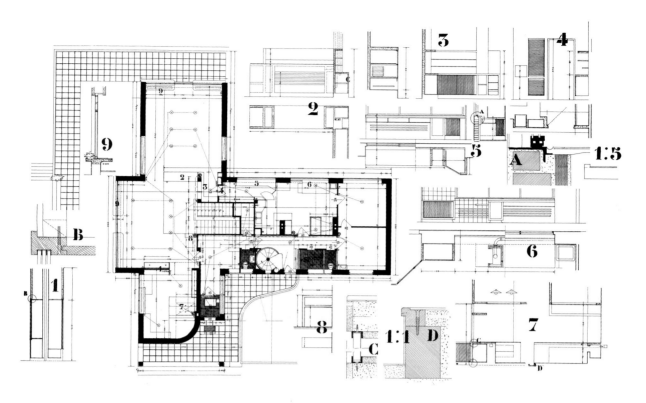

detailing at IIT Chicago. Yorke leant back somewhat languidly (it was after lunch) and said, 'Why can't we produce some details that Mies could copy?'.

I do not recall any acrimony in these encounters with Yorke. On reflection, perhaps he liked the challenge and the implication that we were reminding him of the basics of the modern movement, particularly in its continental manifestation. The plant room for the workshop block in Leeds was probably our first *cause célébre*. Normally, and this was the proposition for this case, a steel structure for a roof plant room would have been covered in timber boarding. Instead, we designed exposed Miesian details with glass infill panels suitably insulated. Randall, having satisfied himself that it worked, helped us put it to Yorke who accepted it with little more than a murmur through his pipe. Later we heard from Randall that they had both agreed it was a risk they could take as it couldn't be seen from the streets outside (it was surmounted by, and lower than, the three-storey perimeter buildings). We all laughed, and it was built and formed the prototype of a range of steel structures (architectural steelwork) done by the office over the next decade or more.

Similar acceptance was gained for the exposing of concrete based on Le Corbusier's '*béton brut*'. I cannot recall knowing of any other office where quiet revolution – it was no less – was taking place with so little pain and with no spilling of blood. This is ultimately a tribute to the quality of FRS Yorke, whose remarkable human gifts encouraged us to develop ideas against the general run of the office – and with increasing risk to the office's reputation if they failed (some did, of course). Had Yorke held very strong ideas himself, other than those based on quality and sound practice, it would have been impossible to create such radical change. Had he not had the gifts of courage and toughness in helping the changes to come about, they couldn't have happened either. At times it could have been uncomfortable for him, but I am certain that very privately he was excited.

Yorke, for all his social gifts, easy good manners, amusing gentle sense of humour and generosity of spirit, was a very private person. It was as if his extrovert personality, his wide range of friends and his genuine bonhomie masked to some extent a private, lonely and possibly disappointed man. This is not an original observation, nor is it uncommon among similar phlegmatic personalities. I am sure that it was chemical/genetic not experiential.

After all, he had achieved much of what he must have set out to do as a young architect. Maybe the buildings he first saw and the works of the architects he first met were, in his mind, beyond his own ability to achieve. If this is so, it is all the more remarkable that he settled for influence and guidance of others to achieve other ends. The man was genuinely modest and unaffected, shy perhaps; his intelligence could not have hidden from him that as an architect he was inferior to many of the people with whom he was otherwise on equal terms.

His gifts lay – and this must have been a conscious, very private decision – in his choosing to work with and influence others in the successful pursuit of architecture. While working on Leeds College towards the end of the documentation and drawings of stage one, I was thrilled one day in 1954 when Randall came to my drawing board and said in his direct New Zealand manner, smiling: 'We're going to give you a job on your own.' The job was Haileybury Boys Club in Stepney, east London. For many years several public schools had clubs in the poor areas of London where boys could gain, free, some of the advantages of their more privileged compatriots. This one was run by Haileybury and Imperial Services College of which the prime minister of the previous Labour Government (1945–51) Clement Attlee was an alumnus; he performed a ceremonial opening of the new club some years later.

The project had been in the office for some years. The scheme had been approved and was awaiting finance. This had been raised and was to go ahead with a £15,000 budget. Yorke and Penelope Whiting had produced a scheme and naturally, like all young architects, I proceeded to redesign it; but sensibly (and agreed by Yorke) I kept to the brief in general organisation. The first thing was to reorganise the plan of the 3-foot by 3-foot module, a simple thing to do which immediately created a more orderly plan. Apart from this, and dealing with an uncomfortable junction between the two-storey block and the single-storey clubroom, the rest of my effort was in the elevations. I was unhappy with the given scheme architecturally; it seemed another example of pragmatism and, worse, expediency. The fourth volume of Le Corbusier's *Oeuvre Complète* had just been published (these volumes were as eagerly awaited as hot cross buns or Dickens serial novels in the nineteenth century). Alan Cordingley, who worked in Cyril Mardall's section of the office, came to our section to announce that volume four was out. All he then said was 'See page 174'. Page 174 was in fact *Maisons Jaoul* and, put very simply, fitted exactly into the New Brutalist aesthetic then being bandied about London by the Smithsons.[6]

Anyway, these matters were in the air and I produced a brick and concrete edge beam design, which was to be built. However, it had certain difficulties at the LCC planning department where they literally wanted us to clad it — with vertical timber boarding on the first floor, it was suggested. I was horrified after the meeting with Walter Bor, who was a senior planner for the area and had a revised scheme drawn out by one of his assistants. Yorke backed my scheme to the hilt and, at another meeting with Bor, gently steamrollered the opposition while, in a sense, they weren't looking. It was a vintage Yorke performance. He said, as usual, very little, but there was no doubt about the outcome.

At that time there was a fierce battle of styles ranging in the LCC. On the one hand were the Marxists, in very strong positions in the architectural and planning hierarchy, who were struggling to interpret (literally — there were meetings at Communist Party headquarters) the Stalin/Zhdanov line about the 'people's architecture'. They were mostly modernists in an intellectual crisis, so couldn't go down the route of the Stalinallee housing scheme in Berlin. It ended up approximating Swedish modern. Graeme Shankland argued that though there were contradictions in Swedish society, and that it was still a 'mixed economy', there were lessons for us in its socialist aspirations. On the other side were the various unreconstructed modernists responsible for the various Corbusian and Miesian interpretations of mass-housing architecture. Some of the group were known as the anarchoaesthetes, a euphemism for social fascists, and other Marxist Soviet jargon.

Bor, who I don't believe was especially political, was obviously at that time following the formal line. Yorke was not very political. Most modern architects were on the left, as Yorke was, but in many cases, and certainly in his, politics were rarely discussed. I suppose he would have been on the centre left of the Labour Party, but not a member. He once told me he had marched in Arms for Spain rallies in the 1930s, as indeed had most intellectuals of his generation and background. Again, not uncommonly, he was less than consistent in his social attitudes. No doubt he wished, truly, for a more even and fair distribution of wealth and I never heard him complain strongly against high taxation which, at the time, was the policy of whatever government was in power. But in his attitude to money he was more of the peasant than the idealist. His family seemed to live at the top of their income to maintain their lifestyle, and Yorke's view of practice in the 1920s and 1930s — what he called his milk and buns period — replicated this habit.[7] This, I believe, was a piece of romanticism — he generally lived well with a car, trips abroad and nice places to live.

Randall tells how in 1937 Yorke gave him a raise from £4 a week to £4 10s, provided he moved to a flat in Yorke's house in Tregunter Road and paid 15 shillings a week rent — which of course he did. Rosenberg once told me, with a smile, that Yorke once offered him some space in his barn at Middlefield Farm. The space was no use for the farm, but would be fine to house

FRS Yorke (right) and Werner Duttmann, city planner of Berlin, around the time of Duttmann's invitation to Yorke to contribute to Interbau in 1957.

some of Yorke Rosenberg & Mardell's old archives. It made sense and was accepted, and the documents were duly stored; and then there was a bill for storage. On balance, these were endearing traits, like his distribution of the old white £5 notes at Christmas – somewhat proprietorial in modern terms, but fine at the time on Christmas Eve when drinks were going round the office (much of it from Yorke's many friends in the trade!).

Beryl Hope, who worked with Yorke on a new house in George Street, W1 for the television chef Philip Harben, told me with amusement how in celebration of the job Yorke, Beryl and all the workmen went to a nearby pub.[8] They all bought Yorke drinks, though he stood his own round. I have always like this story, accepting Beryl's interpretation that they liked Yorke and enjoyed working with him – 'Nothing stuck up about him,' one can imagine them saying. They enjoyed drinking with him and he with them.

I can imagine Yorke being sensitive in showing camaraderie and avoiding seeming to be a rich man slumming or buying the drinks because the workmen couldn't afford them. In the English class system, particularly in those days when it was so much stronger, what could have been a minefield for most people in his position was handled without effort with a natural dignity that respected the dignity of others. In fact, Beryl said that she heard one of the workmen say, 'Christ, he don't harf drink a lot' – an economic rather than a moral concern on his part.

Yorke was marvellous company on any social occasion. At whatever level you were eating or drinking his appetite was comprehensive. He once looked up from a large plate of roast beef in the Cheshire Cheese (appropriately Dr Johnson's haunt – there was something Johnsonian about

Yorke), said 'What about it?' and ordered another helping. This was after a dozen oysters! On one occasion he said to me in a tone of modest boasting, 'I don't recall ever having a half bottle of wine'; then, after a pause for reflection, he added, 'Yes, once, but I had just drunk a full bottle of before that'. His appetite was Rabelaisian, no doubt bordering on greed. Someone in the office (Lloyd Smith) said 'Yorke didn't mind what he ate as long as he got a lot!'.[9]

The first time I accompanied Yorke on a trip was in 1956 when we were working on Gatwick airport.[10] We visited airports in Paris and Zurich, and then continued on to Berlin where Yorke had been commissioned to do a housing project for Interbau. He liked old-fashioned rather than grand hotels; although in some ways a stylist, perhaps the peasant streak (money) rather than the pomp put him off the latter. He could certainly have afforded them, but perhaps his somewhat spartan public-school upbringing and his memory of the 'milk and buns' period conditioned him against it. In fact, a real Puritan streak went with the appetite and self-indulgence – a not uncommon phenomenon in the English middle classes. This also went with his work ethic or, more appropriately phrased, activity ethic. He never lazed or lounged, he had to be doing something – work or play; in between aeroplane flights he would be writing postcards. We spent one night in Paris and stayed at the Normandy Hotel close to the Louvre. After several drinks in several bars ('at the zinc') Yorke suggested that we dined at a favourite restaurant of his. I was quite, but only quite, happy about this – and mildly surprised, as I had been there as a student in 1948, taken by an American friend. The point about the restaurant was that for a fixed sum – I've forgotten how much, but very reasonable – you could eat as much as you wanted. Drink was extra, and we drank heavily of the *vin de table*. The trip was memorable, not only for the study of airports but for the opportunity I had to observe and enjoy the sort of things Yorke liked – which, luckily, were the kind of things I liked. I say 'luckily' because he, despite an air of democracy, was totally selfish and you were offered what he wanted to do next as if it were the natural and obvious choice.

Three observations come to mind: an introduction to Kirschwasser in Switzerland; an introduction to snails (one dozen) and the frightful smell of garlic in the bathroom afterwards; and an introduction to *eisbein* in Berlin. This is a huge pork knuckle with pease pudding and sauerkraut and potatoes, rather Rabelaisian, even heroic. We had two *eisbein*, one ordered immediately after the other. In Berlin we stayed at the Kempinski, then not fully restored to grandeur. We shared a bathroom and I asked if he had any talcum powder; his shocked sneer at such a pansy request showed the obvious masculine side of his nature – public school, cold baths and no heating!

It's strange but, despite being away with Yorke for five nights, I can hardly remember any conversations about architecture. I must have asked about the 1930s and the architects he knew, but perhaps I didn't. Perhaps there was reserve on both sides. Lots of fun and jokes and meals and drinks, but no memorable conversation.

The Interbau of 1955–7 had commissioned Yorke to design some houses in the Hansa Viertel in Berlin. It was a prestigious appointment – others asked were Aalto, Niemeyer, Taut, Gropius and Le Corbusier. Their houses were mostly built, but Yorke's never got very far. I got the impression that there was some embarrassment – perhaps Yorke didn't really want to do them, perhaps they didn't like the proposals. At least Yorke's relationship with Werner Duttman, as city architect and collaborator, was excellent. Duttman was an Anglophile who had been a prisoner of war in England towards the end of the war and had studied planning under Thomas Sharpe at Durham. He was also a full-blooded bon viveur, very bright, very intelligent, close in many ways to Yorke himself. They got on famously, but the design of the houses was never developed very far before being abandoned.

In the summer of 1954, at one of the office meetings held every three to four months to discuss jobs and so on, Yorke and Randall agreed to a suggestion by one of the assistants, Roger

Tomalin, to have an internal competition to encourage design ideas from the drawing office. It was open to anyone in Yorke's group and Yorke and Randall would judge it. They gave out the brief to anyone interested. Kitch and I decided to do it together and so did two other assistants. The brief was a new one just in from Worcester County Council, for a college of further education at Bromsgrove, Worcestershire. The only rule was that the work was not to be done in office hours. Kitch and I won it. I don't remember whether there was a prize (if so it was very small, but that wasn't the point). The job was eventually built in line with our proposals. Some people had (not unreasonably) a rather cynical view that the office got it on the cheap. We thought, however, that it was a bold and imaginative idea on the part of Yorke and Randall and one I doubt many offices would have entertained at the time.

The only controversy I recall during the course of the job was the use of certain colours, particularly black and particularly in the boiler-house complex. Yorke didn't like it, but we argued without acrimony and in the end he agreed. Somehow, I don't think he was particularly interested in the job – or he was confident we could do it and if he didn't like it he could say, 'I told you so, at the time'. He once said (not over this issue, and quite gently) that he thought I could be 'rather rude'. Thinking back to this period, I can understand why he said it – I must have been tiresome on occasion.

In October 1955 Yorke called me on the intercom, a relatively new device in the office, with three red lighted buttons for Yorke, Rosenberg and Mardall in addition to the office-floor call buttons. I went up the two floors to his office. He was leaning back looking amused and content. He showed me a piece of paper – foolscap, two pages. It was the brief – that short – for Gatwick Airport. He said in his characteristically casual manner that he would like me to do it with him – 'What about it?' I was delighted of course. He had within the last two weeks hinted, obliquely, that I should be clearing my lines as there might be a big job coming in, but this was really exciting. I naturally and stutteringly indicated assent and that was the end of the first conversation.

I read the brief, and 'brief' it was. It was to develop the airport. A small airport existed, a very advanced design of the 1930s, but this one was to be on a new site and would become the second airport for London (Heathrow, by Yorke's great friend Gibberd, being the first). The brief gave an outline of the main spaces required, but the most important information was the projected passenger figures and the absolute deadline, which was completion for operation by 9 June 1958. The total cost, the biggest part of which was to be a new runway, taxi tracks, telecommunications and the host of support facilities necessary for an international airport, was to be £6 million.

The engineers were Frederick Snow & Partners with whom we had never worked before. I believe Yorke received the commission with Snow's agreement and the backing of the permanent secretary to the Ministry of Transport and Civil Aviation, Sir Alfred le Maitre. Yorke told me he didn't know him well but had given a lecture on modern architecture in the 1930s to a group of people in Clapham, south London, at le Maitre's invitation.

To be made job architect, directly responsible to Yorke, for the most prestigious job the office had ever received was the most flattering and exciting yet daunting prospect I had ever faced. Considering how little I had built, Yorke's confidence was staggering, but the superb quality of the man was in the fact that, whether doing so was calculated or natural, putting me at ease by his very casualness completely implied the confidence he had in my ability and, at the same time, gave me the confidence to accept the job without qualms. I do not know any architect of his generation and his stature who would have taken the same risk. It was remarkable at the time and just as remarkable in retrospect.

During the next two and half years of incredible demands on my resources, completely backed by Yorke during the whole period, as if there was no possibility of failure, I often recalled the remark of a British engineer of the nineteenth century who, asked by an astonished layman, 'How could you built 2,000 miles of railway in South America?' replied: 'Easy. You just built it a foot at a time.' Yorke and I and the team got on very well with the engineers who were running the whole programme and we became lifelong friends with people like Norman Payne (now Sir Norman Payne) who eventually became chairman of the British Airports Authority.

In those days, programming techniques common today (fast track, for instance) and contractual systems to produce complex operations quickly did not exist. It was done with strength of will, optimism and sometimes sheer bloody-mindedness, late working and high morale, and was accompanied by good fun. Sometimes doggedness combined with ignorance or naivety achieves results that calculation of risk and probability couldn't achieve. We all learnt in two and a half years more that we could normally learn in five or ten! Most of my assistants were of my age or slightly younger, several were Canadians and Australians, and for a time Georg Heinrichs from Berlin worked with me on the control tower and fire station.

Randall was a fantastic supporter but let me get on with it, knowing I would ask him for advice when needed. It was certainly the most fulfilling and happiest period of my architectural life and I am in perpetual debt to Yorke for having made it possible. I was fortunate indeed. Yorke and I had one or two battles, the most intense concerning the elevations I produced in mid-1956. I wanted a kind of *brut le Corbusier* elevation, but Yorke dug in and was right. What emerged was better, and there was no ill feeling after the first skirmishes. Yorke's main contribution to Gatwick was as a guide and critic, a facilitator and a steady hand when the going was difficult.

As usual it was Yorke's role to keep an overview, and to help make the achievement of the aims we had set easier, managerially and politically when big guns were required. A typical example was the terrazzo flooring, a very large area of material for the main concourse. The best sample we received was the most expensive, and led to the highest levels of involvement of the Civil Service for obvious reasons of expenditure of further money. Yorke dug his heels in and said, rhetorically: 'If we can't have that, then I'd sooner have granolithic.' Rhetoric won the day and he was right, though the decision smarted in some quarters for years!

In the spring of 1956 Yorke had been thinking of the importance of the coordination and control of the interiors of the terminal building. The scope and scale were absolutely new to the office – passenger areas, check-in desks, lounge, bars, shops, restaurants, etc. He recruited Brian Henderson, and for the next two years Brian and I worked closely together (except for when he was recalled to the army for the Suez crisis) in a way few architects do or can. It was – after we had sorted each other out – an intimate and fruitful relationship that lasted until my retirement as chairman of Yorke Rosenberg & Mardall in 1989. Could Yorke be such a magician that he could see that our chemistry (Brian and I are quite different) could work and that 1+1 = 3? The answer must be 'yes', if it hadn't worked the result would have been woeful, for there would not have been time to change. The end result would not have been remotely as good as it was.

The Airport was opened by the Queen on 9 June 1958. Two small events on this fantastically memorable day relate to Yorke in that they were typical. Early in the day, when final preparations were being made, Brian Henderson and I were having a row with the flower-arranger someone had appointed. We didn't like the arrangement at all. Yorke put his head round the door of the restaurant where the battle was taking place, summed up the situation in a microsecond and disappeared. Very endearingly, he was with several of us and our wives in the pier after the formal opening, just enjoying it all, when a messenger from Sir Frederick Snow came up and said, 'Mr Yorke, don't you remember you're supposed to meet the Queen?' He had forgotten. Or perhaps he hadn't? The day ended with a large and very jolly party – Yorke's flat and then a dinner at the Coq d'Or.

Towards the end of June 1958 Yorke's red buzzer rang and he asked me to 'come up'. He was sitting there smiling, as he had at the Gatwick conversation in October 1955, and, again very casually, he said:, 'We'd like to make you a partner . . . what about it?'. I replied, slightly stunned, 'Yes, marvellous, thanks, but of course it's not like making it on your own.' He dismissed this with a wave of the hand and said, 'Well . . . that's something different'. I shook hands, delighted, and he said there'd be a meeting with the other partners later that afternoon. That meeting took place shortly afterwards with Yorke, Rosenberg and Mardall all looking cheerful and positive. Again, in a characteristic surprise (after the others had shaken hands and welcomed and congratulated me) Yorke said quietly – it was a way with him – 'And we're going to make Randall a partner too'. Randall was away in Leeds. Yorke picked up the telephone and asked for him on site. 'Randall, we've made David a partner and we'd very much like to make you one too.' Randall confirmed next day that he was stunned and that he'd said 'Yes, marvellous,' bursting into tears (Randall is very sentimental and really had not expected it). He went on to say to Yorke, 'By the way, I don't think you're going to like the colours on the workshop block' – or some such displacement remark. Yorke was amused at this. The only inkling I'd had of any such events was a few weeks before when Randall had said to me, 'By the way David, Yorke asked me if I'd mind if you were made a partner and I said, "Not at all as long as he doesn't bugger me about"...'

Yorke and Rosenberg went off on a trip to China the following weekend and Mardall went sailing, which he did every summer. This timing was brilliant as it left Randall and myself time to think about the implications of these shattering events. Two factors were uppermost in our thinking.

1. The arrangement which had worked very successfully for 14 years (since 1944) had to change. Clearly you couldn't continue with three partners, each in a sense having his own office, each with an associate and various levels of assistants, and each doing jobs his way architecturally and managerially, with a loose (however effective) overall control. Randall and I worked on the proposition that the office was one organisation with five partners and that the future would be based on this.

2. Despite the positive and generous manner in which the news was received, inevitably some people were disappointed, in that it implied they would not be made partners and others were understandably nervous of the changes, whatever they would be. This meant a lot of effort on the part of Randall and myself to assuage and help, especially senior people who, both older and more experienced than I, were concerned. That we largely achieved this sometimes painful transition was a credit to the morale of the office, and to the backing of the senior partners for our proposals.

We instituted formal meetings of the partnership to take place every week. When the original three partners returned we had the first meeting of all five partners and our proposals were accepted enthusiastically, though there was much that was painful in the detailed implementation. There is no doubt that making Randall a partner was a Yorke masterstroke. Only he could have seen its vital importance. This is not to imply that Rosenberg and Mardall were not in agreement but I believe it was his idea. Randall, a natural catalyst, was a linchpin in the new arrangements. He was the same age as the others, a friend of Yorke and a pre-war assistant, and was therefore able to help me to adjust to a dramatic transformation in my own role. He was able, because of our historical relationship, to criticise my headstrong desire for change as well as on occasion encourage the others to my point of view provided it was rational and for the good, as he saw it, of the office. I remember once putting a point strongly and Yorke saying 'I don't agree with David, but he's right'. I also remember, some months after the event, saying to Yorke privately: 'Since I became a partner it has been interesting to see how you three have behaved.

Cyril Mardall has made, with grace, the most astonishing transition and has been eager and help-ful to me at all times, whilst Rosenberg (a very complex and emotional man) has made a tremendous effort but not always been able to accept change. You, on the other hand, who mas-terminded it all, have made no change in your attitude at all.' Yorke replied, 'I agree with you. I like it', and poured me a large Scotch.

After the meetings we often had marvellous dinners when much informal business was transacted. Yorke was such a vivid companion that it was always a disappointment for me when he had another engagement, which was quite frequent. They were all good company, but Yorke had a special quality of bonhomie, always interested in conversation irrespective of who was talking. He often summed up others' statements with wit and élan. Much drink was taken and hair was let down. These occasions were purgative, sometimes personally painful, but usually apposite and to very good effect.

Immediately following Gatwick we worked with Frederick Snow on the new international air-port for Kuwait. The brief was shorter than that for Gatwick and called for an international air-port category 1A. We used all our recent experience and Brian Henderson and I worked hard on producing terminal and ancillary buildings, including hangars. Unfortunately, only some of the buildings were completed and the terminal building was not one of them, about which we were very sad. Yorke was involved, but not very closely as it was becoming apparent that he was not

FRS Yorke (second left) with, to his left Randall Evans, David Allford and Cyril Mardall (extreme right, back to camera): c1960, shortly after Allford and Evans became partners of Yorke Rosenberg and Mardall.

well. The signs were a certain loss of energy and interest, though his energy was still more than the average. His voice, never as strong as his personality, was deteriorating and eventually he had an operation to remove a cancer (a tracheotomy). This meant the loss of his larynx. He virtually lost his voice and could only communicate verbally in a gruff whisper. His courage, as one would expect, was fantastic. He still laughed a great deal and communicated his thoughts with what remained of his voice, gestures and writing on bits of paper. Even worse for him was the fact that his condition meant he had great difficulty in eating, though, luckily, less in drinking. We did several competitions at the time, one for Lever Brothers House in Hamburg and the other, invited, for the new Churchill College in Cambridge. Neither were successful but Yorke was interested, though not active, in both.

In all this misfortune the last great event we enjoyed with Yorke was what I called his last trip. In 1960–1 with some development work at Gatwick in the offing, we went on a trip to the latest European airports. The party consisted of Yorke, myself, Brian Henderson, Lister Rogers of Frederick Snow and Dr Clarke of the Ministry of Transport and Civil Aviation. We had, as usual, a marvellous time with Yorke defying his deteriorating health. One night in Rome we left him in a nightclub as he didn't seem to want to go to bed. Next morning (we had an early start) we asked how he was and he replied, 'I'm getting too old to buy sandwiches for the band'.

Understandably we didn't see much of him in the next year or two. We bought a site and built an office for ourselves – possibly the first architects in England to do so. Yorke took a very keen interest in this, especially as it had his office and flat as usual – though now purpose-built as a roof penthouse. He loved it, though he was not there as much as he would have liked after he moved in, in 1961.

We had wanted a new office space since the changes in the partnership and were enjoying a reasonable growth, so the new space was not only needed but, equally important, was a new symbol of our hope in the future. We had talked of taking office space in one of the new blocks then beginning to be completed in London but Yorke hated the idea, thinking they were characterless, anonymous and without residential facilities. He was right and we were lucky to find a site on the edge of the city near Chancery Lane and build what we wanted.

After we moved he spent a good deal of time in hospital at St Thomas's where, naturally, he was a favourite with the nurses. I rarely saw him, but one of the last times we had a conversation was when we discussed the prospect of a new school we were going to do together in Bakewell, Derbyshire. I'm sure this project was something that kept him going mentally. He loved that area as I did, and we talked of the visits we would make and of the fun we would have. At the very beginning I asked him about the Derbyshire County Architect who was responsible for recommending us for the job. Yorke wrote down: 'He is a man who has been looking towards modern architecture all his life and is not sure he's going to like it when he gets there!'

That is almost my last memory of him. He died when I was on holiday in June 1962. Though he was only fifty-five, the sadness of such an early death was perhaps mitigated by the thought that he had lived several normal lifetimes. He packed more into twenty-four hours than any one – myself or others – had known or have since known. He was always active and courageous and had a gargantuan appetite for life so that his energy enthused others and enhanced the lives of everyone in contact with him, whether regularly or briefly. He is still for me the most vivid person I ever met and ever will meet, and I still occasionally have dreams that make him miraculously alive and in the present.

The paradox of the growth and development of the office over the thirty years after Yorke's death is that they were very much in his spirit – yet he would not have liked what happened.

Indeed, with his presence things would, by definition, have been different although the general thrust would have been the same. Either they would have been modified or there would have been conflicts. As I am writing a memoir of Yorke I am not about to give an apologia of what these might have been, although that could be an interesting speculation. Nor am I concerned here with writing the history of the office, other than during my own years of knowing and working with him. The point of mentioning what happened to the office after Yorke, contributes to an understanding of his achievements, his drive and his appetites and vision.

Yorke was a big man in all senses of the phrase, yet his aspirations were essentially nonvisionary. The core of his personality was so strong and self-willed, even self-indulgent, his architectural ambitions so concerned with personal fulfilment, that he was not afraid of following them and taking the next step from wherever he was. His vision, for such it was, was concerned with the good life and not with a theoretical aim or ambition. The aspect of modernism in, say, the vision of Le Corbusier or Gropius was not to his taste. He remained all his life a very personal kind of architect, not unlike his father and not far from the Arts and Crafts movement of which his father had been a part. He was not interested, *per se*, in large organisations or in the management techniques and philosophies that these required. And yet in his own career the very demands of post-war reconstruction and the spread of the ideas of modernism led inevitably to what was at the time (1944–62) a large office. He never showed any resistance to this tendency and just got on with the next job. Intellectually, he obviously accepted that better construction management was a concomitant of the growing size and complexity of the projects and of the office itself.

In 1986 when as a partnership we were considering whether to become a limited company (we in fact became a plc in 1987, the first firm of architects to do so – we were by then a firm of multidisciplinary consultants, architects, engineers, interior designers and planners) I had a flash of memory that Yorke had once given a lecture on the subject of limited companies and architects at an RIBA conference. The next day I asked our librarian to look it up – I recalled it was after 1953 and before 1955.[11] She quickly unearthed it. It was a remarkable document for its time. It was certainly beyond my understanding when I first read it when it was published. Yorke never in my presence referred to it, nor did he do so later at any partnership meetings; he had either forgotten it (unlikely) or thought its time had not come. One can only imagine the sort of effect it had on the profession at the time. Disinterest would. be the reaction of many; most would have thought it irrelevant or even preposterous.[12]

Similarly, Yorke was very keen, as most modern architects were, on close collaboration between the various professionals in the design team, but he never proposed the idea of developing a multidisciplinary practice. Such ideas were in the air in the late 1950s and the 1960s but, again, he may have thought them premature or that they would complicate matters of organisation and management that were difficult enough with the practice of architecture alone. Indeed, the arguments for and against these ideas are still debatable and fascinating, but they do not form part of the matter in this memoir – except to say that Yorke Rosenberg & Mardell took this route and that Yorke would certainly have been interested in the ideas intellectually. Whether he would have enjoyed the opportunities a multidisciplinary practice brought, or been critical or even dismayed by the extra management and complication they caused, is quite impossible to say. Yet in a way he envisaged this kind of practice and, even more importantly, encouraged the open discussion of the ideas that eventually generated such developments. For instance, he went to the USA and visited some of the large firms including SOM in Chicago for whom he had a great respect. I believe his whole approach was a dynamic one and that his style laid the foundation for the growth and development of a large multidisciplinary practice to take place.

David Allford, 1927–97

I still believe, however, he would not personally have enjoyed it. One part of him was still, to the end, steeped in a personal view of architecture and the tradition of craft and professionalism. He was wary of, actively disliked even, the tendency to overorganise and overmanage. He appreciated the need for the rational and the systematic, he was orderly in his editing work and, indeed, could not, for instance, have edited *Specification* from 1935 to 1962 without these qualities. But he was more at home discussing architecture and life with friends and colleagues than with the discipline of modern management. It is perhaps this that made him such an expert fly fisherman (his most passionate hobby); despite his public-school upbringing he seemed never to have had any serious interest in team sports.

Over and above the pioneering work he did for the modern movement in English architecture, it was in my view, his personality, wit and intelligence that made his influence so significant. He was a link between the Arts and Crafts movement up to World War I and the continental modern movement between the two wars. Yorke's sense of the importance of the modern movement he first experienced on the continent, and the single-minded courage and skill with which he brought it to the attention of architects and a new and informed public in this country, laid the foundations for the development of an English school of modern architecture that has become significant, and even formidable, in world terms. I believe all of us owe a debt to Yorke who, among those of his generation, helped form a new architecture in England.

Notes

1. For information on the Braithwaite House, see Chapter 2.
2. Later it became Leeds Polytechnic, and is now Leeds Metropolitan University.
3. Each partner had about 15 to 20 assistants and the office was engaged mostly on publicly funded projects.
4. Penelope Whiting, *The New Small House*, Architectural Press (London), 1951.
5. The office had a well-stocked bar in the sideboard, overlooked Hyde Park and, despite an open fire, was often cold. It attracted Yorke's numerous friends from overseas, including Alvar Aalto. A story runs that as an afternoon of discussing architecture drew on Aalto became restless and eventually, at about 6 pm, asked: 'When do we stop work and start drinking?' Yorke, serious-faced, replied, 'We don't stop work', allowing just enough time for Aalto's face to fall before adding, 'we just start drinking', and produced a large bottle of Scotch. (Editor's note)
6. For an account of the New Brutalism, see Reyner Banham, *The New Brutalism: ethic or aesthetic*, Architectural Press (London), 1966.
7. See Chapter 5.
8. Harben had been the chef at the Isobar, designed by Yorke and Breuer before World War II, in the Isokon Flats in Lawn Road, Hampstead, London, designed by Wells Coates in 1933, where all manner of modernists lived, including Gropius, Breuer, Henry Moore and Agatha Christie.
9. Randall Evans, reportedly, made an even cruder comment. 'Kay would put his dick where I wouldn't put my walking stick,' and he was not referring to Yorke's appetite for pudding.
10. Beryl Allford remembers that the fishmonger Bill Angless, who came to see Allford and Yorke off at London Airport, commented that they were like a pair of farmers rather than modern architects.
11. The lecture 'The Private Architect's Problem' was given at a RIBA conference at Eastbourne in the summer of 1953, and published in the *RIBA Journal* vol 60 (April 1954), pp 225–7. See Chapter 5.
12. Raglan Squire did not think so, or at least did not think so with the hindsight of 30 years. Indeed, he even claimed that he had introduced the theme of becoming a limited company in response to Yorke's request to 'stir things up a bit'. See Raglan Squire, *Portrait of an Architect*, Smyth (Gerrards Cross), 1984, pp 179–80.

SOURCES

Numerous archives hold material by or related to FRS Yorke. The largest single quantity is held at the Royal Institute of British Architects. It includes a selection of his drawings (in the Drawings Collection), and some private papers and correspondence. These entered the institute's collections at different times, the most recent significant addition is over 30 boxes which came from Yorke's old firm, by then known as YRM Architects and Planners, in 1997 when they moved premises. While much of this material relates to the period after Yorke's death in 1962, it did yield a scrapbook he had kept during the 1930s and an almost unbroken run of annual accounts, from 1935 until his death. At the time of writing this collection had not been catalogued, though this is made clear in the references to items from it. Material which entered the institute earlier, including the drawings and personal correspondence, is catalogued and easily accessible.

A second significant archive came into the possession of David Allford from Randall Evans in 1992. Evans had worked with Yorke from 1936 to 1939, and again after 1945, becoming a partner of Yorke, Rosenberg & Mardall in 1958. Additionally his wife and Yorke's wife were sisters. It was perhaps this combination of family and professional associations that led him to collect material, after his death, from the penthouse Yorke occupied in the building at Greystoke Place in the City of London which the firm had built for itself. Evans simply boxed the material and, when David Allford informed him that he was working on a study of Yorke, offered it to him unseen. Primarily it comprises photographs, some of Yorke's work but more illustrations he obtained from other architects. There are also some drawings, short descriptions of projects, family and personal photographs and a few postcards. Allford, with advice from Evelyn Newby, catalogued the material, and it is referred to as the Allford Yorke Archive.

Further archives with relevant material include Eton College, and the Shakespeare Centre in Stratford-upon-Avon (which holds personal and business material of Yorke's clients, the Flower family). Other architects' papers are often illuminating, especially those of people like Sir John Summerson and the Hon Godfrey Samuel, who had a greater penchant than Yorke for keeping their records in order. Both are held at the RIBA, and Samuel's, in particular, is useful for reconstructing early MARS Group affairs. Richard Burton has kindly provided some private family material, including drawings and photographs.

Contemporary publications, especially those by Yorke himself or covering his design work, are another important source. Most were published by the Architectural Press, either as books, the annual *Specification*, or in *The Architectural Review* and *The Architects' Journal*. The principal ones are listed below.

The Modern House, Architectural Press (London), 1934, 1935, 1937, 1943, 1944, 1948, 1951, 1956.
The Modern House in England, Architectural Press (London), 1937, 1944, 1948.
The Modern Flat (with Frederick Gibberd), Architectural Press (London), 1937, 1948, 1950.
Planning for Reconstruction (co-author), Architectural Press (Cheam), 1944.
A Key to Modern Architecture (with Colin Penn), Blackie and Son (London and Glasgow), 1939.
Specification, editor, annually from 1935 until his death, latterly with Penelope Whiting

A selection of the most important periodical articles follows:
The Architects' Journal
Yorke's Writings
'Measured drawing of the facade of Landor House, Warwick', vol 73 (January–June 1931), supplement to issue of 8 April.
'Graphic statics' (with WEJ Budgen), vol 75 (January–June 1931), pp 639ff, 665ff.
'Rebuild the British Industries Fair', vol 77, (January–June 1933), p 234.
'Trade Notes'; weekly column from 22 March 1933 – 29 August 1935.
'The year's work abroad', vol 79 (January–June 1934), p 73.

Reviews of Yorke's writings
Erich Mendelsohn, review of *The Modern House*, vol 80 (July–December 1934), pp 55–60.
Working detail of Torilla, vol 82 (July–December 1936), p 319.
The Architectural Review

Yorke's writings
'From order through disorder to order', vol 70 (July–December 1931), pp 171–8.
'Three new houses', vol 71 (January–June 1932), pp 56–9 (includes Lois Welzenbacher's Haus Rosenbauer).
'Inside the theatre' (Shakespeare Memorial Theatre, Stratford-upon-Avon), vol 71 (January–June 1932), p 216.
Summary of *The Modern House*, vol 76 (July–December), 1934, pp 9–16.
Introduction to *The Modern House in England*, vol 80 (July–December), 1936, pp 237–308.

Reviews of Yorke's buildings
Review of the house at Hatfield (Torilla), vol 78 (July–December 1935), pp 97–9.
Illustrations of cottages at Stratford-upon-Avon, vol 85 (January–June 1939), p 282.
Illustrations of houses at Eton, vol 85 (January–June 1939), p 32.
Illustrations of nursery wing at Shottery Manor and construction of two cottages in Sussex, vol 87 (January–June 1940), pp 111ff, 122ff.
RIBA Journal
Yorke's writings
'The private architect's problem' (April 1954), pp 225–7.

Reviews of Yorke's work
EJ Carter, review of *The Modern House*, vol XLI (1934), pp 929–30.
Spectator
Geoffrey Boumphrey, review of *The Modern House* (17 August 1934), p 231.

Further relevant periodical entries are listed in the footnotes.

Finally, over the twelve-year history of this project there were numerous interviews and discussions with people who had known and worked with Yorke. The most important are listed below.

Interview subjects: Christabel Bielenberg, Randall Evans, Beryl Hope, Barbara MacDonald, Cyril Mardall, Colin Penn, Sir James Richards, Penelope Whiting

SELECT BIBLIOGRAPHY

Abercrombie, Patrick et al, *Greater London Plan* 1944, HMSO, London, 1945

Allan, John, *Lubetkin*, RIBA Publications, London, 1992

Bertram, Anthony, *Design*, Harmondsworth, Penguin, 1938

Bielenberg, Christabel, *The Past is Myself*, Chatto and Windus London, 1968, republished Corgi, 1984

The Road Ahead, Bantam, London, 1992

Blomfield, Reginald, *Modernismus*, Macmillan, London, 1934

Bowley, Marian, *The British Building Industry*, CUP 1966

Campbell, John, *Nye Bevan and the Mirage of British Socialism*, Weidenfeld and Nicholson, London, 1987

Carpenter, Humphrey, *The Brideshead Generation*, Faber, London, 1990

Cherry, Gordon *William Holford*, Mansell, London and New York, 1986

Ciucci, Giorgio, 'The Invention of the Modern Movement' in *Oppositions*, 24 Spring 1981, pp 68–91

Cohn, Laura, *The Door to a Secret Room, a Portrait of Wells Coates*, Scolar Press, Aldershot, 1999

Crawford, Alan, *CR Ashbee*, Yale University Press, London and New Haven, 1985

Dean, David, *The Thirties: Recalling the English Architectural Scene*, Trefoil, London, 1983

Dell, Edmund, *A Strange Eventful History*, HarperCollins, London, 2000.

Driller, Joachim, *Breuer's Houses*, Phaidon, London, 2000

Economist, The, 'The Architect's Dilemma', first published in the *Economist*, 25 July 1953, reprinted in the *RIBA Journal*, April 1954, pp 226–7

Esher, Lionel, *A Broken Wave*, Penguin, Harmondsworth, 1981

Ferguson, Niall (ed), *Virtual History*, Picador, London, 1997

Finnimore, Brian, *Houses from the Factory*, Rivers Oram, London, 1989

Forty, Adrian, 'Common sense and the Picturesque', in Iain Borden and David Dunster, (eds) *Architecture and the Sites of History*, Butterworth Architecture, Oxford, 1995, pp 176–86

'Le Corbusier's British Reputation' in *Le Corbusier Architect of the Century*, edited by Michael Raeburn and Victoria Wilson, The Arts Council, London, 1987, pp 35–41

Words and Buildings, Thames and Hudson, London, 2000

Fry, Maxwell, *Autobiographical Sketches*, Elek, London, 1975

Gatje, Robert, *Marcel Breuer a Memoir*, Monacelli, New York, 2000

Giedion, Sigfried, *Mechanization Takes Command*, OUP, Oxford, 1948, Norton Edition, 1969

Gold, John, 'Commodotie, Firmenes and Delight': modernism, the MARS Group's 'New Architecture' Exhibition (1938) and imagery of the urban future', in *Planning Perspectives*, vol 8, no 4, October 1993, p 357–376

'Creating the Charter of Athens: CIAM and the Functional city, 1933–43', in *Town Planning Review*, vol 69, no 3, July1998, p 225–247

The Experience of Modernity: modern architects and the future city 1928–53, Spon, London, 1997

'The MARS plans for London, 1933–1942: plurality and experimentation in the city plans of the early British Modern Movement', in *Town Planning Review*, vol 66, no 3, July1995, p 243–267

Goldthwaite, Richard, *The Building of Renaissance Florence*, Johns Hopkins University Press, Baltimore and London, 1980

Gropius, Walter, (trans P Morton Shand), *The New Architecture and the Bauhaus*, MIT Press, Cambridge Mass, 1965

Gutman, Robert, *Architectural Practice a Critical View*, Princeton Architectural Press, New York, 1988

Hampson, Martin, *Edgbaston*, Tempus Publishing, Stroud, 1999

Harris, Kenneth, *Attlee*, Weidenfeld and Nicholson, London, 1982

Harrison, Tom, and Charles Madge, *Britain by Mass Observation*, Penguin, Harmondsworth, 1939

Hastings, Hubert de Cronin, *Recent English Domestic Architecture*, The Architectural Press, London

Hilberseimer, Ludwig, 'Die Wohnung Unserer Zeit', in *Die Form* vol 6, no 7, 15 July 1931, pp 249–70

Hillier, Bevis, *Young Betjeman*, John Murray London, 1988

Hilton, Tim, *John Ruskin The Later Years*, Yale University Press, New Haven and London, 2000

Hyman, Isabelle, *Marcel Breuer, Architect*, Abrams, New York, 2001

Isaacs, Reginald, *Gropius*, Bulfinch, an imprint of Little Brown, Boston, Toronto, London, 1991

Jackson, Anthony, *The Politics of Modern Architecture*, Architectural Press, London, 1970

Jackson, TG, and Norman Shaw, (eds), *Architecture: Profession or Art*, Murray, London, 1892

Jones, Douglas V, *Edgbaston As It Was*, Westwood Press, Sutton Coldfield, undated

Jordy, William H, 'The Aftermath of the Bauhaus in America: Gropius, Mies, and Breuer, in *The Intellectual Migration, Europe and America 1930–1960*, edited Donald Fleming and Bernard Bailyn, The Belknap Press of Harvard University Press, Cambridge Mass, 1969, pp 485–543

Kaufmann, Edgar J Jr, *Fallingwater*, the Architectural Press, London, 1986

Korn, Arthur, *History Builds the Town*, Lund Humphries, London, 1955

Land, Tim, *Eton Renewed*, John Murray, London, 1994

Landau, Roy, 'A History of Modern Architecture that still needs to be Written', in *AA Files* 29, Spring 1991, pp 49–54

Le Corbusier, *Vers Une Architecture*, published in English as *Towards a New Architecture*, trans Frederick Etchells, John Rodker, London, 1927

Lloyd, John, 'Media Manifesto', in *Prospect*, October 2002, pp 48–53.

Lloyd, Nathaniel, *A History of the English House*, The Architectural Press London, 1931

Lubbock, Jules, *The Tyranny of Taste: the politics of architecture and design in Britain 1550–1960* Yale University Press and the Paul Mellon Centre for British Art, New Haven and London, 1995

MacGrath, Raymond, *Twentieth Century Houses*, Faber, London, 1934

McCoy, Esther, *Blueprints for Modern Living*, MoCA, Los Angeles, 1990

McIntyre, Ian, *The Expense of Glory – a Life of John Reith*, Harper Collins, London, 2000

Macleod, Iain, *Neville Chamberlain* Muller, London, 1961

Martin, JL (Leslie), Ben Nicholson and Naum Gabo, *Circle: International Survey of Constructive Art*, Faber & Faber, London, 1937

Mowl, Timothy, *Stylistic Cold Wars, Betjeman versus Pevsner*, John Murray, London, 2000

Mumford, Eric, *The CIAM Discourse on Urbanism 1928–60*, MIT, Cambridge Mass, 2000

Muthesius, Herman, *Das Englische Haus*, Wasmuth Verlag, Berlin, 1904–5

Oliver, Paul, Ian Davis and Ian Bentley, *Dunroamin*, Barrie and Jenkins, London, 1981, reprinted Pimlico, 1994

Pevsner, Nikolaus, *Pioneers of Modern Design*, first published as *Pioneers of the Modern Movement* Faber, London, 1936

Phillips, Randal, *The Modern English House*, Country Life, London, 1927

Powell, Kenneth (ed), *Collaborations The Architecture of ABK*, August Birkhauser, London, 2002

Powers, Alan, *In the Line of Development*, RIBA Heinz Gallery, London, 1992

Serge Chermayeff, RIBA Publications, London, 2001

Pringle, Marian, *The Theatres of Stratford-upon-Avon*, Stratford-upon-Avon Historical Society, 1993

Rasmussen, Steen Eiler, *London: The Unique City*, Jonathan Cape, London, 1934

Richards, JM, *An Introduction to Modern Architecture*, Penguin, Harmondsworth, 1940

Memoirs of an Unjust Fella, Weidenfeld and Nicholson, London, 1980

'The Regency Precedent', in *The Architects' Journal*, vol 78 12 October 1933, p 455

Richardson, Albert and H Donaldson Eberlein, *The Smaller English House of the Later Renaissance 1660–1830*, Batsford, London, 1925

Richardson, Margaret, in *Architects of the Arts and Crafts Movement* Trefoil Press, London, 1983

Roberts, Andrew, in *The Holy Fox, a Biography of Lord Halifax* Weidenfeld and Nicholson, London, 1991

Robinson, Andrew, *The Man Who Decoded Linear B* Thames and Hudson, London, 2002

RIBA, *Strategic Study of the Profession*, Phases 3 and 4, 1995

Schildt, Goran, *Alvar Aalto in his own Words*, Otava, Helsinki, 1997

Shand, P Morton, 'Scenario for a Human Drama' in *The Architectural Review* vol 76, pp 9–16, to which Shand provided a foreword. The series continued with 'Immediate Background' August 1934. pp 39–42, 'Peter Behrens' September 1934 pp 83–9, 'Van der Velde to Wagner' October 1934 pp131–4, 'Glasgow interlude' vol 77 January 1935, pp 23–6 and 'Machine-à-Habiter to the house of character' March 1935, pp 61–4

Shonfield, Katherine, *Walls Have Feelings*, Routledge, London, 2000

Sloan Jr, Alfred P, *My Years with General Motors*, Pan, London, 1967

Spence, Basil, *Phoenix at Coventry*, Geoffrey Bles, London 1962

Spector, Tom, *The Ethical Architect*, Princeton Architectural Press, New York, 2001

Squire, Raglan, *Portrait of an Architect*, Smythe, Gerrards Cross, 1984

Stamp, Gavin (ed), *Britain in the Thirties*, Architectural Design, London, 1979

Stevens, Garry, *The Favoured Circle*, MIT Press, Cambridge Mass, 1998

Summerson, John (ed), *Concerning Architecture*, Allen Lane, London, 1968

John Nash Allen & Unwin, London, 1935

Swenarton, Mark, *Artisans and Architects*, Heinemann, London, 1989.

Tatchell, Sydney, 'Architectural Practice', *RIBA Journal*, September 1935, vol XLII, pp 1103–5

Taut, Bruno, *Modern Architecture*, The Studio, London, 1929

Taylor, SJ, *The Great Outsiders, Northcliffe, Rothermere and the Daily Mail*, Weidenfeld and Nicholson, London, 1996

Thompson, J Lee, *Northcliffe, Press Baron in Politics 1865–1922*, John Murray, London, 2000

Thompson, Paul, *William Butterfield*, Routledge and Kegan Paul London, 1971

Twentieth Century Society, *Twentieth Century Architecture*, vol 1 and 2, 1994 and 1996

Watkin, David, *Morality and Architecture*, first published in 1977, reissued in revised form as *Morality and Architecture Revisited*, John Murray, London, 2001

The Rise of Architectural History, Architectural Press, London, 1980

Weinreb, B, *The Small English House*, B Weinreb Architectural Books, London, 1977

Wilk, Christopher, *Marcel Breuer Furniture and Interiors*, the Architectural Press, London, 1981

Wilson, Colin St John, *The Other Tradition of Modern Architecture*, Academy Editions, London, 1995

Yerbury, Francis, *Modern European Buildings*, Gollancz, London, 1928
Swedish Architecture of the Twentieth Century, Benn, London, 1925

Yorke Rosenberg Mardall, *The Architecture of Yorke Rosenberg Mardall 1944–1972* (with an introduction by Reyner Banham), Lund Humphries, London, 1972

INDEX

Figures in italics indicate captions. 'Y' indicates Francis Reginald Stevens Yorke and 'YRM' Yorke, Rosenberg & Mardall.